Contents

Finding Your Best Starting Point .... **vii**

Finding the Best Starting Point for You vii • New Features in Microsoft
Works Suite 2001 ix • Corrections, Comments, and Help ix • Visit Our
World Wide Web Site x

Using the Book's CD-ROM .... **xi**

System Requirements xi • Installing the Practice Files xii • Using the
Practice Files xiii • Viewing the Multimedia Demos xiv • Uninstalling
the Practice Files xiv • Need Help with the Practice Files? xv

Conventions and Features in This Book .... **xvii**

UNIT 1   Getting Started   1

Lesson 1   Introducing Microsoft Works..**3**

Exploring Microsoft Works 3 • Starting with a Task 6 • Starting with a
Program 11 • Starting from the History Tab 14 • Getting Help 15 •
Changing or Hiding the Office Assistant 19 • Lesson Wrap-Up 19 • Quick
Reference 20

Lesson 2   Creating a Letter...**23**

Creating a Document 24 • Using Word Menus and Toolbars 28 • Enter-
ing and Editing Text 29 • Finding and Replacing Text 32 • Formatting
Text 34 • Saving and Printing a Document 38 • Installing a Printer 41 •
Lesson Wrap-Up 41 • Quick Reference 42

Lesson 3   Keeping Track of Contacts **45**

Storing Contact Information 46 • Sorting Contacts 49 • Organizing
Contacts 51 • Sharing Contacts 55 • Using Identities 58 • Printing
Contacts 58 • Lesson Wrap-Up 60 • Quick Reference 60

Lesson 4   **Communicating on the Internet**..**63**

> What Is the Internet? 64 • Establishing an Internet Connection 64 •
> Finding People and Information on the Internet 65 • Personalizing
> Internet Explorer 70 • Controlling Security in Internet Explorer 72 •
> What Is Outlook Express? 76 • Sending E-Mail Messages 79 •
> Managing E-Mail Messages 82 • Cleaning Out Your Mailbox 85 •
> Lesson Wrap-Up 85 • Quick Reference 85

Unit 2   **Managing Your Information**   **89**

Lesson 5   **Managing Your Schedule**..**91**

> Starting and Viewing a Calendar 91 • Adding Appointments and
> Events 93 • Adding Birthdays and Holidays 97 • Managing a
> Calendar 98 • Sharing a Calendar 102 • Saving Calendar Items in
> Other Formats 104 • Lesson Wrap-Up 104 • Quick Reference 105

Lesson 6   **Tracking a Budget**...**107**

> What Is a Spreadsheet? 107 • Creating and Saving a Spreadsheet 109 •
> Entering Text and Numbers 112 • Performing Calculations 115 •
> Presenting Data in a Chart 120 • Previewing and Printing a Spread-
> sheet 123 • Lesson Wrap-Up 126 • Quick Reference 126

Lesson 7   **Creating a Mass Mailing**...**129**

> What Is a Mail Merge? 130 • Setting Up a Form Letter 134 • Viewing
> and Printing Merged Data 137 • Working with Other Data Sources 139 •
> Customizing the Merge Results 139 • Filtering and Sorting Names
> and Addresses 141 • Creating Labels and Envelopes 143 • Printing
> Envelopes 147 • Lesson Wrap-Up 147 • Quick Reference 148

Lesson 8   **Working with Databases**...**151**

> What Is a Database? 151 • Creating a Database 152 • Entering Infor-
> mation 156 • Formatting a Database Form 159 • Finding and Sorting
> Information 159 • Filtering Database Information 161 • Printing Data-
> base Information 164 • Modifying a Report 166 • Lesson
> Wrap-Up 168 • Quick Reference 168

Lesson 9   **Creating a Newsletter**..**171**

Creating a Newsletter Using a Wizard 172 • What Is Lorem Ipsum? 176 • Adding Text to a Newsletter 176 • Modifying Document Formatting 179 • Enhancing a Document with Pictures 183 • Working with Pictures 187 • Lesson Wrap-Up 188 • Quick Reference 188

Unit 3   **Integrating Other Tasks**   **191**

Lesson 10   **Managing Accounts and Investments**...**193**

Setting Up Accounts in Microsoft Money 194 • Entering Transactions 198 • Tips for Entering Transactions 201 • Scheduling a Recurring Transaction 202 • Tracking Investments 203 • Reporting Financial Health 207 • Lesson Wrap-Up 209 • Using Money Files 210 • Quick Reference 210

Lesson 11   **Creating an Invitation**..**213**

Starting with a Built-In Design 213 • Starting a Print Project from Scratch 216 • Working with Pictures 217 • Formatting Text 222 • Saving and Printing Your Invitation 227 • Lesson Wrap-Up 230 • Quick Reference 230

Lesson 12   **Planning Trips and Finding Information**.......................................**233**

Locating Information in Encarta Encyclopedia 233 • Planning a Route with Streets & Trips 238 • Lesson Wrap-Up 243 • Quick Reference 243

Index..**245**

Finding Your Best Starting Point

With Microsoft Works Suite 2001, you have all the tools you need to make the most of your home computer. Works is a collection of programs with built-in tasks for creating both fun and serious projects, such as letters, budgets, invitations, inventories, checklists, school reports, and more. This book provides a step-by-step tour of common tasks in Works so that you can learn how to get the great results you want.

important

The Works Suite 2001 software is not provided on this book's CD-ROM. To complete the lessons in this book, you will first need to purchase and install Works Suite 2001.

Finding the Best Starting Point for You

This book is designed for people who are learning Works for the first time as well as people who have experience with earlier versions of Works and are now upgrading. If you have Works Suite 2001, you can follow all of the lessons in the book. If you have Works 6.0, the lessons that require Microsoft Word (Lessons 2, 7, and 9) and other programs that are included only with Works Suite (Lessons 10 through 12) do not apply. For details about the programs included in each version of Works, see the section "Exploring Microsoft Works" in Lesson 1, "Introducing Microsoft Works." Use the table on the next page to find your best starting point in this book.

important

This book is designed for use with Microsoft Works Suite 2001 running on Microsoft Windows 95 or later. To see which version of Works you're running, check the product package. If you have a previous version of Works or Works Suite, a *Step by Step* book that matches your software is probably available. Please visit our World Wide Web site at *http://mspress.microsoft.com* or call 1–800–MSPRESS (1–800–677–7377) for more information.

If you are	Follow these steps
New to Works to Works Suite 2001	**1** Install the practice files. See "Using the Book's CD-ROM" later in this book. **2** To learn basic Works skills, complete Lesson 1. To learn basic skills for using Microsoft Word 2000 (included with Works Suite 2001), complete Lesson 2. **3** Work through the remaining lessons in any order.

If you are	Follow these steps
Upgrading from a previous version of Works or Works Suite	**1** Learn about the new features of Works 2001 that are covered in this book. See the following section, "New Features in Microsoft Works Suite 2001." **2** Install the practice files. See "Using the Book's CD-ROM" later in this book. **3** Complete the lessons that cover the topics you need. To locate information about general topics, see the table of contents. To locate a specific topic or feature, see the index.

If you are	Follow these steps
Referencing this book after working through the lessons	**1** Locate information about specific commands, features, or topics in the index, or see the table of contents to locate information about general topics. **2** Review each lesson's major tasks in the Quick Reference section at the end of the lesson.

tip

If you're new to a Works Suite program and want help getting started, click its Help menu and see if the Quick Tours command is available. If it is, click the command to start an introductory tour about using the program. Not all programs included with Works Suite feature a Quick Tour.

New Features in Microsoft Works Suite 2001

The following table lists the major new features in Microsoft Works Suite 2001 that are covered in this book. The table shows the lesson in which you can learn about each feature. You can also use this book's index to find specific information about a feature or task.

To learn how to	See
Format documents and text in Word 2000 with the Format Gallery	Lesson 9
Browse the Web with the latest version of Microsoft Internet Explorer	Lesson 4
Send e-mail messages with the latest version of Microsoft Outlook Express	Lesson 4
Store text, pictures, and sounds with the Works Portfolio	Lesson 9
Create fun print projects with Microsoft Picture It! Publishing (formerly Microsoft Picture It! and Microsoft Home Publishing)	Lesson 11

Corrections, Comments, and Help

Every effort has been made to ensure the accuracy of this book and its CD-ROM. Microsoft Press provides corrections and additional content for its books through the World Wide Web at

http://mspress.microsoft.com/support/

If you have comments, questions, or ideas regarding this book or the CD-ROM, please send them to us.

Send e-mail to

mspinput@microsoft.com

Or send postal mail to

Microsoft Press
Attn: Step by Step Editor
One Microsoft Way
Redmond, WA 98052-6399

Please note that product support for Works Suite 2001 is not offered through the above addresses.

For support information regarding Microsoft Works, visit the Microsoft Product Support Services Web site at

http://support.microsoft.com/directory/

Microsoft also provides information about Microsoft Works at

http://www.microsoft.com/works/

Visit Our World Wide Web Site

We invite you to visit the Microsoft Press Web site at the following location:

http://mspress.microsoft.com

You'll find descriptions for all of our books, information about ordering titles, notices of special features and events, additional content for Microsoft Press books, and much more.

You can also find out the latest in software developments and news from Microsoft Corporation by visiting the following Web site:

http://www.microsoft.com

Using the Book's CD-ROM

The CD-ROM inside the back cover of this book contains the practice files that you'll use as you work through the exercises in the book and multimedia files that demonstrate some of the exercises. By using the practice files, you can concentrate on learning the tasks and save time while working through a lesson. With the practice files and the step-by-step instructions in the lessons, you'll learn by doing, which is an easy and effective way to acquire and remember new skills.

important

The Microsoft Works Suite 2001 software is not provided on this book's CD-ROM. To complete the lessons in this book, you will first need to purchase and install Works Suite 2001.

System Requirements

To complete the lessons in this book, you must have the following software installed on your computer:

- Microsoft Windows 95, Windows 98, Windows Millennium Edition, or Windows 2000
- Microsoft Works Suite 2001

important

This book is designed for use with Microsoft Works Suite 2001 for Microsoft Windows 95 or later. To see which version of Works you're running, check the product package. If your software is not compatible with this book, a *Step by Step* book that matches your software is probably available. Please visit our World Wide Web site at *http://mspress.microsoft.com* or call 1–800–MSPRESS (1–800–677–7377) for more information.

Installing the Practice Files

Practice files icon

Follow these steps to install the practice files on your computer's hard disk so that you can use them with the exercises in this book.

1   If your computer isn't on, turn it on now.

2   If you're using Windows 2000, press Ctrl+Alt+Del to display a dialog box asking for your user name and password. If you are using Windows 95, Windows 98, or Windows Millennium Edition, you will see this dialog box only if your computer is connected to a network.

3   If necessary, type your user name and password in the appropriate boxes, and then click OK.

4   Remove the CD-ROM from the package inside the back cover of this book and insert it in the CD-ROM drive of your computer.

A start window should appear automatically.

If the start window does not appear, browse the files on the CD-ROM and double-click StartCD.exe.

The options in the start window include browsing the multimedia demo files, installing the practice files, and opening the Microsoft Press Support Web site.

5   In the list of options, click Install Practice Files.

The setup program window appears.

6   Follow the instructions that appear on the screen.

The setup program creates a folder named Works Suite 2001 SBS Practice and copies the practice files into this folder. The setup program also creates a shortcut to the practice folder on the desktop.

For best results in using the practice files with this book, keep the preselected location of the practice folder. Depending on the version of Windows that you are using, the practice folder is created in one of the following locations:

■   Windows 95, Windows 98, or Windows Millennium Edition

C:\My Documents\Works Suite 2001 SBS Practice

■   Windows 2000

C:\Documents and Settings\<*user name*>\My Documents\Works Suite 2001 SBS Practice

After the setup program is finished installing the practice files, the start window is again displayed.

Close

7   To close the start window, click the Close button on the title bar.

8   If you are finished with the CD-ROM, remove the it from your CD-ROM drive and replace it in the package inside the back cover of the book.

tip

If your computer is set up to connect to the Internet, you can visit the Microsoft Press Web site at *http://mspress.microsoft.com* and the Microsoft Press Support Web site at *http://mspress.micrsoft.com/support/*.

Using the Practice Files

 Practice files for the lesson

Some lessons in this book require the use of a practice file and some do not. At the beginning of each lesson that uses a practice file, you'll see the practice files icon, and the lesson will include explicit steps for how to open the correct file. The practice files and the lessons are designed with a real-world scenario in mind, so you can easily apply the skills you learn. In this book, a fictional volunteer committee is organizing an effort to restore a neighborhood park. To practice using Microsoft Word with Works Suite, you'll write a letter and create a newsletter about the group's activities.

Some of the practice files have names that end with the word *Final*. These files are not used to complete the lesson; instead, they show how the resulting file should look once the lesson is successfully completed. The following table lists the practice files included on this book's CD-ROM that are needed to complete the lessons.

Lesson folder	Practice file
Lesson01	No practice files
Lesson02	Letter to Uncle Steve.doc, a letter to practice editing
Lesson03	Addresses.wab, a file to add sample addresses to your Address Book
Lesson04	Six e-mail messages (.eml files) to use with Outlook Express Restoration Project Article.doc, a file to attach to an e-mail message
Lesson05	No practice files
Lesson06	No practice files
Lesson07	Oak Park Mailing List.doc, a data source for a mass mailing Volunteer Solicitation Letter.doc, a form letter
Lesson08	No practice files
Lesson09	Restoration Project Article.doc, an article for a newsletter Oak Park News - One Column.doc, a partially complete newsletter Friends.jpg, a picture for a newsletter
Lesson10	No practice files
Lesson11	Trail.jpg, a picture for an invitation
Lesson12	No practice files

Viewing the Multimedia Demos

Throughout this book, you will see icons for multimedia demos for particular exercises. The multimedia demos are located in the Demos folder on this book's CD-ROM and are not installed on your hard disk. To view the demos, you must have a multimedia player installed, such as Windows Media Player, and your computer must be capable of playing sound.

> **tip**
> For best results when viewing the demos, set your screen resolution to 800 by 600 or higher.

Use the following steps to play a demo.

Multimedia demo icon

1   Insert the CD-ROM in your CD-ROM drive.

A start window should appear automatically.

If the start window does not appear, browse the files on the CD-ROM and double-click StartCD.exe.

2   In the list of options, click Browse Multimedia Demos.

The multimedia demos in the Demos folder on the CD-ROM are listed.

3   Double-click the demo you want to view.

Your media player plays the multimedia demo.

Close

After the demo is finished, click the Close button on the media player title bar.

> **tip**
> For the latest information on Microsoft Windows Media Player, visit the Windows Media Web site at the following location: *http://www.microsoft.com/ windows/windowsmedia/*.

Uninstalling the Practice Files

Use the following steps when you want to delete the practice files added to your hard disk by the setup program.

important

Be aware that uninstalling the practice files will also delete any files that you have saved in the Works Suite 2001 SBS Practice folder.

1   On the Windows taskbar, click the Start button, point to Settings, and then click Control Panel.

2   Double-click Add/Remove Programs.

The Add/Remove Programs Properties dialog box appears.

3   In the list of installed programs, click Works Suite 2001 SBS Practice, and then click Add/Remove or Change/Remove.

A confirmation message appears.

4   Click Yes.

The practice files are uninstalled.

5   Close the Add/Remove Programs Properties dialog box.

6   Close the Control Panel window.

Need Help with the Practice Files?

Every effort has been made to ensure the accuracy of this book and the contents of its CD-ROM. If you do run into a problem, Microsoft Press provides corrections for its books through the World Wide Web at

http://mspress.microsoft.com/support/

We invite you to visit the Microsoft Press Web site at

http://mspress.microsoft.com

You'll find descriptions for all of our books, information about ordering titles, notices of special features and events, additional content for Microsoft Press books, and much more.

Conventions and Features in This Book

You can save time when you use this book by understanding how it was designed. Please take a moment to read the following list, which points out helpful conventions and features that you might want to use.

- Hands-on exercises for you to follow are given in numbered lists of steps (1, 2, and so on). A round bullet (●) indicates an exercise that has only one step.

- Text that you are to type appears in **bold**. When a new term is used for the first time, that word also appears in **bold**.

- Buttons or icons that you are to click appear in the margin when it might not be clear what those buttons or icons look like.

- A plus sign (+) between two key names means that you must press those keys at the same time. For example, *Press Alt+Tab* means that you hold down the Alt key while you press the Tab key.

- The movie icon in the margin alerts you that the book's CD-ROM includes a multimedia demo that demonstrates the task described at that place in the book. For more information about the demos, see "Viewing the Multimedia Demos" in the "Using the Book's CD-ROM" section at the beginning of the book.

Practice files for the lesson

- The practice files icon in the margin provides information about the files that you'll need to complete that lesson. You can install all the practice files from this book's CD-ROM. For more information about installing the practice files, see the section "Using the Book's CD-ROM" at the beginning of the book.

- You can get a quick review of how to perform the tasks you learned by reading the Quick Reference at the end of each lesson.

UNIT 1

Getting Started

LESSON

1

Introducing Microsoft Works

ESTIMATED
TIME
20 min.

In this lesson, you will learn how to:
- ✔ *Start and work in Microsoft Works.*
- ✔ *Begin a new task.*
- ✔ *Launch a Microsoft Works program.*
- ✔ *Work with files and documents you've saved before.*
- ✔ *Get answers from online Help.*

Microsoft Works

Microsoft Works is many programs in one, all designed to help you get the most out of your home computer. Works includes all the tools you need to create letters, greeting cards, school reports, mailing labels, budgets, checklists, and more. You can also use Works to access the Internet and e-mail, schedule and track appointments, balance your checkbook, perform research, and plan a vacation. Whatever your task, Works makes it simple by providing preformatted templates and step-by-step wizards that guide you to polished results.

This book can help you take advantage of all that Works has to offer. In this lesson, you'll be introduced to the components of Works, find out about different ways that you can get started, and practice using Works Help to answer questions that arise while you work.

Exploring Microsoft Works

Microsoft Works provides a set of programs that help you perform the tasks you do most often with your computer. In Works, you can choose what you want to do from a list of common tasks, such as sending an e-mail message, creating a letter, or researching a school paper. Works then starts the appropriate program for your task and can even guide you in setting up the type of document you want to create.

When you start Works, you can begin with the Works Task Launcher, a home page from which you can start new tasks, launch programs, and view a history of the documents you've already created. When you start with a task, Works determines which program you need to work in and then opens it. When you start with a program, you can create a new, blank document of the type created by that program, such as a word processing document, a spreadsheet, or a database. You can also start from a document you've already created.

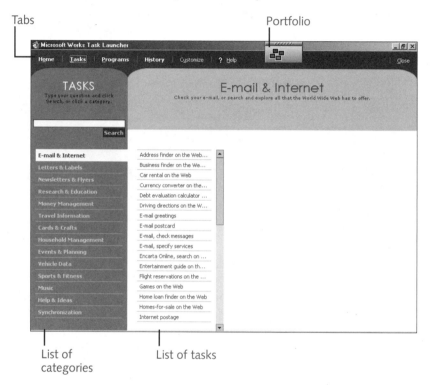

Some of the core components of Works include the following:

- Microsoft Word, a word processing program that you can use to write letters, reports, and documents of any length. (Only Works Suite includes Word. Works 6.0 includes Works Word Processor instead of Word as its word processing program.)

- Works Spreadsheet, a tool you can use to create budgets, financial worksheets, graphs and charts, lists, and tables of all kinds.

- Works Database, a tool for organizing quantities of information and creating data entry forms.

- Works Calendar, a tool for keeping track of appointments and important dates.

- Works Portfolio, a window on your screen into which you can paste text, pictures, and just about anything else you copy from other programs and the Internet.
- Microsoft Internet Explorer, which provides access to the World Wide Web and MSN.
- Templates and wizards, which help you get polished results every time, no matter what type of document you're creating.

The following table summarizes the components that come with Works Suite 2001 and Works 6.0.

tip
To see which version of Works you have, see your product package.

Component	Works Suite 2001	Works 6.0
Works Word Processor		✔
Word 2000	✔	
Works Spreadsheet	✔	✔
Works Database	✔	✔
Works Calendar	✔	✔
Windows Address Book	✔	✔
Works Portfolio	✔	✔
MSN integration	✔	✔
Internet Explorer 5.5	✔	✔
Outlook Express 5.5	✔	✔
Encarta Encyclopedia Standard 2001	✔	
Streets & Trips 2001	✔	
Picture It! Publishing 2001	✔	
Money 2001 Standard Edition	✔	
FoneSync 3.1	✔	

important
This book is designed to work with Works Suite 2001. If your version is Works 6.0, you can follow many but not all the lessons. Lessons 2, 7, and 9 through 12 require components that are not included with Works 6.0.

Starting with a Task

*Microsoft
Works Suite*

Even if you don't know exactly which Works program you need to use, you get going in Works by starting with a task. A task is anything you want to do in Works: write a letter, balance the household budget, plan a party, surf the Web, or something else.

You can start Works from the Microsoft Works Suite icon on your Windows desktop or from the list of programs on the Windows Start menu. As the illustration below shows, the Start menu includes two entries for Microsoft Works: one that starts the Task Launcher and one that opens a submenu of programs included with Works.

To see a multi-media demo about the Task Launcher, double-click the Use Task Launcher icon in the Demos folder on the book's CD-ROM.

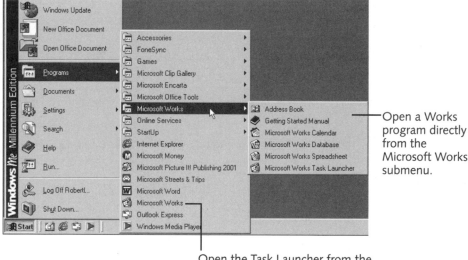

Open a Works program directly from the Microsoft Works submenu.

Open the Task Launcher from the Microsoft Works command.

To identify the task you want to perform, you use the Task Launcher. In the Task Launcher, tasks are grouped into categories, such as Letters & Labels and Household Management. When you choose a category, Works displays a list of tasks to choose from.

In this exercise, you browse the list of tasks in the Task Launcher and then start a task that creates a garage sale flyer. Next you use the Search box in the Task Launcher to locate a particular task.

1   On the taskbar, click the Start button, point to Programs, and then click Microsoft Works.

When you start Works for the first time after installation, Works displays the Microsoft End User License Agreement dialog box.

2   If the Microsoft End User License Agreement dialog box appears, review the agreement. If you accept the agreement, click I Agree.

If you clicked I Agree, the Microsoft Product Registration dialog box appears.

3   If the Microsoft Product Registration dialog box appears and you want to register Works now, click Register Now and follow the instructions in the registration wizard. Otherwise, click Register Later.

The home page of the Task Launcher opens. The Portfolio continues to be displayed.

To close the Portfolio, click to expand it, click the Tasks menu, and then click Close.

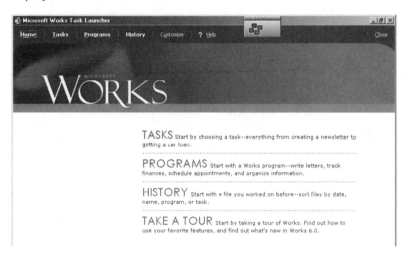

4   Click the Tasks tab.

Categories of Works tasks are listed on the left. Tasks for the first category are listed on the right.

5   In the list of tasks, click Newsletters & Flyers.

Tasks for creating newsletters and flyers are listed on the right.

6   Click the Flyers task.

A description of this task appears to the right.

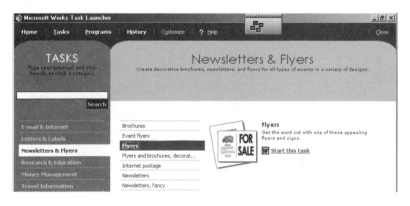

7   Click Start This Task.

The Works Flyers Wizard appears and displays options for choosing a topic. Behind the wizard, Word 2000 starts.

tip

The first time you start Word, product key and registration dialog boxes might be displayed.

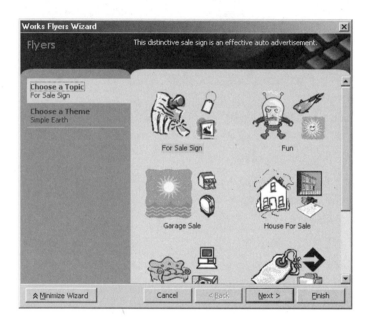

8   Click Garage Sale, and then click Next.

Options for choosing a formatting theme with fonts and colors appear. Behind the wizard, your selections appear in the Word document.

9   Click Finish.

The wizard closes, and Word displays a garage sale flyer that you can customize.

Introducing Microsoft Works

Save

10 To save the flyer so that you can work on it later, click the Save button on the Standard toolbar.

The Save As dialog box opens. In the File Name box, Word suggests a name based on the first line of text in the document.

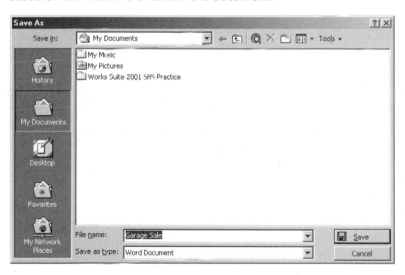

For details about installing the practice files, see "Using the Book's CD-ROM" at the beginning of this book.

11 Make sure the Save In box shows My Documents or browse to the location where you installed this book's practice files.

12   Double-click the Works Suite 2001 SBS Practice folder, and then double-click the Lesson01 folder.

If you did not install this book's practice files or you want to save your work in a different location, browse to the folder you want.

13   In the File Name box, type **My Garage Sale Flyer**.

14   Click Save to save the document.

The Word title bar changes to show the new filename.

15   On the File menu, click Exit.

Word closes, and the Task Launcher is displayed.

If the Task Launcher does not appear, click Microsoft Works Task Launcher on the taskbar.

16   In the Search box, type **recipe**.

17   Click the Search button.

Works lists the search results on the right.

18   Under Search Results, click Recipe Book.

A description of this task appears to the right.

19   Click Start This Task.

The Works Recipe Book Wizard appears and displays options for choosing a style of recipe book. Behind the wizard, Works Database opens and displays the selected recipe style.

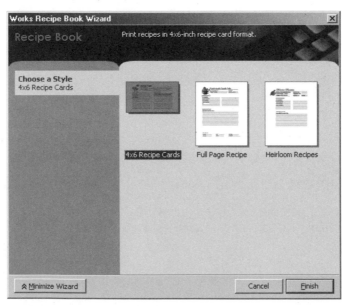

20   Click Full Page Recipe, and then click Finish.

The wizard closes, and Works Database displays a recipe that you can customize.

Notice that even though the recipe book is a Works Database document and the garage sale flyer is a Word document, many of the same toolbar buttons are available. Similar toolbars make it easy to work in different Works programs.

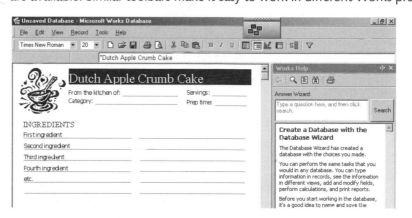

Save

21   To save the recipe book so that you can work on it later, click the Save button on the toolbar.

The Save As dialog box opens.

22   Make sure the Save In box shows My Documents.

23   Double-click the Works Suite 2001 SBS Practice folder, and then double-click the Lesson01 folder.

If you did not install the practice files or you want to save your work in a different location, browse to the folder you want.

24   In the File Name box, type **My Recipe Book**, and then click Save.

The Works Database title bar changes to show the new filename.

Close

25   On the Database title bar, click the Close button.

Works Database and the recipe book close, and the Task Launcher is displayed.

Starting with a Program

When you know which program you want to use to do something, or you just want to start from scratch, you can use the Task Launcher to start a program. In the Task Launcher, the Programs tab lets you go directly to the programs—Word, Works Spreadsheet, Works Database, Works Calendar, Address Book, the Portfolio, and others.

In the Task Launcher, the Programs tab shows you all the programs you can start and also lists tasks associated with the program you select. These are the same tasks that appear on the Tasks tab, organized instead by program. You can use the Programs tab to learn which programs are used for different types of tasks.

The Task Launcher offers an easy way to start a Works program, and that's the method this book uses. But, you can also use the Start menu to start a program. When you click the Start button and point to Programs, the Microsoft Works submenu that appears includes a list of the programs you can open.

In this exercise, you use the Programs tab of the Task Launcher to start Word and then Works Spreadsheet.

Programs

1   In the Task Launcher, click the Programs tab.

All Works programs are listed on the left, and the first program, Word, is selected. Tasks associated with Word appear on the right.

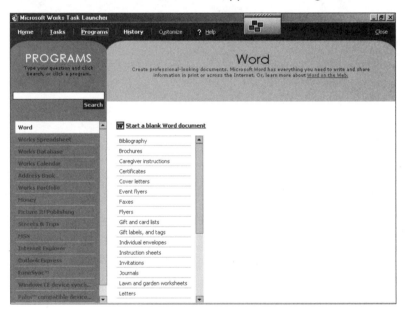

2   Click Start A Blank Word Document.

Word opens in a new window with a blank document.

Toolbars
Menu bar   Title bar

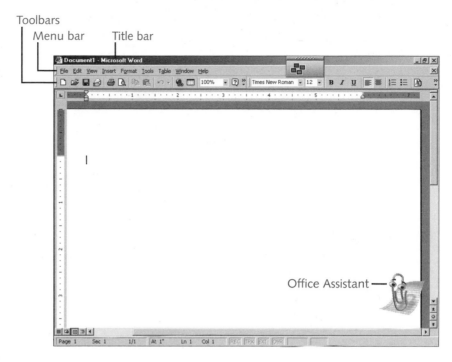

*If the Office
Assistant is not
visible on your
computer, your
screen will not
exactly match
this illustration.*

Close

3   On the Word title bar, click the Close button.

Word closes, and the Programs page of the Task Launcher is displayed.

4   In the list of programs on the left, click Works Spreadsheet.

Tasks associated with Works Spreadsheet are listed on the right.

5   Click Start A Blank Spreadsheet.

Works Spreadsheet opens in a new window with an empty spreadsheet.

Toolbar
Menu bar   Title bar   Works Help

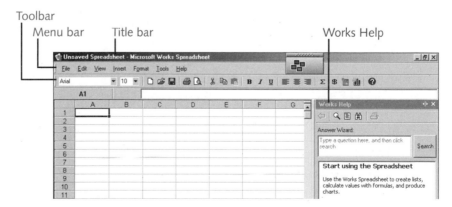

Close

6   On the Works Spreadsheet title bar, click the Close button.

Works Spreadsheet closes, and the Task Launcher is displayed.

Starting from the History Tab

After you create documents with a Works program, you can quickly find them again in the Task Launcher. The History tab lists up to 500 documents. Every time you create a new document with Works, it is added to the History list. When you want to work with a document again, you can click its name in this list to open it.

Date that the document was last saved   Task and program used to create the document

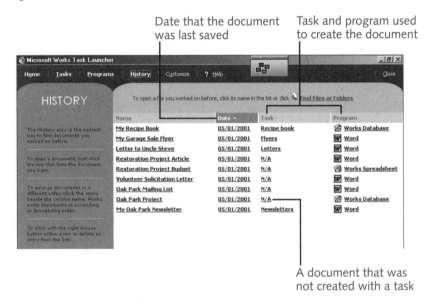

A document that was not created with a task

The entries in the History list are just shortcuts to your documents. The documents themselves are stored on your computer's hard disk in the location you specified when you saved them. When you no longer need to work on a document, you can delete its entry from the History list. Works deletes only the shortcut in the History list, not the document itself.

To make it easier to find documents, especially if you have many entries in the History list, you can sort entries in the list by name, date, task, or program. The History list does not contain those tasks that did not result in a document, such as browsing the Internet or checking e-mail.

In this exercise, you explore the History tab, open a document from the History list, and then delete an entry from the History list.

History

1   In the Task Launcher, click the History tab.

All documents that you have created with Works programs are listed in the order that you created them.

Name	Date ▾	Task	Program
My Recipe Book	05/01/2001	Recipe book	Works Database
My Garage Sale Flyer	05/01/2001	Flyers	W Word

2   To change the order in which the files appear, click the arrow to the right of the Date column header.

Works sorts the files in descending order by date. Now the My Garage Sale Flyer file appears first.

3   Click My Garage Sale Flyer.

Word starts and opens the flyer you saved earlier in this lesson.

Close

4   On the Word title bar, click the Close button.

Word closes, and the History tab of the Task Launcher appears again.

5   In the History list, right-click My Recipe Book.

A shortcut menu appears.

6   Click Delete.

7   In the message box that is displayed, asking if you want to delete this item, click Yes.

Works deletes the shortcut to My Recipe Book but does not delete the document from the Lesson01 folder, where you saved it.

Getting Help

When you don't know how to do something, you can ask Works Help. Works Help is a complete online reference tool with information about all the Works features and how to use them. You can get help by asking the Answer Wizard, scanning the complete table of contents, or searching the index for a topic. Any of these methods can lead you to an answer, so you can use the method that you like best.

When you're working in a Works program, such as Works Spreadsheet, Works Help displays topics about only that program's tasks and features. When you're working in Word, the Office Assistant and Word Help work together to provide answers to your questions. The Office Assistant is intended as a friendly way to find the topic you want in Word Help. If you hide the Office Assistant, you can still display all the topics in Word Help.

In this exercise, you use different methods in Works Help to locate a particular topic. Then you switch to Word to work with the Office Assistant and Word Help.

1 If the Works Help pane is not already visible in the Task Launcher, click Help, and then click Microsoft Works Help.

Works Help appears.

Answer Wizard box —

Help topic —

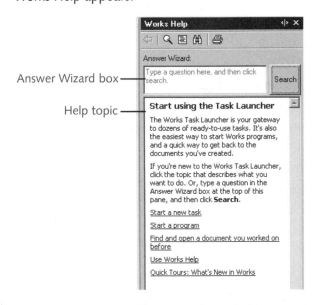

It doesn't matter whether you type uppercase or lowercase letters when you ask the Answer Wizard a question.

2 In the Answer Wizard box, type **how do i open a document?**

3 Click the Search button.

Works displays a list of topics about starting documents.

4 Click Start A Blank Document.

Works displays the Help topic of this name.

5 On the Works Help toolbar, click the Back button.

Works displays the last Help screen you viewed.

Back

6 Click Open A Document You Worked On Before.

Works displays the Help topic.

7   Under the Help topic title, click the blue text *Where are my documents listed?*

Works expands the Help topic with an explanation of the History list.

Resize Help

8   On the Works Help title bar, click the Resize Help button to change the width of the Help pane, and then click the Resize Help button again to restore the original width.

Contents

9   On the Works Help toolbar, click the Contents button.

The Task Launcher table of contents is displayed.

10   Click Find Tasks And Documents, and then click Find Documents.

Works displays a list of Help topics about finding documents.

11   Click Find And Open A Document You Worked On Before.

Works displays the Help topic you displayed earlier when you used the Answer Wizard.

Index

12   On the Works toolbar, click the Index button.

A search box and a list of keywords appear.

13   In the box that says *Type a word to search the index*, type **open**.

As you type, Works searches the keyword list for a match and then displays topics about documents in the Topics Found box.

14   In the Topics Found box, click Open A Document You Worked On Before.

Works displays the Help topic you displayed earlier when you used the Answer Wizard and Help Contents.

15   To compare the Help in Works with the Help in Word, in the History area of the Task Launcher, click My Garage Sale Flyer in the History list.

Word opens with the flyer document you opened in an earlier exercise.

If the Office Assistant is not visible, on the Help menu, click Show The Office Assistant.

16   Click the Office Assistant.

The Office Assistant asks what you would like to do and displays a list of possible tasks based on the current state of the open flyer document.

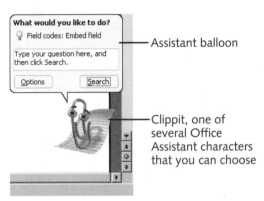

— Assistant balloon

—Clippit, one of several Office Assistant characters that you can choose

17   In the Type Your Question Here box, type **how do i create a letter?** and then click Search.

The Office Assistant displays a list of topics about creating letters.

18   Click Create A Letter.

Word Help opens and displays the Create A Letter topic.

19   On the Word Help toolbar, click the Show button.

Show

The Word Help window expands to show tabs for Contents, Answer Wizard, and Index, just like the options in Works Help.

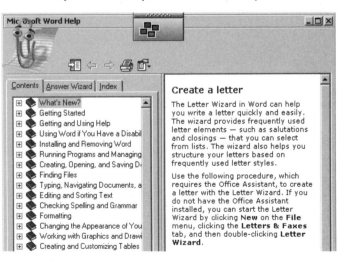

Close

20   On the Word Help title bar, click the Close button.

The Word Help window is closed, and the flyer expands to fill the entire screen. The Office Assistant moves to the corner of the window.

21   On the Help menu, click Hide The Office Assistant.

If the Office Assistant displays a message about turning off the Office Assistant, click No, Just Hide Me.

The Office Assistant is hidden.

22   On the Help menu, click Microsoft Word Help.

The Office Assistant reappears and asks what you would like to do.

23   Click anywhere in the garage sale flyer away from the Office Assistant.

The Assistant balloon goes away, but the Office Assistant remains attentive in the corner of the window.

Changing or Hiding the Office Assistant

The ever-vigilant Office Assistant can be helpful when you're trying to learn a new program. When it is turned on, it monitors your actions in the document and can provide tips for working more efficiently. When you first install Works and Word 2000, the Office Assistant is Clippit, the flexible paper clip. You can choose a different character to act as your assistant. Sometimes, though, you need to see the entire screen or work without interruption. You can turn the Office Assistant off so that it never appears when you work in Word.

To change or turn off the Office Assistant, click the Office Assistant, and then click the Options button. Then:

- If you want to change the character, click the Gallery tab, and then click the Next button. When you see a character you like, click OK.

- If you want to turn off the Office Assistant, click the Options tab, clear the Use The Office Assistant check box, and then click OK.

Lesson Wrap-Up

To finish the lesson:

Close

1   On the Word File menu, click Exit. Or, on the title bar of the Word window, click the Close button.

If a message box appears, asking whether you want to save the changes you made, click No.

Word closes, and the Task Launcher appears.

Close Help

Works Portfolio

To open the Portfolio, click the Programs tab in the Task Launcher, click Works Portfolio, and then click Start Works Portfolio.

2   In the Works Help pane of the Task Launcher click the Close Help button.

The Works Help pane closes.

3   In the Task Launcher, click Close.

4   If you want to close the Portfolio, click to expand it, click the Tasks menu, and then click Close.

The Portfolio closes.

Quick Reference

To start the Task Launcher

●   On the Windows taskbar, click Start, point to Programs, and then click Microsoft Works.

To use the Task Launcher to start a task

1   In the Task Launcher, click the Tasks tab.

2   Click a category on the left, and then click the task you want in the list to the right.

3   Click Start This Task.

To use the Task Launcher to start a program

1   In the Task Launcher, click the Programs tab.

2   In the list of programs on the left, click a program.

3   On the right, click the link to start the program.

To start a Works program without the Task Launcher

●   On the Windows taskbar, click Start, point to Programs, and then click the program you want.

To use the Task Launcher to start Word

1   In the Task Launcher, click the Programs tab.

2   In the list of programs, click Word, and then click Start A Blank Word Document.

To open a document you've already created

1   In the Task Launcher, click the History tab.

2   In the list of documents, click the name of the document you want to open.

To display Works Help

●   Click Help, and then click Microsoft Works Help.

To ask the Answer Wizard for help

1   If the Answer Wizard is not visible, click the Answer Wizard button on the
     Works Help toolbar.

2   In the Answer Wizard box, type your question, and then click Search.

To search the Works Help index for a topic

1   On the Works Help toolbar, click the Index button.

2   In the box at the top, type a keyword, and then click a topic name in the Top-
     ics Found box.

To display the Works Help Contents

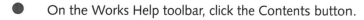

●   On the Works Help toolbar, click the Contents button.

To display the Office Assistant in Word

●   On the Help menu, click Show Office Assistant.

To temporarily hide the Office Assistant in Word

●   On the Help menu, click Hide Office Assistant.

To permanently hide the Office Assistant in Word

1   Click the Office Assistant, and then click the Options button.

2   In the Office Assistant dialog box, click the Options tab, clear the Use The
     Office Assistant check box, and then click OK.

To close the Portfolio

●   Click to expand it, click the Tasks menu, and then click Close.

To open the Portfolio

1   In the Task Launcher, click the Programs tab.

2   In the list of programs, click Works Portfolio, and then click Start Works
     Portfolio.

2

Creating a Letter

In this lesson, you will learn how to:

✔ *Create a document from scratch.*

✔ *Use the Letter Wizard to write a letter.*

✔ *Enter and edit text.*

✔ *Find and replace text.*

✔ *Format the text on a page.*

✔ *Save and print a document.*

**ESTIMATED TIME
35 min.**

Nothing beats a word processing program for typing. Whether you're creating a quick letter or writing your thousand-page memoirs, Microsoft Word can help you organize your thoughts, choose a good-looking document format, and spell and use grammar correctly. Word even checks your typing by fixing some mistakes as you go. It's a powerful program that professionals have used for years, and now Microsoft Works Suite users can take advantage of all that Word offers.

This lesson introduces Word by means of a simple and common task: writing a letter. You'll see how to start from a blank page and get a head start on your letter by using a wizard. Then you'll learn how to enter, edit, and format text and save and print the results.

**Practice files
for the lesson**

This lesson uses the practice files that you installed from this book's CD-ROM. For details about installing the practice files, see "Using the Book's CD-ROM" at the beginning of this book.

Creating a Document

To see a multimedia demo about creating a document using a wizard, double-click the Create Letter icon in the Demos folder on the book's CD-ROM.

People have used Word to write novels, letters, invoices, legal briefs, school reports, and just about anything else you can think to write. Anything you create in Word is a **document**. A highly versatile program, Word can help you start any document with predesigned **templates** and intelligent **wizards** that set up the page layout and formatting for you and sometimes even supply the text. To create a document, all you have to do is type your text.

Many wizards let you specify a **theme**. A theme is a set of unified design elements, such as fonts and colors, that define the overall appearance of a document.

If you like, you can start Word with a blank page—the equivalent of a clean sheet of paper in a typewriter—and immediately begin to type. The blinking vertical line on the page, called the **insertion point**, shows you where the text you type will appear on the page. As a Works user, you can use the Works Task Launcher together with Word to create many types of documents, either from scratch or based on a timesaving template or wizard.

In this exercise, you create a letter using both of these methods. First you start a new, blank document in Word. Then you use the Task Launcher to start the Works Letter Wizard, which prompts you for information and then creates a letter for you in Word.

1   On the taskbar, click the Start button, point to Programs, and then click Microsoft Works.

The Works Task Launcher opens.

Programs

2   Click the Programs tab.

All Works programs are listed in the Task Launcher.

3   In the list of programs, click Word.

Tasks for Word are listed on the right.

---

important

If you installed Microsoft Works 6.0 (rather than Microsoft Works Suite 2001), Microsoft Word does not appear in the Task Launcher. Instead, you'll see the Works Word Processor, which is the program that Works 6.0 uses for word processing tasks. For details about creating a letter using the Works Word Processor, search Works Help for *letter*.

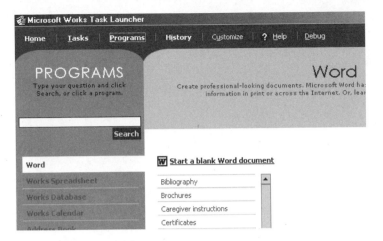

4   Click Start A Blank Word Document.

Word opens with a new, blank document.

If the Office Assistant is disabled on your computer, your screen will not exactly match the following illustration.

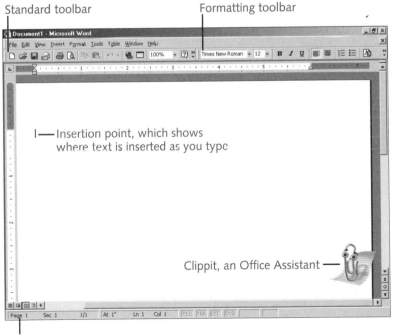

Standard toolbar   Formatting toolbar

I— Insertion point, which shows where text is inserted as you type

Clippit, an Office Assistant —

Status bar

To restore the Office Assistant, click Show The Office Assistant on the Help menu.

Microsoft Works

5   If the Office Assistant appears, on the Help menu, click Hide The Office Assistant.

The Office Assistant goes away. For the purposes of this lesson, the Office Assistant will not be shown in any illustrations.

6   On the taskbar, click Microsoft Works Task Launcher.

The Task Launcher appears.

7   Click the Tasks tab.

Categories of tasks appear on the left, and tasks for the selected category appear on the right.

8   Under Tasks, click Letters & Labels.

Tasks for the Letters & Labels category appear.

9   In the list of tasks, click Letters.

A description of the Letters task appears.

10   Click Start This Task.

The Microsoft Word program window opens, and the Works Letter Wizard is displayed. The wizard asks you to choose a layout.

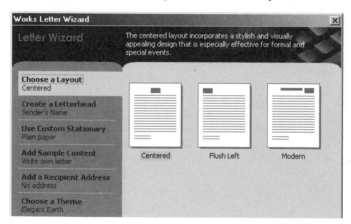

11   Click the Centered layout, and then click Next.

Options for creating a letterhead appear.

12   In the Sender's Name box, select the sample text, and then type **Elizabeth Boyle**.

If you make a mistake as you type the information, press the Backspace key to delete the error, and then type the correct text.

13   In the Return Address box, select the sample text, type **123 South Oak Drive**, press the Enter key, and then type **Sacramento, CA 32607**.

tip

You can click the Address Book button to the right of the Sender's Name box to select contact information that you've already stored in Address Book. For details about Address Book, see Lesson 3, "Keeping Track of Contacts."

14   In the Phone And Fax Numbers box, select the sample text, and then press the Delete key.

15   In the E-Mail Address box, select the sample text, and then press Delete.

16   Click Next.

Options for using custom stationery appear.

17   Keep the current setting to use plain paper, and then click Next.

Options for adding sample content appear.

18   Keep the current setting to write your own letter, and then click Next.

Options for adding a recipient's address appear.

19   Keep the current setting to not include a recipient's address, and then click Next.

Options for a choosing a theme appear.

20   Drag the Font Set slider to the left until the Simple font set is selected, and then drag the Color Set slider to the right until the Summer color set is selected.

21   Click Finish.

Word creates a formatted letter that includes the information you typed. The wizard inserts today's date. Your screen should look similar to the one on the following page.

Creating a Letter

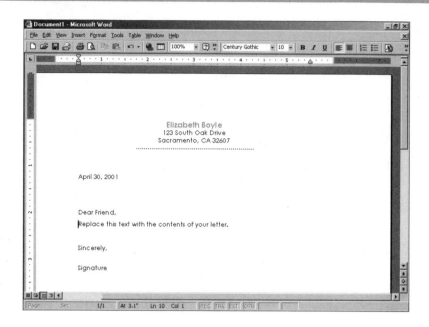

Using Word Menus and Toolbars

Although Microsoft Word contains a great many task-specific commands, you won't see them all at once on the menus and toolbars. Instead, when you first start Word, it displays only the most frequently used commands and toolbar buttons. As you work, Word adds the commands and buttons that you use to personalize the menus and toolbars.

More Buttons

You can expand menus and toolbars to see all the commands and buttons by clicking the arrows located at the bottom of a menu and the More Buttons button at the end of a toolbar. If you stop using a command for a while, Word stops showing it.

In case you're wondering, Word behaves this way for several reasons. By personalizing the menus and toolbars, Word works the way you do. In addition, this behavior keeps the menus and toolbars—and your work area—reasonably uncluttered, which in turn makes it easier to learn and use Word.

If you prefer to work with the full set of menu commands visible at all times, you can specify this option. On the Tools menu, click Customize, and then click the Options tab. Clear the Menus Show Recently Used Commands First check box, and then click OK.

Entering and Editing Text

Typing in Word has definite advantages over using a typewriter. To begin with, Word is designed to correct certain common errors, such as typing *teh* instead of *the*. You may find it a little disconcerting at first to find Word making corrections as you type, but if you're like most people, you'll soon come to rely on it. In addition, Word has a built-in Spelling And Grammar checker. When it is activated, Word underlines potentially misspelled words with a red wavy line and possible grammatical errors with a green wavy line.

For the typos that Word cannot automatically correct, you can always press the Backspace key and then type again. But what if you accidentally delete an entire paragraph? Word lets you undo the damage with the Undo command, which reverses the last change you made.

Making changes to text is called **editing**. When you want to edit something you've typed, you first **select** the text you want to change and then choose an action to work on the selection. For example, to delete a word, you must first select the word and then press Delete.

In this exercise, you type the text of a brief personal letter. Then, rather than type the entire letter, you work with a sample file to practice selecting, editing, and adding text.

important

This exercise requires you to open a sample letter, which you copied to your hard disk when you installed the book's practice files. In the My Documents folder, you will see a folder named Works Suite 2001 SBS Practice, which contains folders of sample files for each lesson.

Right-pointing arrow

1   Move the mouse in the margin to the left of the word *Signature* until you see a right-pointing arrow, and then click once.

The word *Signature* is highlighted, indicating that it is selected.

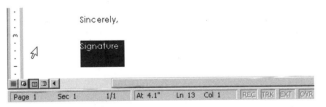

I-beam pointer

2 Press Delete.

The text is removed.

3 Position the pointer (which changes to an I-beam) over the word *Friend*, and then double-click.

The text is selected. Any subsequent text that you type replaces the selected text.

4 Type **Steve**.

If you make a typing mistake, press Backspace to delete it.

5 Drag over the text *Replace this text with the contents of your letter.* to select the line.

6 Press Delete.

The text is deleted.

7 On the Standard toolbar, click the Undo button.

The text is reinserted.

Undo

8 On the Edit menu, click Redo Clear.

The text is again deleted.

To undo the last several actions you performed, repeatedly click the Undo button or press Ctrl+Z.

tip

If the Redo Clear command is not listed on the Edit menu, you probably haven't used the Redo command recently. On the Edit menu, click the down arrow at the bottom of the menu to expand it, and then click Redo Clear. Word deletes the text and adds the Redo command to your Edit menu.

9 Type **hello** and then press the Spacebar.

Word automatically replaces the lowercase "h" with an uppercase "H" to start the sentence.

10 Type **from sunny California!** and then press Enter.

When you press Enter, Word starts a new paragraph. Instead of typing the rest of the letter, next you'll open a sample letter file.

11 To open the sample letter, click the Open button on the Standard toolbar.

The Open dialog box appears.

Open

12 Make sure the Look In box shows My Documents.

*For details
about install-
ing the prac-
tice files, see
"Using the
Book's
CD-ROM" at
the beginning
of this book.*

13 Double-click the Works Suite 2001 SBS Practice folder, and then double-click
the Lesson02 folder.

If you do not see Works Suite 2001 SBS Practice in the list of folders, browse
to the location where you installed the practice files.

14 Click Letter To Uncle Steve.doc, and then click Open.

A complete draft of the letter opens in a new window. Word indicates sus-
pected spelling and grammar errors with wavy underlines. On the Windows
taskbar, at least two Word tasks now appear. Your screen should look similar
to the following illustration.

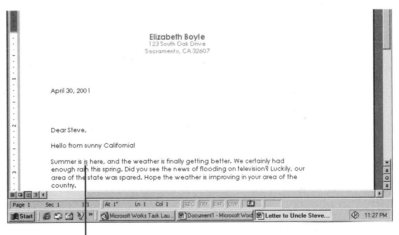

Word indicates possible errors with wavy underlines.

15   In the second paragraph, right-click the word *is* that appears with a wavy red underline.

A shortcut menu appears with commands for correcting spelling errors.

16   Click Delete Repeated Word.

Word corrects the duplicate word by deleting it.

17   Drag the scroll bar down to view the bottom of the letter, click just to the left of the word *Look* with the I-beam pointer, and then press Enter.

Word inserts a new line.

18   Press the Up Arrow key.

The insertion point moves to the start of the blank line.

19   Type **As we discussed, I'm sending my special order:** and then press Enter.

20   Type **Organic carrots** and press Enter, type **Ruby chard** and press Enter, and then type **Baby corn**.

The new lines of text appear above the paragraph that starts with the word *Look*. Your screen should look similar to the following illustration.

> know, and we can converse online! How exciting! My e-mail address
> Liz@sample.microsoft.com.
>
> As we discussed, I'm sending my special order:
>
> Organic carrots
>
> Ruby chard
>
> Baby corn
>
> Look forward to hearing from you. Say hello to the kids!

tip

Word's ability to correct misspelled words as you type is called the **AutoCorrect** feature. You can customize AutoCorrect to recognize the words that you tend to type incorrectly and delete any entries that you do not want AutoCorrect to change. You can even have AutoCorrect recognize abbreviations, such as your initials, so that it will complete the word or phrase for you. To see the AutoCorrect entries, on the Tools menu, click AutoCorrect. For more information, search Word Help for *AutoCorrect*.

Finding and Replacing Text

With Word, it's easy to locate and edit specific words or phrases in your document. You can even find all instances of a particular word or phrase and change each instance to something else. For example, you can locate every occurrence of *Fred* in a document and change it to *Barney*. In a long document particularly, this ability to find and replace text is a big time-saver.

In this exercise, you search for all instances of a word so that you can replace the text.

1   Hold down the Ctrl key, and then press the Home key.

Word moves the insertion point to the top of the document.

2   On the Edit menu, click Find.

The Find And Replace dialog box appears.

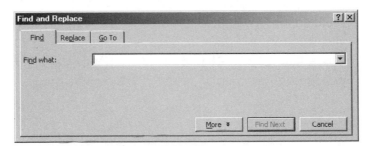

3   In the Find What box, type **PC**, and then click Find Next.

In the document behind the Find And Replace dialog box, Word finds the first instance of the word *PC* and selects it.

4   Click the Replace tab.

Options for replacing the found text are displayed.

5   Click the More button.

Search options appear in the Find And Replace dialog box, and the More button changes to the Less button.

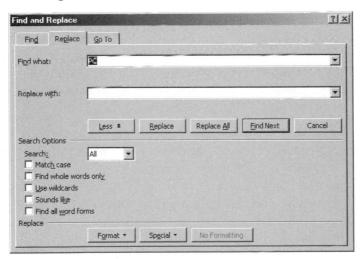

6   In the Replace With box, type **computer**.

7   Select the Match Case check box.

This option ensures that Word will find only the instances of the word *PC* that are uppercase.

8   Click Replace.

Word replaces the first instance of the word *PC* with *computer* and then moves to the next instance.

9   Click Replace.

Word displays a message box indicating that it has finished searching the document.

10   Click OK, and then click Close in the Find And Replace dialog box.

Word moves the insertion point to the top of the document

tip

In addition to text, Word can search for all kinds of special characters and formats, such as the tab character or a word formatted as italic. These advanced capabilities are especially useful in documents that are longer or more complex than this lesson's letter. For details, search Word Help for *finding and replacing text*.

Formatting Text

The visual design that a document uses is its **format**, which includes the style and layout of the text on the page. When you start Word with a template or a wizard, as you did by using the Letter Wizard, Word formats the new document for you using the options you selected. Even so, you can apply different formats to personalize your document. For example, you can change the way text looks by applying a different font or color, and you can adjust the margins and other page layout settings.

More Buttons

The easiest way to format your document is to use the buttons on the Formatting toolbar. Normally, this toolbar is docked at the top of the Word window. When you first install Word, some of the formatting buttons might not be visible until you click the More Buttons button. The buttons on the Formatting toolbar give the same result as the commands on the Format menu and provide a quick way to change the font; apply a style, such as boldface or italics; format a list with numbers or bullet characters; indent paragraphs; and so on.

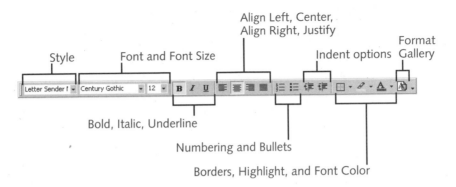

Style   Font and Font Size   Align Left, Center, Align Right, Justify   Indent options   Format Gallery

Bold, Italic, Underline

Numbering and Bullets

Borders, Highlight, and Font Color

Word provides some very sophisticated formatting options that are described in later lessons, such as multiple-column layouts for newsletters and styles for Web pages. In this exercise, you customize the letter's format by choosing a different font and color for the letterhead, creating a bulleted list, and changing the page margins.

1   At the top of the letter, select the words *Elizabeth Boyle*.

Font

2   On the Formatting toolbar, click the Font arrow.

A list of the fonts installed on your computer appears.

3   Scroll in the list, and then click Papyrus or another available font.

Word formats the text using the Papyrus font. The name remains selected.

Font Color

4   On the Formatting toolbar, click the Font Color arrow, and then click blue.

Word changes the text color to blue. The name remains selected.

important

If the Font Color button is not visible, click More Buttons on the Formatting toolbar to see the Font Color button.

More Buttons

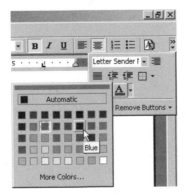

5   Click anywhere on the screen to cancel the selection.

The newly formatted letterhead should look like this:

6   Scroll down, position the mouse to the left of the words *Organic carrots*, and then select this line and the next two lines.

The three lines are selected.

Bullets

7   On the Formatting toolbar, click the Bullets button.

Word formats each line as an item in a bulleted list. The lines remain selected.

8   On the Format menu, click Bullets And Numbering.

The Bullets And Numbering dialog box appears and displays the Bulleted tab.

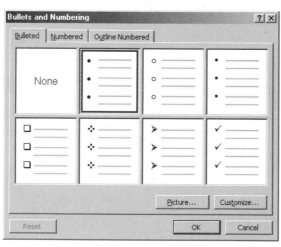

9   Click the diamond style bullet shown in the bottom row (second option from the left), and then click OK.

Word formats the bullet style to reflect your new choice.

10 To adjust the page margins, on the File menu, click Page Setup.

The Page Setup dialog box appears and displays the Margins tab.

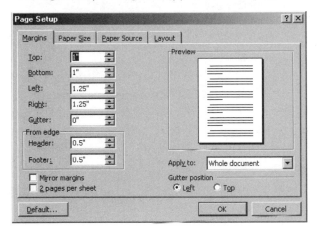

11 In the Left box, click the up arrow three times to increase the left margin to 1.5".

In the Preview area, the picture changes to show what the document will look like with the new setting.

12 In the Right box, repeat the previous step to increase the right margin to 1.5".

The Preview area reflects the new setting.

13 Click the Paper Size tab.

You can use this tab to change paper size and orientation.

14 Under Orientation, note that the current setting specifies Portrait, so the short edge of the paper is the top of the page.

If you wanted to print a document that was wider than it was long, you would use the Landscape option.

15 Click the Paper Source tab.

You can use this tab to specify the feed tray on your printer.

16 Click the Layout tab.

You can use this tab to lay out more complex types of documents.

17 Click OK.

Word applies the new margins to the letter.

Saving and Printing a Document

For most documents, saving and printing your work are key steps. As you create or change a document, your work is held in the computer's temporary memory. To store your document for future use, you must give it a name and save it to a hard disk, a floppy disk, or a network drive. The first time you save a new document, you will give it a name and specify where you want to store it. After that, Word automatically updates the file in that location each time you save it.

Printing a document first requires that you have a printer installed on your system. (If you don't, see the sidebar "Installing a Printer" later in this section.) To make sure your document looks the way you want before you commit your printer paper and toner, you can preview it in the Print Preview window. Unless you have a printer capable of printing color, you will not be able to print the lovely colors that you add to documents.

In this exercise, you save the letter you modified in the previous exercises with a new name. You store it in a subfolder of the Works Suite 2001 SBS Practice folder on your hard disk. Then you preview and print the letter.

1   On the File menu, click Save As.

The Save As dialog box opens.

2   In the File Name box, type **Letter to Uncle Steve New**.

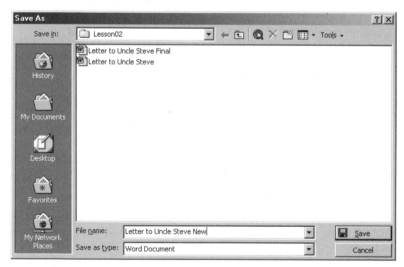

3   In the Save In box, make sure that the Lesson02 folder is selected.

If you want to save your work in a different location, browse to the folder you want.

4 Click Save to save the document with the new name.

The Word title bar changes to show the new filename.

Print Preview

5 On the Standard toolbar, click the Print Preview button.

important

If the Print Preview button is not visible, click More Buttons on the Standard toolbar to see the Print Preview button. You can also click Print Preview on the File menu.

More Buttons

The letter appears in the Preview window as shown. The Print Preview toolbar is displayed, which contains buttons you can use while previewing a document.

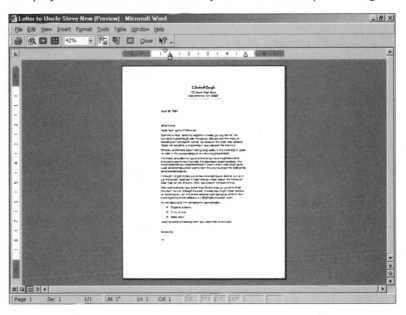

Zoom In pointer

6 To zoom in for a better view, position the pointer over the text in the document, and then click.

The view is magnified. The pointer changes to the Zoom Out pointer.

Zoom Out pointer

7 Click the text to zoom out.

8 On the Print Preview toolbar, click the Close button.

Print preview closes, and the document is displayed in print layout view.

tip

Print layout is just one of several **views** that you can use in Word to display your document in different ways. For example, Word includes the following views: normal, Web layout, print layout, and outline. For more information about Word views, search Word Help for *views*.

9   On the File menu, click Print.

The Print dialog box appears.

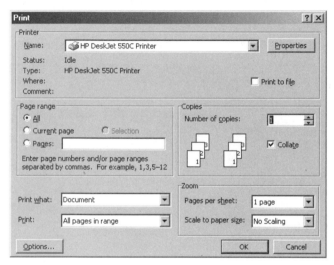

10   Click the Name arrow, and then click a printer.

If you have only one printer, you won't see any other options in the Name box.

11   Under Print Range, keep the current option (All).

All the pages of the letter will be printed.

12   Click OK.

Word prints your letter.

Installing a Printer

When you buy a printer, the manufacturer typically provides installation instructions. After you've plugged the printer into the appropriate port and wall outlet, you must tell Windows where to find it.

1 On the Windows taskbar, click the Start button, point to Settings, and then click Printers.

The Printers window opens.

2 Double-click the Add Printer icon.

The Add Printer Wizard appears.

3 Follow the instructions in the wizard.

On a typical home computer, you would choose Local Printer on the first wizard screen, identify the manufacturer and model on the next screen, specify the computer port that you connected the printer to, provide a name for the printer as you want it to appear in other programs, and then finish. You might need to insert your Windows CD-ROM or the disk provided by the printer's manufacturer to complete the installation procedure.

Add Printer

Lesson Wrap-Up

To finish the lesson:

1 To close all the Word windows, on the File menu, click Exit.

If a message box appears, asking whether you want to save the changes you made to Letter To Uncle Steve New, click Yes.

If a message box appears, asking whether you want to save the changes you made to Document1, click No.

Word closes, and the Task Launcher appears.

2 In the Task Launcher, click the Close button on the title bar.

Close

If the Task Launcher does not appear, click Microsoft Works Task Launcher on the taskbar.

Quick Reference

To start Word and create a new document from scratch

Programs

1   In the Task Launcher, click the Programs tab.

2   Under Programs, click Word, and then click Start A Blank Word Document.

To create a letter using the Letter Wizard

Tasks

1   In the Task Launcher, click the Tasks tab.

2   Under Tasks, click Letters & Labels, and then in the list of tasks, click Letters.

3   Click Start This Task.

4   In the Works Letter Wizard, follow the instructions on the screen, and then click Finish.

To select text

1   Position the pointer to the left of the text.

2   Drag to the right.

To delete text

1   Select the text you want to delete.

2   Press the Delete key.

To reverse your last action

●   On the Edit menu, click Undo. Or click the Undo button on the Standard toolbar.

To restore the last action you reversed

●   On the Edit menu, click Redo. Or click the Redo button on the Standard toolbar.

To scroll through the pages of a long document

●   Slide the scroll bar.

To find text

1   On the Edit menu, click Find.

2   Type an entry in the Find What box, and then click Find Next.

To replace text

1   On the Edit menu, click Replace.

2   Type an entry in the Find What box, type an entry in the Replace With box, and then click one of the replacement buttons.

To expand a menu

● At the bottom of the menu, click the down arrow.

To change the font

1 Select the text you want to change.

2 On the Formatting toolbar, click the Font arrow, and then click a font.

To change the font color

1 Select the text you want to change.

2 On the Formatting toolbar, click the Font Color arrow, and then click a color.

To format text as a bulleted list

1 Select the text you want to format.

2 On the Formatting toolbar, click the Bullets button.

To adjust page margins and layout

1 On the File menu, click Page Setup.

2 On the Margins tab, specify top, bottom, left, and right margins.

3 On the Paper Size tab, specify Portrait or Landscape orientation.

4 Specify other options as required, and then click OK.

To save a new document

1 On the Standard toolbar, click the Save button.

2 Type a filename and a location, and then click Save.

To preview a document before printing

● On the Standard toolbar, click the Print Preview button.

To print a document

● On the File menu, click Print. Or click the Print button on the Standard toolbar.

Creating a Letter

LESSON

3

Keeping Track of Contacts

ESTIMATED TIME 20 min.

In this lesson, you will learn how to:
- ✔ *Store people's contact information in Address Book.*
- ✔ *Sort and organize contacts.*
- ✔ *Use identities to share contacts.*
- ✔ *Print contact information.*

These days, when people tell you how to contact them, the information often includes multiple telephone and cell phone numbers as well as street and e-mail addresses. That's a lot to keep track of, but Windows Address Book can help. When you store your contact information online, you get all the usual advantages of using a computer to organize information. For example, it's quick to search for one person among many, it's easy to change someone's information, and contacts are organized in a consistent way. In addition, you can share the information—that is, when you store contacts in Address Book, the information is accessible from other programs, such as Microsoft Works Calendar and Microsoft Outlook Express, as well as to other people who use your computer.

In this lesson, you'll learn how to enter, organize, and print your contacts, as well as share Address Book with other users of your computer.

 Practice files for the lesson This lesson uses the practice files that you installed from this book's CD-ROM. For details about installing the practice files, see "Using the Book's CD-ROM" at the beginning of this book.

Storing Contact Information

Any person you add to Address Book is a **contact**. In addition to addresses, Address Book can store home and business information, phone and fax numbers, conferencing information, instant messaging addresses, and personal information such as birthdays and anniversaries. You set up your list of contacts in Address Book by adding new names and entering information. After you add a contact to Address Book, you can easily add to and revise the information.

In this exercise, you start Works and open Address Book, add new contact information for Steve Alboucq, and then edit that contact.

> ### important
> This lesson assumes that your Address Book is empty. If you already have contacts listed in your Address Book, the illustrations will not match what you see. You will not lose your contact information by following the steps in these exercises, but you will end up with extra contacts, which you can remove (as described later in this lesson).

1   On the taskbar, click the Start button, point to Programs, and then click Microsoft Works.

The Works Task Launcher opens.

2   Click the Programs tab.

All Works programs are listed in the Task Launcher.

3   Click Address Book.

Tasks for Address Book are listed on the right.

4   Click Start Address Book.

Address Book opens.

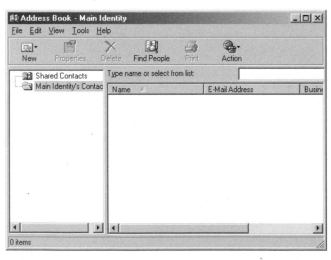

New

5 On the toolbar, click the New button, and then click New Contact.

The Properties dialog box appears and displays the Name tab.

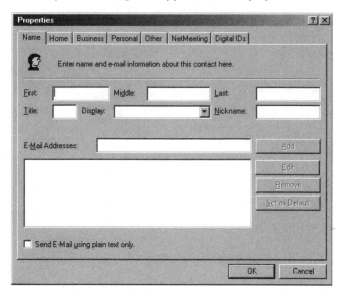

6 In the First box, type **Steve**.

As you type, the name also appears in the Display box. This is the name that Address Book will display in the list of contacts and elsewhere. You can change the display name by typing a different name in the Display box or by selecting a name from the drop-down list.

7 In the Last box, type **Alboucq**.

8 In the E-Mail Addresses box, type **steve@sample.microsoft.com**, and then click Add.

The e-mail address is added to the list.

tip

If a contact has more than one e-mail address, such as one for business and one for home, you can add each one in the E-Mail Addresses box. Use the Set As Default button to select one as the address to use when sending e-mail messages.

9 Click OK.

Steve Alboucq now appears in the list of contact names. Your screen should look something like this:

Built-in folders. Click to display contacts in the folder.

List of contacts

tip

If your Address Book doesn't look like the illustration, make sure it uses Folders And Groups view. To display this view, on the View menu, click Folders And Groups. Then make sure the Main Identity's Contacts folder is selected.

10 In the Address Book list, double-click the name Steve Alboucq.

The Steve Alboucq Properties dialog box appears and opens to the Summary tab.

11 Click the Home tab.

The Home tab displays options for storing home information for this contact.

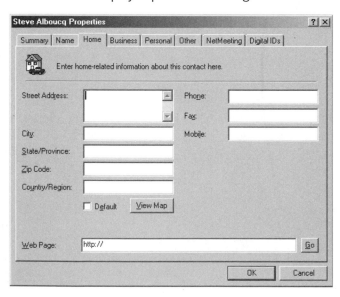

Press the Tab key to move quickly from one field to the next.

12 In the Street Address box, type **4567 Main St.**

13 In the City box, type **Buffalo.**

14 In the State/Province box, type **NY**.

15 In the Zip Code box, type **98052.**

16 In the Phone box, type **(000) 555-0189.**

17 Click OK.

The Properties dialog box for Steve Alboucq is updated.

> ## tip
> If your contact information includes a street address and you have Internet access, you can easily display a map of that address. On the Home or Business tab of a contact's Properties dialog box, click the View Map button to open Expedia Maps in your browser. A printable street map will pinpoint the contact's address.

Sorting Contacts

You can change the order in which Address Book displays names and information. Address Book typically sorts contacts in alphabetical order by first name. You can sort by last name instead, or list the contacts in descending order (Z to A). You can also change the order of the columns. Address Book displays Name, E-Mail, Business Phone, and Home Phone in that order unless you rearrange the columns.

In this exercise, you'll practice sorting a list of contacts. For the purposes of this exercise, you will import contacts from the Addresses.wab file that you installed from this book's CD-ROM.

> ## tip
> The following five steps are designed only to provide sample contacts for you to work with and are not steps you would typically perform while working in Address Book.

1 On the File menu, point to Import, and then click Address Book (WAB).

The Select Address Book File To Import From dialog box appears.

2 Make sure the Look In box shows My Documents.

3   Double-click the Works Suite 2001 SBS Practice folder, and then double-click the Lesson03 folder.

For details about installing the practice files, see "Using the Book's CD-ROM" at the beginning of this book.

If you do not see Works Suite 2001 SBS Practice in the list of folders, browse to the location where you installed the practice files.

4   Select Addresses.wab, and then click Open.

A message box notifies you when the import process is complete.

5   Click OK.

The new contacts are added to Address Book, which now looks something like this:

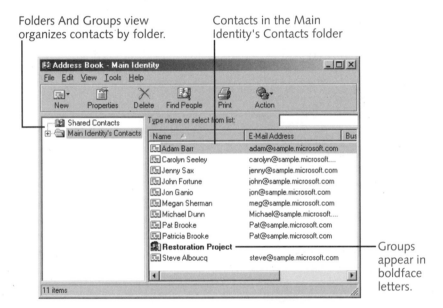

Folders And Groups view organizes contacts by folder.

Contacts in the Main Identity's Contacts folder

Groups appear in boldface letters.

---

tip

If you cannot see all of the Address Book columns, drag a side of the Address Book window to make it wider.

---

6   To change how contact names are sorted, click the Name heading two times.

Each time you click, Address Book changes the sort order of the list of names. The arrow beside Name shows whether the list is in ascending (A to Z) or descending (Z to A) order.

The names are displayed in ascending order by last name.

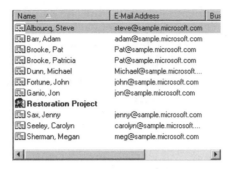

7   Click the Name column heading two more times.

The names are displayed in the original ascending order by first name. You can see that there are two entries for the same person: Patricia Brooke and Pat Brooke.

8   To remove the duplicate contact, in the list of contacts, click Pat Brooke to select the entry.

9   Click the Delete button on the toolbar.

10   Click Yes in the message box asking if you want to delete.

The contact is removed.

tip

After completing this lesson, use the technique in steps 8 through 10 to remove the fictional contacts from your Address Book.

Organizing Contacts

To find and use contacts more easily, you can organize them in a couple of different ways. When you want to communicate with a particular set of your contacts at once, you can organize contacts into a **group** (also known as an "alias" in some programs). Then, anytime you want to send e-mail to everyone in the group, just use the group name instead of typing each contact individually. For example, let's say that you plan to send e-mail frequently to four people in your Address Book to notify them of a project that you're all working on. You can create a group that contains their names.

You can create as many groups as you like. A contact can belong to more than one group. If a contact is no longer associated with a group you've created, you can remove the contact from the group without deleting the contact's information.

Keeping Track of Contacts   3

You can also organize contacts into **subfolders**. Address Book has two folders, which can't be deleted: Shared Contacts and Main Identity's Contacts. As the main user of Address Book, you are the main identity, and so your contacts are stored in the Main Identity's Contacts folder. To further organize a very long list of contacts, you can add a subfolder within the top-level folders and move contacts into it. For example, you can create a subfolder called Soccer and then move all the contacts from your daughter's soccer league into it. That way, when you click the Soccer folder, you'll see a list of just the league participants.

In this exercise, you create a group (alias) for the members of the Oak Park restoration project and then delete the duplicate group, Restoration Project, that was imported with the sample contacts. Next, you create a subfolder in which to store the contact information for the members of the Oak Park restoration project.

New

1   On the toolbar, click the New button, and then click New Group.

The Properties dialog box appears and displays the Group tab.

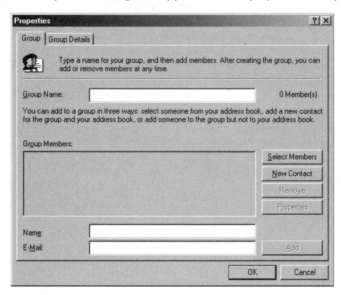

2   In the Group Name box, type **Oak Park Project**.

3   Click the Select Members button.

The Select Group Members dialog box appears.

4   In the list of contacts, click Carolyn Seeley, and then click the Select button.

The name Carolyn Seeley appears in the Members box.

Pressing the Ctrl key while you click lets you select multiple items in a list.

5   In the list of contacts, click Jenny Sax, and then hold down the Ctrl key while you click Megan Sherman, Michael Dunn, and Patricia Brooke.

The four names are selected.

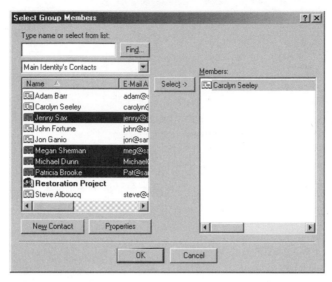

6   Click the Select button.

The four names are added to the Members box.

7   Click OK to close the Select Group Members dialog box.

The Oak Park Project Properties dialog box appears and lists the group members.

8   Click OK.

Address Book creates the group and displays its members as follows:

When a group name is selected ...

... the group members are displayed.

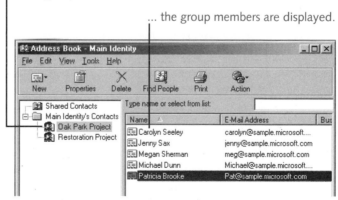

9   Click the Main Identity's Contacts folder.

The complete list of contacts appears, including the Oak Park Project group that you just created.

In Address Book, groups are always displayed in boldface type.

10 To delete a contact from a group, in the list of contacts, click Oak Park Project.

Keeping Track of Contacts   3

11   On the toolbar, click the Properties button.

The Oak Park Project Properties dialog box appears.

12   In the Group Members list, click Patricia Brooke.

13   Click the Remove button.

14   Click OK.

The contact is removed from the group, but the individual entry for the contact remains in your Address Book.

15   Click Restoration Project.

When you imported the sample contacts, you also imported this group. The contacts in this group duplicate the Oak Park Project group that you created.

16   Click the Delete button on the toolbar and click Yes in the message box that is displayed.

The Restoration Project group is deleted, but not the contact information for its members.

17   To create a subfolder and move contacts into it, on the toolbar, click the New button, and then click New Folder.

The Properties dialog box appears.

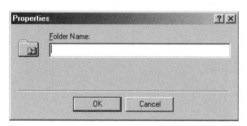

18   In the Folder Name box, type **Oak Park Project Members**, and then click OK.

Under the Main Identity's Contacts folder, Address Book creates an Oak Park Project Members subfolder and selects it. Because this folder has no contacts in it, the contacts list on the right is empty.

19   Click the Main Identity's Contacts folder.

The list of contacts appears on the right.

20   In the list of contacts, click Carolyn Seeley, and then hold down the Ctrl key while you click Jenny Sax, Megan Sherman, and Michael Dunn.

The four contacts are selected.

21   Release the Ctrl key, and then drag the selection to the Oak Park Project Members subfolder.

The contacts are moved into the Oak Park Project Members subfolder.

22   Click the Oak Park Project Members subfolder.

The selected contacts are listed on the right.

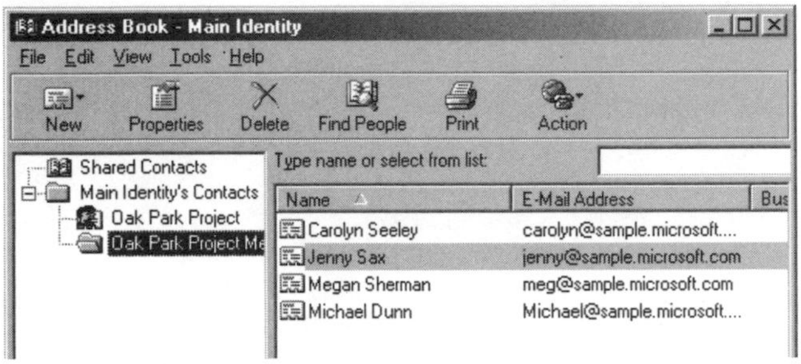

23 Click the Main Identity's Contacts folder.

All the contacts are listed, minus the ones you moved into the Oak Park Project Members subfolder.

Sharing Contacts

When you use Address Book to keep track of contacts, you can share the information you've entered in ways you cannot do with a traditional book-style address book. To begin with, you can share the Address Book program itself with other people using the same computer. Each person can create a unique **identity** to use when he or she is working in Address Book. By logging on with an identity, you see your own e-mail and contacts but not other people's. For example, on a home computer shared by a family, Elizabeth and her son Adam can work in Address Book under their own identities to maintain their contact folders separately.

All the contacts and groups you've created so far are stored in the Main Identity's Contacts folder, which appears on the left side of the Address Book window. Address Book creates this folder for you, the "main identity" using the program. Address Book also creates a Shared Contacts folder. When you want to share your contacts with other Address Book users, you move or copy the contacts to this folder, which everyone can view.

When you create an identity, you can use your own name or assume a mysterious alias, but in any case, each identity has its own contacts folder.

In this exercise, you'll create an identity for Adam and identify yourself as the main identity in Address Book.

1 On the File menu, click Switch Identity.

The Switch Identities dialog box appears.

Keeping Track of Contacts

3

tip
The Switch Identity command does not appear on the File menu if you opened Address Book from within Outlook Express.

2   Click the Manage Identities button.

The Manage Identities dialog box appears.

3   Click the New button.

The New Identity dialog box appears.

4   In the Type Your Name box, type **Adam**, and then click OK.

The Identity Added dialog box appears and prompts you to switch to the new identity.

5   Click No.

The new identity is added to the list in the Manage Identities dialog box.

6   Under the Use This Identity When Starting A Program check box, make sure that Main Identity appears, and then click Close.

The Switch Identities dialog box appears.

7   In the Switch Identities box, make sure that Main Identity is selected, and then click OK.

Address Book now recognizes two user identities, Main Identity and Adam. Because the current identity is still Main Identity, you cannot see Adam's contacts folder.

8   To share a contact with another Address Book identity, in the list of contacts, click Steve Alboucq to select the entry.

9 Drag Steve Alboucq into the Shared Contacts folder.

The contact information is removed from your folder and added to the Shared Contacts folder.

If you cannot see the Shared Contacts folder on the left, on the View menu, click Folders And Groups.

10 To switch to Adam's identity and see the shared contact, on the File menu, click Switch Identity.

The Switch Identities dialog box appears.

11 In the list, click Adam, and then click OK.

The title bar of Address Book changes to "Address Book – Adam" to indicate that Adam is the current identity.

Also, Address Book displays the Adam's Contacts folder. Because it contains no contacts, the list on the right is empty.

12 Click the Shared Contacts folder.

The entry for Steve Alboucq appears in the list of contacts on the right.

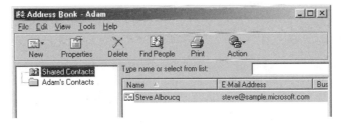

13 On the File menu, click Switch Identity.

The Switch Identities dialog box appears.

14 In the list, select Main Identity, and then click OK.

Address Book displays the Main Identity's Contacts folder.

Using Identities

Creating an identity allows you to share your computer and e-mail with other people. If you used previous versions of Outlook Express, you might have set up user profiles to distinguish among multiple users. Identities have the same purpose. When each user of the computer has his or her own identity, Address Book and Outlook Express display information just for that person. When you log on using identities, you can see your own e-mail and contacts.

In this lesson, you created a new identity for Adam and then switched to this identity. When you switch identities, Address Book and Outlook Express use the new identity until you switch back.

Printing Contacts

Although an address book program offers features that a traditional address book does not, you still sometimes need to see the information in print form. For example, you can print the contents of your Address Book to tuck into your day organizer or post beside the phone. When you want to take your contact information with you, you can print all or part of your Address Book in one of three styles:

- **Memo** prints all the information that you have entered for selected contacts.
- **Business Card** prints only the business information that you entered for selected contacts.
- **Phone Number** prints the name and all phone numbers that you entered for selected contacts.

Address Book formats the printed version for you and sorts the names in the same order that you display them. For the purposes of this lesson, you'll print a single contact's information and then the names and phone numbers of just the people working on the Oak Park restoration project.

1   Click the Shared Contacts folder.

   Address Book displays the shared list of contacts.

2   In the list of contacts, click Steve Alboucq.

3   On the toolbar, click the Print button.

   The Print dialog box appears.

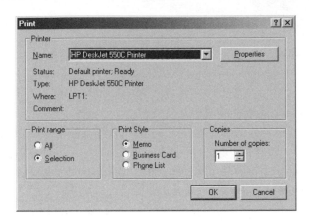

4   Under Print Range, keep the current setting, Selection.

This option prints just the name that you selected.

5   Under Print Style, keep the current setting, Memo.

Address Book will print all the information entered for Steve Alboucq.

6   Click OK.

Address Book formats and prints Steve Alboucq's contact information.

7   To print selected phone numbers from Address Book, click the Oak Park Project Members subfolder.

The contacts for the project are displayed on the right.

8   In the list of contacts, click Carolyn Seeley, and then hold down the Shift key while you click Michael Dunn.

All the names are selected.

9   On the toolbar, click the Print button.

The Print dialog box appears.

10 Under Print Range, keep the current setting, Selection.

Address Book will print just the names you selected.

11 Under Print Style, click Phone List.

Address Book will print a list of names and phone numbers.

12 Click OK.

Address Book formats and prints the selected names and phone numbers.

tip

To print a memo, business cards, or phone numbers for all your contacts, click the Print button, make sure that the All option is selected under Print Range, choose a print style, and then click OK.

Lesson Wrap-Up

To finish the lesson:

Delete

1   To delete the fictional contacts from your list of contacts, click a name to select the entry, and then click the Delete button on the toolbar.

The contact name is removed.

Close

2   On the File menu, click Exit. Or, on the title bar of the Address Book window, click the Close button.

Address Book closes, and the Works Task Launcher appears.

If the Task Launcher does not appear, click Microsoft Works Task Launcher on the taskbar.

3   Click the Close button on the title bar.

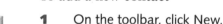

Quick Reference

To add a new contact

New

1   On the toolbar, click New.

2   Click New Contact.

3   Enter the contact's information on the Properties tabs.

To edit contact information

●   In the list, double-click a contact, and then edit the information.

To delete a contact

Delete

●   Click a contact in the list, and then click Delete on the toolbar.

To change how contacts are sorted in the list

●   Click a column heading above the list of contacts.

To create a group

New

1   On the toolbar, click New.

2   Click New Group.

3   Name the group and add members.

To delete a group

●   Click a group name in the list, and then click Delete on the toolbar.

Delete

To create an identity

1   On the File menu, click Switch Identity.

2   Click Manage Identities, and then define properties.

To create a subfolder

1   On the toolbar, click New.

2   Click New Folder.

3   Type a folder name.

To move contacts to a subfolder

1   In the list, hold down Ctrl while you click the contacts that you want.

2   Drag the contacts into the subfolder.

To share contacts with other identities

●   Drag a contact from your folder into the Shared Contacts folder.

To print information for selected contacts

1   In the list, click the contacts that you want.

2   On the toolbar, click Print.

3   Choose the print style you want.

To print information for all contacts

1   On the toolbar, click Print.

2   For the Print Range, select All.

3   Choose the print style that you want.

4

Communicating on the Internet

ESTIMATED TIME 35 min.

In this lesson, you will learn how to:

✔ *Use Microsoft Internet Explorer to communicate on the Internet.*

✔ *Find people and information on the Internet.*

✔ *Personalize Internet Explorer.*

✔ *Change security settings in Internet Explorer.*

✔ *Use Microsoft Outlook Express.*

✔ *Send and receive e-mail messages.*

The Internet delivers a wealth of information to homes and offices everywhere. Microsoft Works can help you take advantage of this rich and sometimes overwhelming resource. As a research tool, the Internet lets you access information on just about any topic. Yet the Internet is larger than the information it hosts. It provides global lines of communication that enable people to send e-mail messages at any time to anyone. Together with Microsoft Internet Explorer and Microsoft Outlook Express, the Internet connects you to people, places, and things around the world.

This lesson introduces you to the rapidly changing world of the Internet and the tools in Works that can help you find what, or whom, you're looking for.

important

This lesson assumes that your computer has access to the Internet and that you have an e-mail account provided through an Internet service provider (ISP).

Practice files for the lesson

This lesson uses the practice files that you installed from this book's CD-ROM. For details about installing the practice files, see "Using the Book's CD-ROM" at the beginning of this book.

What Is the Internet?

Everyone is talking about the Web these days, and with good reason. The World Wide Web, or Web for short, is part of the Internet, a vast global network of computers that are physically connected to one another. The Internet provides the computers and cables that deliver the information—text, images, sounds, and videos—that embodies the Web.

When most people use the Internet, they are really viewing **Web pages** with a **Web browser**. A Web page is a document written in Hypertext Markup Language, or HTML, that can be displayed in graphical format by a program called a Web browser, or simply a browser. For example, Microsoft Internet Explorer is a browser. You can use Internet Explorer to open any HTML document stored on your computer, but to view Web pages, the computer must have an established Internet connection.

When you browse a collection of related Web pages, such as those at *http://www. microsoft.com*, you are viewing a **Web site**. Typically, the first page you see when you go to a Web site is its **home page**. Your browser can also have a home page, which you can specify. A browser's home page is simply the page you see when you first start the browser. When a Web site, such as *http://www.msn.com*, acts as a gateway to other Web sites, it is sometimes referred to as a **portal**.

The unique value that Works brings to your Web forays is that the Works Task Launcher functions as something of a portal. It contains **links** to the types of information people typically look for, such as news, maps, mortgage rates, shopping directories, and so on. For the purposes of the following exercises, you'll use the Task Launcher to open the MSN home page in Internet Explorer. Although you can also start Internet Explorer directly from the Windows desktop, by using the Task Launcher's built-in links, you don't have to know the address of a site to view it.

Establishing an Internet Connection

Network connections are complex, which can make it frustrating for even the most enthusiastic computer fan to set up Internet access. The physical equipment that you need in addition to your computer is a modem and a phone line. Then you need an account with an ISP to enable the connection through your phone line.

(continued)

continued

You can use the Internet Connection Wizard both to sign up for a service and to connect your computer to the Internet. If you already have an Internet account with an ISP, you can use the wizard to tell Internet Explorer your account information.

*Connect To
The Internet*

1   On the Windows desktop, double-click the Connect To The Internet icon.

        The Internet Connect Wizard opens.

tip

If you don't see the Connect To The Internet icon on the desktop, you can check two other places. Click the Start button, point to Programs, point to Accessories, point to Communications, and then click Internet Connection Wizard. Or click the Start button, point to Programs, point to Internet Explorer, and then click Internet Connection Wizard.

2   Click the connection option for the setup you want to use, and then follow the instructions on the screen.

Finding People and Information on the Internet

Despite all the portals designed to link you to frequently requested information, it can still be tricky to locate the particular Web site you want. That's because you need to know the address of the Web page that contains the information. Each Web page has a unique Web address called a Uniform Resource Locator, or **URL**. You've probably seen or heard URLs in print ads and commercials. For example, *http://www.microsoft.com* is the URL for Microsoft Corporation. The *http* part specifies Hypertext Transfer Protocol, a protocol for accessing Web pages, and *www.microsoft.com* identifies the computer that stores the Web pages.

How do you locate the address you want? That's where a good **search engine** comes in handy. You type a keyword, a phrase, or even a person's name into the search engine, and it tries to locate Web sites that contain that information. It then displays links to the sites it found.

Communicating on the Internet 4

Many Web sites include their own search engines. In fact, the sheer number of search tools can be daunting in itself. In the next exercise, you use a couple of different search tools built into Works, the MSN Web site, and Internet Explorer. These are not the only methods you can use by any means. However, the intention of this exercise is to introduce you to a couple of easily accessible methods.

1   On the taskbar, click the Start button, point to Programs, and then click Microsoft Works.

The Works Task Launcher opens.

2   Click the Programs tab.

All Works programs are listed in the Task Launcher.

3   Click MSN.

The Task Launcher displays a list of Web-related tasks.

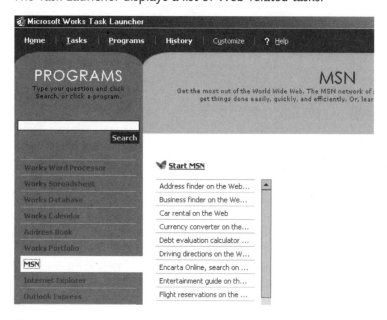

4   Click Start MSN.

The MSN home page appears as shown on the facing page.

tip

If the Internet Connection Wizard appears, contact your ISP for details about setting up Internet Explorer.

Many Web pages change daily, so the sample Web pages shown in this lesson will likely differ from the ones you see.

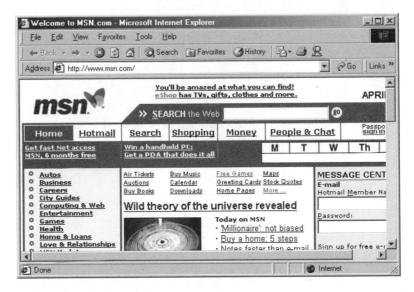

From the MSN home page, you can explore various topics and search for information. However, for the purposes of this exercise, you'll look at another way to display the search options available on the MSN site.

5   On the Windows taskbar, click Microsoft Works Task Launcher to display the Task Launcher again.

Tasks

6   Click the Tasks tab.

7   Click E-Mail & Internet, and in the task list in the right pane, scroll down and click Web Search.

8   Click Start This Task.

Internet Explorer appears and displays the MSN Web Search page.

Maximize

9   If the Internet Explorer window is not maximized, click the Maximize button on the title bar.

10 In the Search The Web For box, type **landscaping** and then click the Search button.

11 If a message box is displayed, asking if you want to continue because it is possible for others to see information you send, click Yes.

MSN displays a list of sites that include the word *landscaping,* as shown on the following page. Because sites change frequently, your results will not match.

tip

To make the search results more specific, type several keywords in the Search The Web For box.

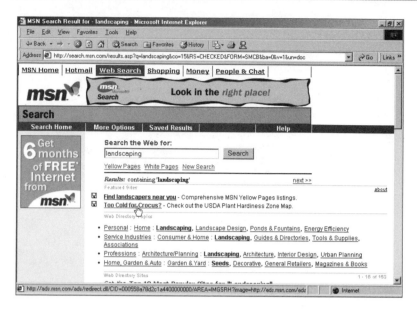

12   Click the Too Cold For Crocus link if it appears. If not, click a link that interests you.

If you click the Too Cold For Crocus link, the United States Department of Agriculture site is displayed, as shown below.

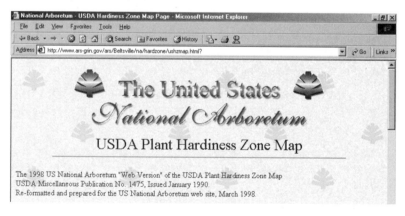

13   On the Standard Buttons toolbar, click the Search button.

The Search pane appears in the left side of the window.

14   Click the Find A Person's Address option.

The Search pane changes to display boxes for entering an address.

15   Under Search For, type the name of someone whose address you want to find in the First Name, Last Name, and, optionally, City and State/Province boxes.

For example, if you wanted to search for Megan Sherman, a fictional volunteer with the Oak Park restoration project, you would type something like this:

16 Click the Search button.

Your browser's search engine locates any matches it can find and then displays the results. Because your browser can be set to use any of several search engines, results will vary. Some matching names might have additional information, including a link to a map that pinpoints the person's address.

17 To close the Search pane, click the Search button on the Standard Buttons toolbar again.

The Search pane is hidden, and the current Web page fills the screen.

Close

If the Task Launcher does not appear, click Microsoft Works Task Launcher on the taskbar.

18 To close Internet Explorer, click the Close button on the title bar.

Internet Explorer closes, and the Task Launcher appears.

tip

One Web site that's easy to find is the Microsoft Works product site. It offers the latest product information as well as detailed how-to articles and tips for getting the most out of Works. On the Tasks tab of the Task Launcher, click E-Mail & Internet, click Works Web Site, and then click Start This Task. Or start Internet Explorer, and then in the Address box, type **www.microsoft.com/works**.

Personalizing Internet Explorer

Internet Explorer can help you return to the Web sites you particularly like. One way it does this is through its home page. You can specify any page you want to appear when you start Internet Explorer. In addition, Internet Explorer can save URLs on its Favorites menu. Then, when you want to view a particular site again, you can click its name on the menu just as you would choose other menu commands. You can even create your own folders on the Favorites menu in which to store groups of URLs. For example, you can create a Vacation folder in which to save links to Web sites about palm trees and sunny beaches.

In this exercise, you personalize Internet Explorer by setting its home page to the National Weather Service Web site. Then you add a Web page to the browser's Favorites menu in a new folder that you create.

1   In the Task Launcher, click the Programs tab.

All Works programs are listed in the Task Launcher.

2   In the list of programs, click Internet Explorer.

Works displays a list of Web-related tasks.

3   Click Start Internet Explorer.

Internet Explorer appears and displays your default home page, which might be MSN, a home page supplied by your ISP, or a page that you have specified.

4   In the Address box, type **http://www.microsoft.com** and then press the Enter key.

The Microsoft home page appears.

tip

When you type a Web address, you can start with the character that comes after *http://*. Unless you type something different for the first part of the address, Internet Explorer assumes you want to start with *http://*.

5   In the list of links on the left side of the screen, under Customer Sites, click Home & Personal.

If you cannot locate this link, in the Address box, type **http://www.microsoft.com/insider** and then press the Enter key.

The Microsoft Insider page appears.

6   To add this page to your list of favorites, on the Favorites menu, click Add To Favorites.

The Add Favorite dialog box appears.

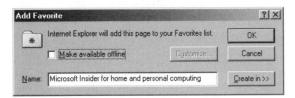

7   To shorten the display name, in the Name box, select the words *for home and personal computing* and then press the Delete key.

Now the Name box reads *Microsoft Insider*.

8   Click the Create In button.

A list of Favorites folders appears.

9   Click the New Folder button.

The Create New Folder dialog box appears.

10   In the Folder Name box, type **Oak Park Project**, and then click OK.

In the Add Favorite dialog box, the Oak Park Project folder now appears selected under the Favorites folder.

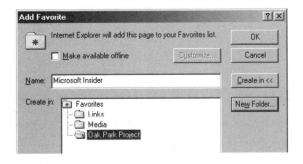

11   Click OK.

Internet Explorer places the link to the Microsoft Insider page in the Oak Park Project folder.

12   On the Favorites menu, click Oak Park Project.

The submenu displays the link for Microsoft Insider.

13   Click outside the menu to close it.

14   In the Address box, type **http://www.nws.noaa.gov** and then click Go.

The National Weather Service site appears.

15   On the Tools menu, click Internet Options.

The Internet Options dialog box appears and displays the General tab.

16   Under Home Page, click the Use Current button.

The Address box now displays *http://www.nws.noaa.gov/*.

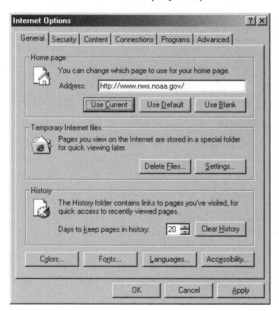

17   Click OK.

The next time you start Internet Explorer, the first page that appears will be the National Weather Service site.

Controlling Security in Internet Explorer

The Web is somewhat utopian in its lack of boundaries. Anyone can view just about any Web site and download just about anything. Clearly, not all information is suitable for all viewers, particularly on a home computer shared by both adults and children, and not all content is safe to download. The **Content Advisor** and **security zones** are two mechanisms built into Internet Explore that give you control over the types of Web content that your computer can gain access to.

Content Advisor works with a rating system that is used by some Web sites. If you turn on Content Advisor, only rated content that meets or exceeds your criteria can be viewed. You can adjust the settings and even protect access to Content Advisor itself with a password. For example, you can specify the Web sites that other people using your computer can view and adjust the ratings settings to reflect what you think is appropriate content in each of four areas: language, nudity, sex, and violence.

Security zones are a different matter. They help you determine whether the content you open or download on the Web is safe for your computer. Internet Explorer provides four security zones: Internet, local intranet, trusted, and restricted. You can assign Web sites to a zone and set its security level. For example, if you assign a Web site to the trusted zone, that means you believe you can download or run files from that site without worrying about damage to your computer or data. If you assign a site to the restricted zone, Internet Explorer always prompts you before allowing you to download or run files from the site.

In this exercise, you examine these security options in Internet Explorer without changing the current settings. The goal of this exercise is simply to show you how you would change them if you wanted to.

1   On the Internet Explorer Tools menu, click Internet Options.

The Internet Options dialog box appears and displays the General tab.

> **tip**
> You can also open the Internet Options dialog box by opening the Internet Options Control Panel. To open Control Panel, click Start, point to Settings, and click Control Panel.

2   Click the Content tab.

Options for the Content Advisor appear in the top area.

3   Click the Enable button.

The Content Advisor dialog box appears and opens the Ratings tab, on which you can set rating levels for adult content. Content Advisor is set to the most conservative (least likely to offend) settings when you first turn it on. You can adjust rating levels by selecting a category and adjusting the slider.

Communicating on the Internet   4

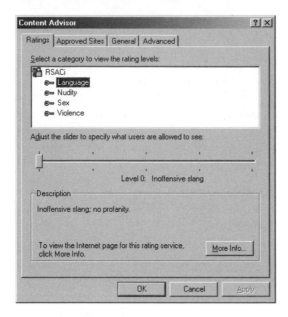

4   Click the Approved Sites tab.

On this tab, you can type a URL and specify whether other people can always or never view it, regardless of how the site's contents are rated.

5   Click the General tab.

On this tab, you can specify whether others can view unrated Web sites as well as set a Supervisor password that prevents other users from changing Content Advisor settings.

6   Click the Advanced tab.

On this tab, you can specify the ratings bureau and ratings rules you use to control whether rated content can be viewed.

tip

Not all Internet content is rated. Keep in mind, if you choose to allow other people to view unrated sites on your computer, that some of those sites might contain inappropriate material.

7   Click Cancel to return to the Internet Options dialog box.

8   Click the Security tab.

Options for setting security levels for the Internet zone are displayed.

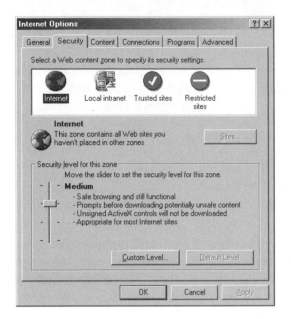

Trusted Sites

9 Click Trusted Sites.

Options for setting security levels for trusted sites are displayed.

10 Click the Sites button.

The Trusted Sites dialog box appears, in which you can type the URL for sites you want to add to this zone—that is, sites from which you can download files and run programs.

11 Click Cancel to close the Trusted Sites dialog box.

The Internet Options dialog box is displayed. Under Security Level For This Zone, the slider is typically set to Low.

12 Click Restricted Sites.

The security level is typically set to High for this zone.

Restricted Sites

13 Click Cancel.

No Content Advisor or security zone settings are changed.

14 To close Internet Explorer, click the Close button on the title bar.

The browser closes, and the Task Launcher is displayed.

Close

If the Task Launcher does not appear, click Microsoft Works Task Launcher on the taskbar.

15 To close the Task Launcher, click the Close button on the title bar.

What Is Outlook Express?

It's worth getting Internet access if only to send and receive e-mail messages, those electronic postcards that require neither paper nor stamps. More and more people have e-mail accounts, making it easier than ever to keep in touch through this convenient medium. Outlook Express is a program that uses your Internet connection to send and receive e-mail messages. The Outlook Express icon is installed right on the Windows desktop for easy access, but you can also start the program through the Task Launcher.

When you start Outlook Express for the first time, the Internet Connection Wizard appears, asking you for information about your e-mail account. Your ISP can give you the correct values to enter in the wizard.

For the purposes of this exercise, you will use practice e-mail messages to work with Outlook Express. In real life, e-mail messages arrive over the Internet and show up in your Inbox, a process that this book cannot simulate. Instead, you will drag sample e-mail messages that you installed from this book's CD-ROM to your Outlook Express Inbox.

Outlook Express

1   On the Windows desktop, double-click the Outlook Express icon.

If you use a different program for e-mail, a message appears, asking if you want to make Outlook Express your default client. Click No.

If a dialog box appears, asking you for your logon information, type your e-mail user name and password and click OK.

The Outlook Express startup screen appears.

If your screen looks different from this, in the Folders list, click Outlook Express.

Startup pane

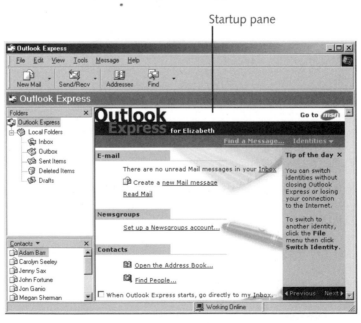

2   At the bottom of the startup pane, select the check box labeled When Outlook Express Starts, Go Directly To My Inbox.

The next time you start Outlook Express, you'll see all the e-mail messages in
your Inbox at a glance and bypass the startup screen.

3   In the Folders list on the left side of the window, click Inbox.

tip
If the Inbox is not displayed, click the plus sign (+) to the left of the Local
Folders folder to expand it, and then click Inbox.

In the upper right pane, Outlook Express displays all the e-mail messages in
your Inbox. Below, in the preview pane, Outlook Express displays the contents of the currently selected message.

Folders list showing e-mail folders

Message list showing e-mail messages in the Inbox

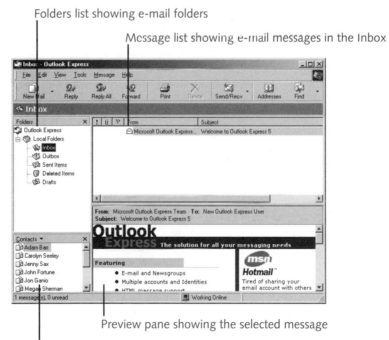

Preview pane showing the selected message

Contacts pane showing contacts you entered in
Address Book in the previous lesson

4   On the desktop, right-click My Computer, and then click Explore on the
shortcut menu.

Windows Explorer opens on top of the Outlook Express window. Windows
Explorer displays the contents of My Computer.

For details about installing the practice files, see "Using the Book's CD-ROM" at the beginning of this book.

5   In the left pane, locate the folder in which you installed the practice files.

Depending on your version of Windows, the preselected practice folder location will vary.

- Windows 95, Windows 98, Windows Millennium Edition:

  C:\My Documents\Works Suite 2001 SBS Practice

- Windows 2000:

  C:\Documents and Settings\<username>\My Documents\Works Suite 2001 SBS Practice

6   Open the Lesson04 folder.

The contents of the folder are displayed in the right pane.

7   On the View menu, click List.

8   Right-click a blank area on the taskbar, and then click Tile Windows Vertically.

The Windows Explorer and Outlook Express windows are now arranged side by side. Your screen should look similar to the following illustration:

To select all the messages at once, click the first message, and then hold down the Shift key while clicking the last message.

9   In Windows Explorer, hold down the Ctrl key while you click each practice e-mail message file, indicated by an envelope icon.

The six e-mail message files are selected.

10 Drag the selected files from the Lesson04 folder to your Outlook Express Inbox.

The messages now appear in the Outlook Express Inbox.

Close

11 On the Windows Explorer title bar, click the Close button.

Windows Explorer closes, and Outlook Express remains open.

Maximize

12 On the Outlook Express title bar, click the Maximize button.

Outlook Express fills the screen, which now should look similar to this:

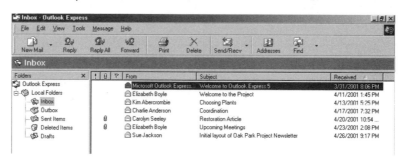

Sending E-Mail Messages

To see a multimedia demo about sending an e-mail message, double-click the Send E-Mail icon in the Demos folder on the book's CD-ROM.

The quickest way to address an e-mail message is to choose one of your contacts. Outlook Express shares contact information with Address Book. When you used Address Book in Lesson 3 to store contact information, you created contacts that now appear in Outlook Express. In addition, when you reply to an e-mail message that someone sends you, that person's information is added to your list of contacts.

When you send an e-mail message, you can **attach** one or more files, such as Word documents, digital photographs, or any other files you want to share. Outlook Express sends the files as attachments that the recipient can save or open using the program the files were created in.

In this exercise, you use your Address Book contacts to find the e-mail address of someone to send e-mail to. Then you attach a file to your message before sending it.

Addresses

tip
You can display your Address Book and make changes to it from within Outlook Express. Just click the Addresses button on the Outlook Express toolbar.

1   On the toolbar, click the New Mail button.

The New Message window opens.

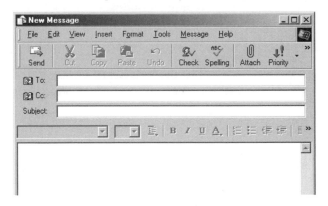

2   In the To box, type **someone@microsoft.com**.

tip

To send mail to more than one person, separate each e-mail address with a comma (,) or a semicolon (;) in the To box.

3   In the Subject box, type **Test**.

The New Message title bar changes to display the subject text.

4   In the message area, type **This is a test.**

Your screen should look similar to the following illustration.

5   On the toolbar of your message, click the Send button.

Outlook Express sends your message to *someone@microsoft.com*, a real e-mail account provided for just this purpose. The account will send an automated reply in response.

6   To address a new message using your contact information, in the Contacts pane in the lower left corner of the Outlook Express window, right-click Patricia Brooke. On the shortcut menu, click Send E-Mail.

The New Message window opens, and Outlook Express inserts *Patricia Brooke* in the To box.

7   On the Standard Buttons toolbar, click the Attach button.

The Insert Attachment dialog box appears.

If you cannot see the Attach button, widen the New Message window until the button is visible.

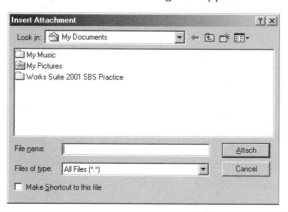

8   Make sure the Look In box shows My Documents.

9   Double-click the Works Suite 2001 SBS Practice folder, and then double-click the Lesson04 folder.

If you do not see Works Suite 2001 SBS Practice in the list of folders, browse to the location where you installed the practice files.

10   Click Restoration Project Article.doc, and then click Attach.

In the message window, a new Attach box appears under the Subject box and displays the filename you just selected. Your screen should look similar to the following:

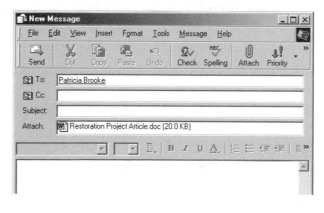

In the real world, the next step would be to write a subject line and text and then send the e-mail message. However, for the purposes of this exercise, you will cancel the message.

Close

11 On the New Message title bar, click the Close button.

A message appears, asking if you want to save changes to this message.

12 Click No.

The message is canceled.

Managing E-Mail Messages

Because the Internet never sleeps, it can deliver mail to you around the clock. You will receive your mail even if your computer is not turned on. The next time you turn it on and start Outlook Express, it polls the Internet to see if you received anything and then displays new messages in your Inbox. You can also manually look for new mail by clicking the Send/Recv button on the Outlook Express toolbar.

After you read an e-mail message, you may want to reply to it, file it away for future reference, or delete it. You can create folders within the Inbox in which to organize messages you want to save. When you don't need to save a message, you can move it into the Deleted Items folder, which preserves the message until you decide to permanently remove it (in much the same way you use the Recycle Bin on the Windows desktop to remove unwanted items).

In this exercise, you reply to an e-mail message that you received, organize the contents of your Inbox into a new folder, and delete unnecessary messages.

1 In your Inbox, click the message from Carolyn Seeley with the subject *Restoration Article*.

The preview pane displays the message, which includes an attachment as indicated by the paper clip icon.

Attachments

2 Click the Attachments button in the preview pane.

A shortcut menu appears with commands for working with attachments.

3 Click Restoration Project Article.doc.

Microsoft Word opens and displays the restoration article.

If you don't have Word installed, an Open Attachment Warning dialog box is displayed. Click the Open It option and click OK. The restoration article will be opened in WordPad.

Close

4 On the Microsoft Word title bar, click the Close button.

Word closes, and the Outlook Express window appears again.

5 On the toolbar, click the Reply button.

A new message window opens that is addressed to Carolyn Seeley. Outlook Express creates a subject line based on the original message's subject and inserts the text of the original message in the message area.

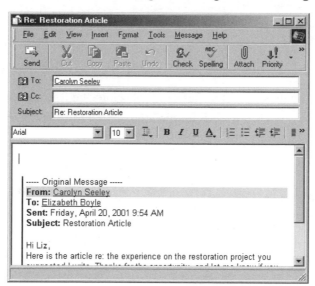

6 Type **Thank you! You'll be hearing from me soon with more information.**

Your message appears above the original message.

In the real world, the next step would be to click the Send button. However, for the purposes of this exercise, you can cancel the message.

Close

7 On the Re: Restoration Article title bar, click the Close button.

A message appears, asking if you want to save changes to this message.

8 Click No.

The message is canceled.

9 To create a folder in which to store the message from Carolyn Seeley, on the File menu, point to Folder, and then click New.

The Create Folder dialog box appears.

10 In the Folder Name box, type **Restoration Project**, and then click OK.

In the Folders list, a new folder named Restoration Project appears under Inbox. Your Folders list should look similar to the illustration on the following page.

11   Drag the message from Carolyn Seeley into the Restoration Project folder.

The message is moved from the Inbox and into the new folder.

Copy pointer

tip
If you want to make a copy of the message, hold down the Ctrl key while dragging it to the folder. The pointer icon will include a small plus sign, indicating that the message will be copied instead of moved.

12   Click the Restoration Project folder.

The message from Carolyn Seeley appears.

13   Click the Inbox folder.

The contents of your Inbox are displayed.

14   Click the message from Elizabeth Boyle with the subject *Welcome to the Project.*

15   On the toolbar, click the Delete button.

The message is removed from the Inbox and moved to the Deleted Items folder.

16   Click the Deleted Items folder.

The message you deleted appears.

17   Right-click the Deleted Items folder.

A shortcut menu appears with commands for working in this folder, including the Empty 'Deleted Items' Folder command, which you can use to permanently delete e-mail messages.

18   Click the Inbox folder.

The contents of your Inbox are displayed.

Cleaning Out Your Mailbox

Outlook Express preserves incoming and outbound e-mail messages so that you never unintentionally lose a message. As noted in the previous exercise, even when you delete a message, it is not permanently removed but merely moved to a different folder. To permanently delete a message, you need to delete it from the Deleted Items folder.

Outlook Express also saves a copy of the messages you send unless you tell it not to. The Sent Items folder contains all your outbound e-mail messages. If someone doesn't receive a message you send—and network glitches do happen—you can retrieve a copy of the message from the Sent Items folder and send it again.

Lesson Wrap-Up

To finish the lesson:

Delete

1   If Outlook Express is the program you use to send and receive e-mail messages, you may want to delete the sample e-mail messages that were added during this exercise. To do this, select the messages, and then click Delete on the toolbar.

Deleted messages are removed from the Inbox and moved to the Deleted Items folder.

Close

2   To close Outlook Express, on the File menu, click Exit. Or on the title bar of the Outlook Express window, click the Close button.

Quick Reference

To view Web pages on the Internet

Programs

1   In the Task Launcher, click the Programs tab.

2   Click MSN, and then click Start MSN.

3   To view a specific Web page, type its address in the Address box.

To find a piece of information on the Internet

1   In the Task Launcher, click the Tasks tab, click E-Mail & Internet, click Web Search, and then click Start This Task.

2   In the Search The Web For box, type a keyword or phrase.

To find a person on the Internet

1   On the Standard Buttons toolbar in Internet Explorer, click the Search button.

2   In the Search pane, click Find A Person's Address, type the name and location of the person you're looking for, and then click Search.

To add a Web page to the Internet Explorer Favorites menu

1   In Internet Explorer, display the Web page you want.

2   On the Favorites menu, click Add To Favorites, and then click the folder that you want to store the link in.

To change your browser's home page

1   In Internet Explorer, display the Web page you want to use as your home page.

2   On the Tools menu, click Internet Options, and then under Home Page, click Use Current.

To enable Content Advisor

1   On the Tools menu in Internet Explorer, click Internet Options.

2   Click the Content Tab.

3   Click Enable, and then choose the settings you want.

To customize security levels for Internet zones

1   On the Tools menu in Internet Explorer, click Internet Options.

2   Click the Security tab, and then click the zone that you want to set the security level for.

3   Move the slider up for a higher level of security or down for a lower level of security.

To send an e-mail message

1   On the Outlook Express toolbar, click New Mail.

2   In the To box, type the e-mail name of each recipient, separating names with a comma or a semicolon.

3   In the Subject box, type a message title.

4   Type the message, and then click the Send button on the New Message toolbar.

To attach a file to an e-mail message

1   On the new message's toolbar, click Attach, and then locate the file you want to attach.

2   Select the file, and then click Attach.

To read an e-mail message

1   Click the Inbox icon in the Folders list.

2   To view the message in the preview pane, click the message in the message list.

3   To view the message in a separate window, double-click the message in the message list.

To reply to an e-mail message

1   Select the message you want to reply to.

2   On the toolbar, click Reply.

3   Type your message, and then click Send.

To create a new folder in Outlook Express

1   On the File menu, point to Folder, and then click New.

2   In the Folder Name box, type the name, and then select the location for the new folder.

To move an e-mail message into a folder

1   In the message list, select the message you want to move.

2   Drag it to the folder.

UNIT 2

Managing Your Information

5

Managing Your Schedule

**ESTIMATED
TIME
25 min.**

In this lesson, you will learn how to:

✔ *Work in different views of your calendar.*

✔ *Schedule various types of appointments.*

✔ *Add birthdays and holidays.*

✔ *Selectively view calendar contents.*

✔ *Set a reminder for an appointment.*

✔ *Share your calendar in e-mail.*

Now you can discover the tool that many businesspeople have come to rely on: an online calendar. Microsoft Works Calendar displays your day, week, or month at a glance. You can use it to track appointments and even remind you of important dates with an on-screen note—minutes, hours, or days in advance. With built-in categories that let you selectively display appointments, Works Calendar can help you sort through family, work, and other obligations quickly.

In this lesson, you'll use Works Calendar to schedule and organize family and community commitments. You'll also filter appointments and set an appointment reminder. Finally, you'll learn how you can share a calendar, by sending appointment notices in e-mail and saving calendar information in different formats.

Starting and Viewing a Calendar

You can start Works Calendar in any of several ways, but when you start from the Works Task Launcher, you can use shortcuts to common tasks. For example, you can search for an appointment. In this exercise, you'll start Works Calendar, which displays today's appointments just like a daily organizer. You can quickly change the view to show a week or a month at a time instead.

In this exercise, you start Works Calendar and view it in different ways.

1   On the taskbar, click the Start button, point to Programs, and then click Microsoft Works.

Microsoft Works Task Launcher opens.

2   Click the Programs tab.

All Works programs are listed in the Task Launcher.

3   Click Works Calendar.

Tasks for Works Calendar are listed.

4   Click Start The Calendar.

5   If a message appears, asking if you want to make Works Calendar the default calendar, click No.

6   If a message appears, informing you about updating Works Calendar with birthdays and anniversaries stored in Address Book, click OK.

Works Calendar opens to today's appointments. If someone has previously used Works Calendar, your screen might show a different view. To display today's appointments, click the View Day button on the toolbar.

View Day

7   If the Works Help pane is open, on the Works Help title bar, click the Close Help button.

Close Help

Later, when you work in Works Calendar on your own, you might want to keep the Help pane open. For the purposes of this lesson, you'll find it easier to work in Works Calendar if the entire screen is available.

The screen now looks something like this:

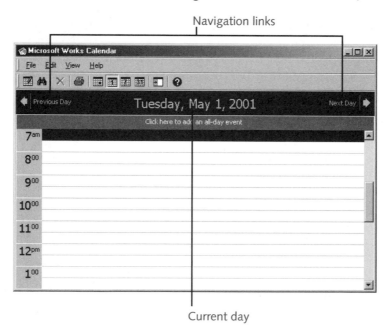

Navigation links

Current day

View Week

8   On the toolbar, click the View Week button.

The current week's calendar appears with today's date highlighted.

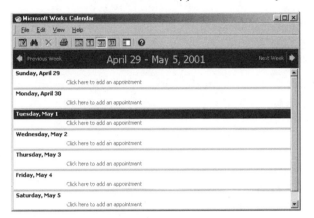

View Month

9   On the toolbar, click the View Month button.

The current month's calendar appears with today's date highlighted.

Adding Appointments and Events

Before you add items to your calendar, it helps to understand the distinction that Works Calendar makes between the terms *appointment* and *event*.

■   An **appointment** is anything that takes place at a specific time of day, such as a community council meeting on Tuesday at 7 P.M. or a luncheon at noon.

■   An **event** is anything that is not associated with a specific time of day, such as someone's birthday, or an activity that occurs for more than one day, such as a week-long summer computer camp.

Managing Your Schedule

5

You can add appointments and events in any Works Calendar view. The view you use depends on what's most convenient for you. Whichever view you prefer, you can add, change, copy, move, and delete any type of appointment or event. In addition, you can schedule regularly occurring items, called **recurring appointments,** with a single command. For example, monthly book club meetings or weekly piano lessons qualify as recurring appointments.

In this exercise, you create and work with a fictional family appointment and then add a recurring community meeting for the increasingly active Oak Park project. In the next exercise, you'll create an event to add a birthday to the calendar.

New
Appointment

1   On the toolbar, click the New Appointment button.

The New Appointment dialog box appears.

2   In the Title box, type **Adam's Kick Boxing Lesson**.

3   Click the Appointment Starts date arrow.

A small monthly calendar appears as shown below.

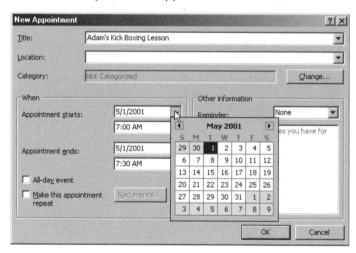

4   Click the right or left arrow to display the calendar for May 2001, and then click Saturday, May 19.

The small calendar closes, and the date you selected is displayed.

5   Click the Appointment Starts time box arrow, and then scroll to and click 2:00 PM.

6   In the Appointment Ends date box, leave the current setting.

Works Calendar automatically updates the end date using your selection for the start date.

7   Click the Appointment Ends time arrow, and then click 3:00 PM.

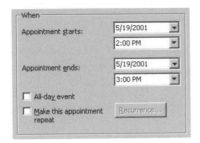

8   Click OK.

The appointment is added to the calendar. If your calendar is showing a different month, you won't see the appointment.

9   To display the May 2001 calendar, in the black border at the top of the month, click the month name to display a list, and then click May 2001.

The May 2001 calendar appears with the kick boxing lesson appointment.

Because only a small amount of text fits in this view of the calendar, the appointment title you entered is truncated. If you pause the pointer over the appointment, however, a tip displays the full text.

Your calendar now looks something like this:

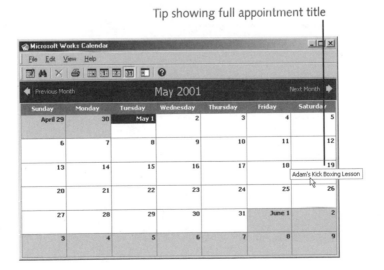

Tip showing full appointment title

10 To copy the appointment you just created, hold down the Ctrl key, and then drag the appointment down onto the following Saturday, May 26.

The calendar now displays two copies of the appointment.

Delete

You can delete appointments in any Calendar view.

11 To delete the kick boxing appointment on May 19th, click the appointment, and then click the Delete button on the toolbar.

A message appears, asking if you want to delete the selected item permanently.

12 Click Yes.

The May 19 appointment no longer appears.

New Appointment

13 To create a recurring appointment, on the toolbar, click the New Appointment button.

The New Appointment dialog box appears.

14 Enter the following appointment details:

- In the Title box, type **Planning Meeting**.

- In the Location box, type **City Hall**.

- In the Appointment Starts date box, click Monday, April 30, 2001.

- In the Appointment Starts time box, click 7:00 PM.

- In the Appointment Ends date box, leave the current setting (4/30/2001).

- In the Appointment Ends time box, click 9:00 PM.

15 Select the Make This Appointment Repeat check box.

Under When, details about the recurring appointment appear, and the Recurrence button becomes available.

16 Click the Recurrence button.

The Recurrence Options dialog box appears.

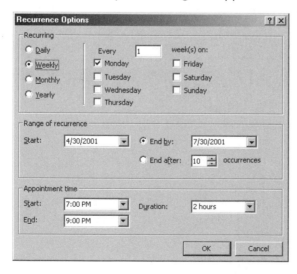

17   Under Recurring, make sure the Weekly option is selected.

To the right, options appear for setting weekly recurrence. Leave the current settings for Every 1 Week On Monday.

18   Under Range Of Recurrence, choose End After, and then click the down arrow to change the number to 6 occurrences.

19   Click OK to close the Recurrence Options dialog box.

20   In the New Appointment dialog box, click OK.

Works Calendar adds the planning meeting to the calendar for six consecutive Mondays.

Adding Birthdays and Holidays

You can add important dates, such as birthdays and anniversaries, to your calendar as all-day events. Another type of special occasion that Works Calendar can display is holidays. With one command, Works can add all the holidays for a given country to your calendar.

In this exercise, you add a birthday and holidays to your calendar.

New Appointment

1   On the toolbar, click the New Appointment button.

The New Appointment dialog box appears.

2   In the Title box, type **Uncle Steve's Birthday**.

3   Under When, select the All-Day Event check box.

The appointment time boxes are removed. In Works Calendar, an event has no start or end time by definition.

> ## tip
> If you want a birthday event to occur every year, you can make it a yearly recurring appointment.

4   Click the Appointment Starts date arrow, and then click July 3.

5   Click OK.

> ## tip
> If you have already entered birthdays and anniversaries in Address Book, you can quickly add them to your calendar by clicking Birthdays on the Edit menu.

6   On the Edit menu, click Add Holidays.

The Add Holidays To Calendar dialog box appears.

7   In the box of countries, scroll down, and then select the United States check box.

8   Click OK.

After a few seconds, a message box indicates that the holidays have been added to your calendar.

9   Click OK.

The holidays now appear on your calendar, which looks something like this:

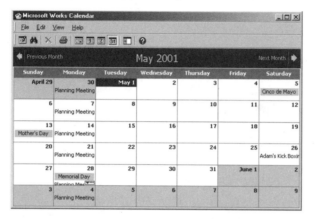

> **tip**
> To remove individual holidays, click the holiday, and then click the Delete button on the toolbar. To view your calendar without holidays, use a category filter as described in the next exercise.

Managing a Calendar

The flexibility to view and filter appointments is the reason many people enjoy using an online calendar program. For example, in Works Calendar you can selectively view appointments by **category,** such as only birthdays or special occasions. Another great benefit—especially if you spend a lot of time in front of your computer—is the ability to have Works Calendar remind you of upcoming appointments.

Works Calendar recognizes many categories. You can assign any appointment or event to a category, such as Education, Entertainment, Medical, or Sports. Assigning to a category is an extra step that helps you later when you want to view your appointments based on the category you assigned them to. You can also create your own categories for appointments that don't belong in any of the ones that Works Calendar provides.

When you set a **reminder** for an appointment, Works Calendar displays a message on your screen in advance of the appointment. Works Calendar doesn't even have to be open, although Microsoft Windows must be running. You specify how far in advance of the appointment you want to be reminded, and Works Calendar takes care of the rest.

In this exercise, you assign Adam's kick boxing lesson to the Sports category and create a new category to which you assign the recurring Oak Park project meetings. Then you filter the view to show only certain appointments. You also set a reminder for the project meeting.

1   In the calendar, double-click the appointment for Adam's kick boxing lesson on May 26.

The Edit Appointment dialog box appears.

2   Click the Change button.

The Choose Categories dialog box appears.

3   Under Select Categories, select the Sports check box (scroll down if necessary), and then click OK.

In the Edit Appointment dialog box, *Sports* appears in the Category box.

> **tip**
> If you create an event to mark someone's birthday, you can assign the event to the Birthday category. Then you can filter the view to show just the upcoming birthdays.

4   Click OK.

5   To create a new category, in the calendar, double-click the Planning Meeting appointment for Monday, April 30, 2001.

Because this is a recurring appointment, a message box appears and asks you whether to open this occurrence or open the series.

6   Click Open The Series, and then click OK.

The Edit Appointment dialog box appears.

7   Click the Change button to display the Choose Categories dialog box.

8   Click the Edit Categories button.

The Edit Categories dialog box appears.

9   Type **Oak Park Project**.

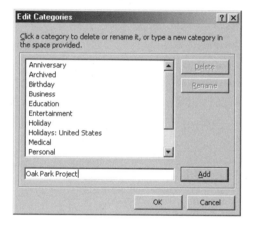

10   Click Add.

A new category, Oak Park Project, appears in the category list.

11   Click OK.

12   In the Choose Categories dialog box, select the Oak Park Project check box, and then click OK.

In the Edit Appointment dialog box, *Oak Park Project* appears in the Category box.

13   To set a reminder for this meeting, under Other Information, click the Reminder arrow, and then click 1 Hour.

14   In the Reminder box, type **Go to City Hall!**

15   Click OK.

An hour before the scheduled appointment, Works Calendar displays a reminder on your screen like this:

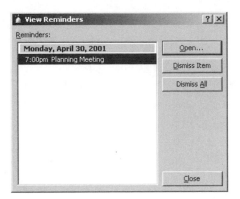

If your computer is turned off when a scheduled reminder is due, you won't see it until the next time you turn on your computer and start Microsoft Windows.

Category Filter

16 To display appointments based on category, on the toolbar, click the Category Filter button.

The Category Filter appears on the left side of the calendar, which currently displays all your appointments and holidays.

17 In the category list, clear both the Holidays: United States check box and the Sports check box.

The calendar now displays only the planning meetings, not the holidays or the kick boxing lesson. Note that the filter is applied to the entire calendar, not just the current month.

Your screen should look similar to the following illustration:

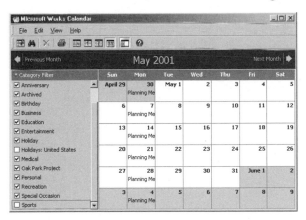

Sharing a Calendar

After you've entered appointments into your calendar, you can then share the results by sending appointment notices to other people in e-mail. Works Calendar saves the appointments you want to send as files in two formats:

- Calendar, the file format used by Works Calendar and other calendar programs. The file has a .vcs extension. The recipient of your e-mail message can import the calendar information from this file into his or her Works Calendar by using the Import command on the File menu.

- HTML, the file format used by Web browsers. Many other programs, such as Microsoft Word, can open this format as well. The file has an .htm extension.

For example, you can notify other committee members of the recurring project planning meetings by sending your calendar appointments to them. To ensure that you send only specific appointments, and not all the appointments and holidays in a given time period, you must first filter your calendar to show just the appointments you want to send. As a result of the previous exercise, your calendar is already filtered to show only the planning meetings.

In this exercise, you send calendar information in e-mail. This exercise assumes your e-mail program is already configured.

1   On the File menu, click Send.

The Send To E-Mail dialog box appears.

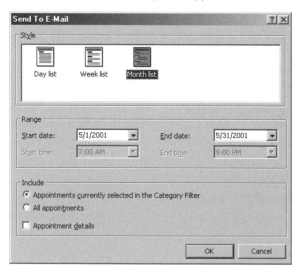

2   Under Range, set Start Date to April 30, 2001.

3   Set End Date to June 4, 2001.

4 Under Include, leave the current setting to send only those appointments that are currently selected in the Category Filter.

5 Click OK.

Depending on how your computer is configured, your e-mail program opens or the Choose Profile dialog box appears. If the Choose Profile dialog box appears, click your e-mail program in the list, and then click OK.

When your e-mail program opens, it creates a new message and attaches two files: Calendar.htm and Calendar.vcs. If you use Microsoft Outlook Express, the screen looks like this:

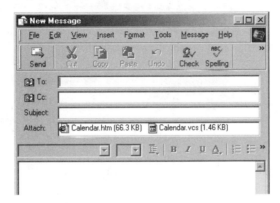

For details about how to send e-mail, see Lesson 4, "Communicating on the Internet."

6 Continue as you would to send any e-mail message.

Works sends two copies of the appointment so that your e-mail recipient can print or use the format that works best. For example, if your recipient opens the Calendar.htm file, he or she will see something like this:

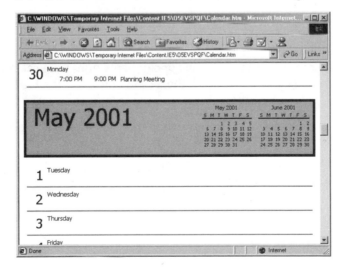

7   To display the calendar again and restore the holidays, click the Microsoft Works Calendar window (or select it on the taskbar).

8   In the Category Filter list, select the Holidays: United States and Sports check boxes.

The holidays and sport appointments appear again in the calendar.

Category Filter

9   On the toolbar, click the Category Filter button to hide the list of categories.

Saving Calendar Items in Other Formats

In addition to exporting calendar information in vCalendar and HTML formats, you can also save and share your calendar items in tab-delimited text format. "Tab-delimited" means that each calendar item is separated by tab characters, a common format that other programs can import. You can then import the file into another calendar program that doesn't recognize the vCalendar format, or into a database or spreadsheet program. You can even open the file in Works Spreadsheet or Works Database.

To export your calendar, click the Export command on the File menu, and then click the format you want. A dialog box for that format is displayed, allowing you to specify options for exporting your calendar. For details on saving your calendar in different formats, search the Works Help index for *export*.

Lesson Wrap-Up

To finish the lesson:

Delete

1   To delete any of the fictional appointments from your calendar, click an appointment, and then click the Delete button on the toolbar.

The appointment is removed.

Close

2   On the File menu, click Exit. Or, on the title bar of the Works Calendar window, click the Close button.

The Works Task Launcher appears.

If the Works Task Launcher does not appear, click Microsoft Works Task Launcher on the taskbar.

3   Click the Close button on the title bar.

Quick Reference

To show today's appointments

●   On the toolbar, click the Go To Today button.

To change views

●   On the toolbar, click the View Day, View Week, or View Month button.

To view a specific date or month

1   Click the date or the name of the month at the top of the calendar.

2   Click the date in the displayed calendar or list.

To add an appointment

1   On the toolbar, click New Appointment.

2   Enter a name, date, and time range.

To copy an appointment

●   Hold down the Ctrl key while you drag an appointment to a new date.

To delete an appointment

●   On the calendar, click an appointment, and then click the Delete button on the toolbar.

To add an event or a birthday

1   On the toolbar, click New Appointment.

2   Enter a name and date.

3   Select the All-Day Event check box.

To create a recurring appointment

1   On the toolbar, click New Appointment.

2   Enter appointment details and select the Make This Appointment Repeat check box.

3   Click Recurrence, and then specify recurrence options.

To add holidays

1   On the Edit menu, click Add Holidays.

2   Select a country.

To assign a category

1   In the calendar, double-click an appointment.

2   Click Change, select a category, and then click OK.

Managing Your Schedule

5

To create a category

1   In the calendar, double-click an appointment.

2   Click Change, click Edit Categories, type a category name, click Add, and then click OK.

To view appointments by category

1   On the toolbar, click Category Filter.

2   Select or clear the categories to show or hide appointments.

To send a calendar in e-mail

1   On the Edit menu, click Send.

2   Enter a date range, specify whether to include all or filtered appointments, and then click OK.

6

Tracking a Budget

ESTIMATED TIME
30 min.

In this lesson, you will learn how to:

✔ *Create a spreadsheet with a wizard or from scratch.*

✔ *Enter text and numbers in a spreadsheet.*

✔ *Perform calculations.*

✔ *Chart your data.*

✔ *Preview, print, and save charts and spreadsheets.*

Since spreadsheet programs became widely available, people have used them for tables, lists, and calculations of all kinds, from simple home budgets to elaborate bookkeeping systems. Spreadsheet programs are so versatile that some people even use them for writing letters!

Works Spreadsheet can help you track a budget, of course, but you can also use it to store medical records, chart sports team statistics, and even plan your next trip. Works Spreadsheet functions something like a combination of word processor and calculator, with tools for both recording information and calculating data. For this reason, Works Spreadsheet is a great tool for organizing and storing all kinds of information.

In this lesson, you'll learn how to work in a spreadsheet to enter and edit the type of simple budget information that a treasurer for the fictional Oak Park restoration project would create.

What Is a Spreadsheet?

A **spreadsheet** is simply a grid of columns and rows, similar to a ledger sheet used by an accountant. If you've ever used an accounting ledger or even your checkbook register, you are already acquainted with a spreadsheet. At its heart, a spreadsheet is a table in which you organize figures in **rows** and **columns** and perform calculations. When you open Works Spreadsheet, you see a grid. Each box where a row and a column of the grid intersect is a **cell** that can contain text, numbers, or formulas. These cells differentiate Works Spreadsheet from a word processor. Although you can format and print text in both types of programs, Works Spreadsheet is designed specifically for working with text and numbers in calculations.

In general, you use Works Spreadsheet to

■ Calculate, compare, and evaluate numbers

■ Chart information

■ Create simple lists and checklists

Works makes it easy to figure out when to use a spreadsheet. You just scan the list of tasks in the Task Launcher and start the task that matches what you want to do. With tasks for creating moving lists, student schedules, graphs and charts, and more, the Task Launcher automatically creates a spreadsheet with typical data that you can customize for your projects. For example, you can start the Financial Worksheets task to set up a budget spreadsheet complete with data that you can quickly personalize. When you can't find a task that matches what you want, you can always start a spreadsheet from scratch, such as the project budget shown below.

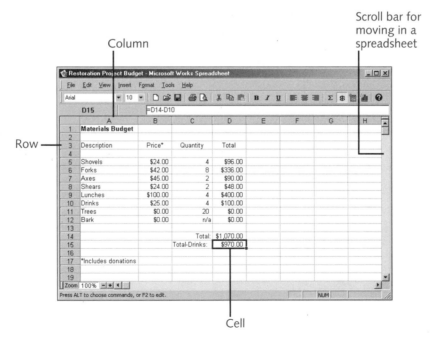

> **tip**
> Sometimes you might see the term *spreadsheet* used to refer to a spreadsheet program and the term *worksheet* used to refer to the document created by a spreadsheet program. In this book, however, we'll use the term *spreadsheet program* to refer to the program and the term *spreadsheet* to refer to the document.

Creating and Saving a Spreadsheet

When you choose a Works task that requires a spreadsheet, a program called a **wizard** appears and asks you questions about the task that you want to complete. Based on your answers, the wizard creates a spreadsheet for you with appropriate sample text and data, which you can replace with your information. For example, when you start the Home Improvement Worksheets task, a wizard appears that asks you to choose a budget, a maintenance checklist, or a work record, and then it creates one of these three types of spreadsheets.

When you start Works Spreadsheet directly, you see a blank spreadsheet with numerous unformatted empty rows and columns. To fill in the blanks, you click in a cell and type. What you type is stored in that cell.

In this exercise, you start two new spreadsheets: one by using a wizard and the other by starting a new, blank spreadsheet. You save the blank spreadsheet to use in subsequent exercises.

1   On the taskbar, click the Start button, point to Programs, and then click Microsoft Works.

The Works Task Launcher opens.

2   Click the Tasks tab.

Categories of tasks appear on the left, and tasks for the selected category appear on the right.

3   Under Tasks, click Money Management.

Tasks for the Money Management category appear.

4   In the list of tasks, click Financial Worksheets.

A description of this task appears.

5   Click Start This Task.

The Works Financial Worksheets Wizard is displayed. The wizard asks you to choose a style.

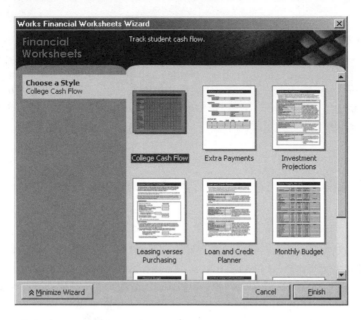

6   Click the Monthly Budget style, and then click Finish.

Works Spreadsheet opens with a spreadsheet named Home Budget, Monthly.

Currently selected cell

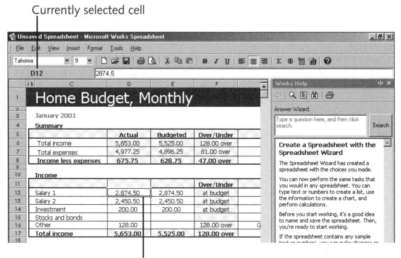

You can type over the sample data supplied by
the wizard to personalize the spreadsheet.

Because the goal of this lesson is to create a project budget, you can see that
the wizard's results have more detail than you need, as well as a home focus
that is not entirely appropriate.

Close

7 To close the spreadsheet, on the Works Spreadsheet title bar, click the Close button.

A message box appears, asking if you want to save changes.

8 Click No.

The Task Launcher is displayed. If the Task Launcher does not appear, click Microsoft Works Task Launcher on the taskbar.

Programs

To create a new, blank spreadsheet while in Works Spreadsheet, click New on the toolbar.

9 To start a new, blank spreadsheet, click the Programs tab.

All Works programs are listed in the Task Launcher.

10 In the list of programs, click Works Spreadsheet.

Tasks for Works Spreadsheet are listed on the right.

11 Click Start A Blank Spreadsheet.

Works Spreadsheet opens with a new, blank spreadsheet.

Close Help

To restore the Works Help pane, click Works Help on the Help menu.

12 If the Works Help pane is open, click the Close Help button on the Works Help title bar to display more of the spreadsheet.

The Help pane is hidden, and the spreadsheet fills the screen.

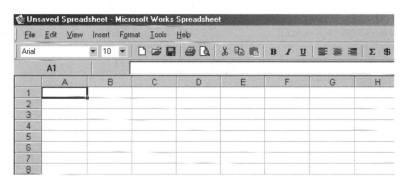

Save

13 To save this spreadsheet, click the Save button on the toolbar.

The Save As dialog box opens.

14 In the Save In box, make sure that the My Documents folder is selected.

For details about installing the practice files, see "Using the Book's CD-ROM" at the beginning of this book.

15 Double-click the Works Suite 2001 Practice folder, and then double-click the Lesson06 folder.

If you want to save your work in a different location, browse to the folder you want.

16 In the File Name box, type **Restoration Project Budget**.

17 Click Save to save the document.

The Works Spreadsheet title bar changes to show the new filename.

Tracking a Budget

Entering Text and Numbers

Whether you start from a task wizard or from scratch, the resulting spreadsheet contains vertical columns, identified by a unique letter, and horizontal rows, identified by a unique number. You can identify each cell in a spreadsheet by its **cell reference**, which consists of the column letter and row number. For example, the cell reference for the cell at the top left of the spreadsheet is A1 because it is in column A, row 1.

To see a multimedia demo about editing a spreadsheet, double-click the Edit Spreadsheet icon in the Demos folder on the book's CD-ROM.

To work with a cell, you must first select it by clicking in the cell or by using the arrow keys or the Tab key to move to the cell. By selecting a cell, you make it the **active cell**, which Works Spreadsheet highlights with a black border. Works Spreadsheet always displays the cell reference of the current active cell at the top of the spreadsheet. To the right of the cell reference is the **formula bar**, which displays the active cell's contents. To enter new or edit existing information in a cell, you type in the formula bar, which looks like a text box. When you click in the formula bar, buttons appear for canceling, entering, and getting help with formulas.

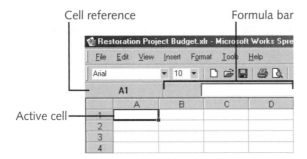

You can **format** a cell to change its appearance and the way Works Spreadsheet evaluates its contents. For example, you can format a cell containing the text *Total* to make the text appear bold and to align the text in the center. If a cell contains a number, such as 12, you can format the cell as currency so that Works Spreadsheet displays and evaluates the value as *$12.00*. Works Spreadsheet includes other number formats as well, such as percent and fraction.

Although only one cell can be active at a time, you can select a group of cells, called a **cell range**. When you work with a cell range, you can quickly repeat text and numbers across columns or down rows.

In this exercise, you select and move among cells in the spreadsheet and then add and format text and numbers.

1   Note that cell A1 is already the active cell and is highlighted with a thick black border.

If A1 is not highlighted, click the cell to make it the active cell.

2   Click in the formula bar, and then type **Materials Budget**.

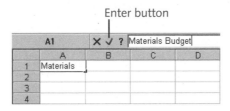

Enter button

3   Click the Enter button on the formula bar.

Enter

The formula bar's contents are added to cell A1, but the text is longer than the cell's width.

4   On the toolbar, click the Bold button.

Bold

The text is formatted in bold type.

5   To resize the column so that all the text fits, point in the center of the column A label, and then double-click.

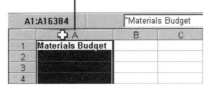

Double-click a column header to change the column width to fit the contents.

Column A widens to show all the text in cell A1.

6   To add labels to the spreadsheet, click cell A3, and then type **Description**.

Cell A3 becomes the active cell, and the text appears in the formula bar as you type.

7   Press the Right Arrow key.

Cell B3 becomes the active cell.

8   Type **Price***, and then press the Tab key.

Cell C3 becomes the active cell.

9   Type **Quantity**.

10   To fill in the details, click cell A5, and then type **Shovels**.

11   Press Tab, and then type **24**.

12   Press Tab, and then type **4**.

13   To enter the remaining items, use the technique in steps 10 through 12 to type the Description, Price, and Quantity information shown in the table on the following page.

*To enter num-
bers quickly,
use your key-
board's keypad.*

Description	Price	Quantity
Forks	42	8
Axes	45	2
Shears	24	2
Lunches	100	4
Drinks	25	4
Trees	0	20
Bark	0	n/a

Your spreadsheet should now look similar to the following illustration.

Text is automatically left-aligned.

Numbers are automatically right-aligned.

	A	B	C	D
1	**Materials Budget**			
2				
3	Description	Price*	Quantity	
4				
5	Shovels	24	4	
6	Forks	42	8	
7	Axes	45	2	
8	Shears	24	2	
9	Lunches	100	4	
10	Drinks	25	4	
11	Trees	0	20	
12	Bark	0	n/a	
13				
14				

Restoration Project Budget.xlr - Microsoft Works Spreadsheet
File Edit View Insert Format Tools Help
Arial   10
C12   "n/a

14   To align the text entries in the Quantity column with the number entries, click cell C12.

Cell C12 (the cell containing the text *n/a*) becomes the active cell.

15   On the toolbar, click the Right Align button.

Works Spreadsheet right-aligns the contents of cell C12.

Right Align

16   To format the numbers in the Price column as dollars, drag from cell B5 to cell B12 to select the cells.

Works Spreadsheet highlights the cells to show that they are selected.

Currency

17   On the toolbar, click the Currency button.

Works Spreadsheet formats the numbers as dollars.

	A	B	C
1	**Materials Budget**		
2			
3	Description	Price*	Quantity
4			
5	Shovels	$24.00	4
6	Forks	$42.00	8
7	Axes	$45.00	2
8	Shears	$24.00	2
9	Lunches	$100.00	4
10	Drinks	$25.00	4
11	Trees	$0.00	20
12	Bark	$0.00	n/a
13			

18   Click cell A17, type ***Includes donations**, and then press the Enter key.

The text is added to cell A17, and A18 becomes the active cell.

19   To save your changes, on the toolbar, click the Save button.

Save

tip

When you work in a spreadsheet, it's often quicker to use keyboard shortcuts rather than the mouse to move among the columns and rows. For example, you can use the arrow keys to move to adjacent cells. That way, you don't have to move your hand off the keyboard when you switch from typing numbers to moving the cell reference. For a complete list of keyboard shortcuts available in Works, search Works Help for *keyboard shortcuts*.

Performing Calculations

Although a spreadsheet is a great place to type a quick list or table, it's an even better place to perform quick calculations. For example, you can add all the numbers in a row or column, or subtract the results of one cell from the contents of another. To calculate a new result, you write an equation called a **formula**.

For example, *=A1+B1* is a simple formula that adds the contents of cell A1 to the contents of cell B1. The equal sign (=) tells Works Spreadsheet that you're typing a formula, and not just text. The plus sign (+) is one of many mathematical operators, which also include the minus sign (–), multiplication symbol (*), and division symbol (/).

If you type this formula in cell C1, you'll see the result of the calculation in the cell and the formula itself in the formula bar. For example, if A1 is 1 and B1 is 2, the result displayed in C1 is 3. Sometimes it's easier to find errors or track cell references if you show the formula in a cell. You can toggle the view of a spreadsheet to show results or formulas. Unless you change the view, Works Spreadsheet displays results, but you can change this by clicking Formulas on the View menu.

6

Tracking a Budget

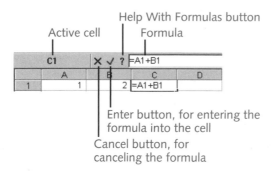

Active cell

Help With Formulas button

Formula

Enter button, for entering the
formula into the cell

Cancel button, for
canceling the formula

When you want to calculate something a little more complicated than the sum of
two cells, you can use a **function**. A function performs a specific calculation on
the cells you specify. For example, the SUM function totals a group of cells that
you select. Works Spreadsheet can also perform more advanced financial, statisti-
cal, and mathematical functions, including everything from loan payment rates to
cosines.

To help you create formulas, Works Spreadsheet includes the Easy Calc tool. With
this tool, you can quickly create a simple formula or set up a more advanced formula that uses one of the built-in functions.

In this exercise, you write a formula to calculate row and column totals, copy a
formula to other cells, and then create a formula that contains a function.

1 Click cell D3, and then type **Total**.

D3 becomes the active cell, with the value *Total*.

Center Align

2 To format the labels, drag from cell B3 to cell D3, and then click the Center
Align button on the toolbar.

Works Spreadsheet centers the Price, Quantity, and Total labels.

3 To enter a formula that calculates the subtotal for shovels, click in cell D5, and
then type **=B5*C5**.

Because you typed an equal sign (=) first, Works Spreadsheet interprets the
text as a formula. The asterisk (*) is the symbol for multiplication.

Enter

4   Click the Enter button on the formula bar.

Works Spreadsheet evaluates the formula and displays the result in cell D5.

D5	=B5*C5		
	A	B	C	D
1	Materials Budget			
2				
3	Description	Price*	Quantity	Total
4				
5	Shovels	$24.00	4	96
6	Forks	$42.00	8	

Fill handle

5   To quickly copy this formula for each item, click cell D5 to display the selection border.

FILL

6   Drag the small square in the lower right corner of the cell, called the fill handle, down from cell D5 to cell D12.

The pointer changes to the Fill pointer as you drag. When you release the mouse button, the formula in cell D5 is copied to each cell in the selection range. Works Spreadsheet updates the cell references in each formula, so the correct total for each item is displayed.

	A	B	C	D
1	Materials Budget			
2				
3	Description	Price*	Quantity	Total
4				
5	Shovels	$24.00	4	96
6	Forks	$42.00	8	336
7	Axes	$45.00	2	90
8	Shears	$24.00	2	48
9	Lunches	$100.00	4	400
10	Drinks	$25.00	4	100
11	Trees	$0.00	20	0
12	Bark	$0.00	n/a	0
13				FILL

7   To see how Works Spreadsheet updated the formula, click cell D6, and then view the formula bar.

Cell references are
updated for each
cell in the range.

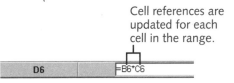

D6	=B6*C6	

Works Spreadsheet updated the cell references in the copied formula to
=*B6*C6* for this cell. Works Spreadsheet similarly edited the cell addresses for
each formula in the range you repeated.

Tracking a Budget   6

8   To format the subtotals, click column header D.

All cells in column D are selected.

Currency

9   On the toolbar, click the Currency button.

Works Spreadsheet formats the numbers as dollars but does not change the format of cell D3 (containing the text *Total*).

Right Align

10   To create a grand total, click cell C14, type **Total:** and then click the Right Align button.

Works Spreadsheet adds the text to cell C14 and right-aligns it.

AutoSum

11   Click cell D14, and then click the AutoSum button on the toolbar.

Works Spreadsheet selects the range of cells under the Total heading and displays a formula that uses the SUM function to add all the numbers in the selection.

If the cells selected by AutoSum are not the ones you want, select the correct cells.

The SUM function adds the cell values in a range.   A colon (:) is used to indicate all the cells between D5 and D13, inclusive.

	D5:D13	X ✓ ?	=SUM(D5:D13)		
	A	B	C	D	
1	**Materials Budget**				
2					
3	Description	Price*	Quantity	Total	
4					
5	Shovels	$24.00	4	$96.00	
6	Forks	$42.00	8	$336.00	
7	Axes	$45.00	2	$90.00	
8	Shears	$24.00	2	$48.00	
9	Lunches	$100.00	4	$400.00	
10	Drinks	$25.00	4	$100.00	
11	Trees	$0.00	20	$0.00	
12	Bark	$0.00	n/a	$0.00	
13					
14			Total:	=SUM(D5:D13)	
15					

Enter

12   Click the Enter button on the formula bar.

Works Spreadsheet evaluates the formula and displays the result in cell D14.

13   To calculate a total that doesn't include drinks, click in cell C15, type **Total–Drinks:** and then click the Enter button on the formula bar.

Works Spreadsheet adds the text to cell C15, but the text is wider than the cell.

14   Double-click the column C header.

All cells in column C are widened to accommodate the text in cell C15.

Easy Calc

15 Click cell D15, and then click the Easy Calc button on the toolbar.
The Easy Calc dialog box appears.

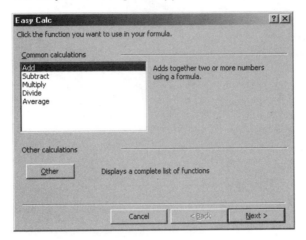

16 Under Common Calculations, click Subtract, and then click Next.
Easy Calc asks you to identify the values you want to subtract.

17 If the Easy Calc dialog box covers up the Price, Quantity, and Total cells, drag the dialog box by its title bar to the right of column D.
Don't worry if the Easy Calc dialog box runs off the screen.

Minimize Dialog

tip
If a cell or range of cells is hidden by the Easy Calc dialog box, click the Minimize Dialog button to the right of the Range box to make the dialog box smaller.

18 In the spreadsheet, click cell D14.
Easy Calc adds the cell reference D14 in the List Of Values box.

19 In the spreadsheet, click cell D10.
Easy Calc adds the minus sign and the cell reference D10 in the List Of Values box.

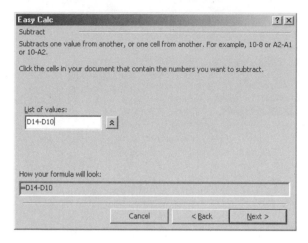

20   In the Easy Calc dialog box, click the Next button.

You might need to drag the dialog box toward the center of the screen first and then click the Next button.

Options for the final result are displayed, showing cell D15 as the place where Easy Calc will insert the result.

21   Click the Finish button.

Easy Calc adds the formula *=D14–D10,* which appears in the formula bar. The result is displayed in cell D15.

Save

22   To save your changes, on the toolbar, click the Save button.

> ## tip
> If you remember your high school algebra, you can write many types of formulas in Works Spreadsheet. For details about creating formulas, type **formulas and functions** in the Answer Wizard in Works Help.

Presenting Data in a Chart

With a chart, you can illustrate, analyze, and interpret data and relationships. A chart depicts spreadsheet data in a visually appealing way that's often easier to understand than rows of numbers. In Works Spreadsheet, a chart is just another way of looking at the same information contained in the spreadsheet.

You can use your spreadsheet data to create many different types of charts, including area, bar, line, pie, stacked line, scatter, radar, combination, and 3-D charts. The type of chart you select depends on how you want to present your data. For example, if you wanted to show values as a percentage of a whole, you would select a pie chart.

Charts make a great addition to documents created in other programs. For example, you can copy a Works Spreadsheet chart to a newsletter created in Word to illustrate an article.

In this exercise, you create a chart of the Oak Park budget information much as you would to present the information to a committee you wanted to impress. You then preview and print the chart.

1   Drag from cell A3 to cell D10.

The range of cells is selected.

New Chart

2   On the toolbar, click the New Chart button.

The New Chart dialog box appears and displays the Basic Options tab.

3   Under Chart Type, click Pie.

A preview of the chart appears in the Preview box.

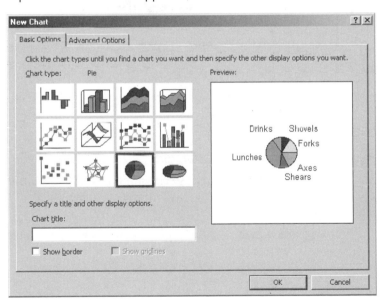

4   In the Chart Title box, type **Cost of Materials**.

The title appears in the Preview box.

5   Click OK.

Works Spreadsheet displays the chart in Chart view, which includes commands and toolbar buttons for working with charts. Your screen should look similar to the following.

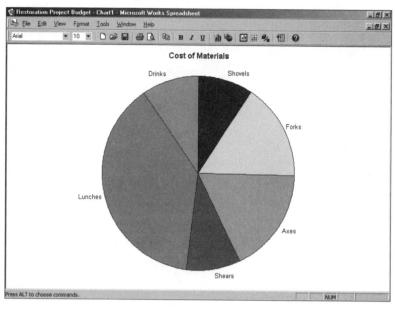

Chart Type

6   To change the chart type, click the Chart Type button on the toolbar.

The Chart Type dialog box appears and displays the Basic Types tab.

7   Under Chart Type, click 3-D Pie, and then click OK.

Works Spreadsheet changes the look of the pie chart.

Save

8   To save your changes so far, click the Save button on the toolbar.

9   To see how the chart looks when printed, click the Print Preview button on the toolbar.

Print Preview

The spreadsheet is displayed in the Print Preview window, and the pointer changes to a magnifying glass when passed over the chart.

important

If your printer is capable of printing color, the preview will be in color. Otherwise, Works Spreadsheet substitutes black lines and patterns for the colors.

ZOOM
Zoom pointer

10   To magnify the view, click on the chart.

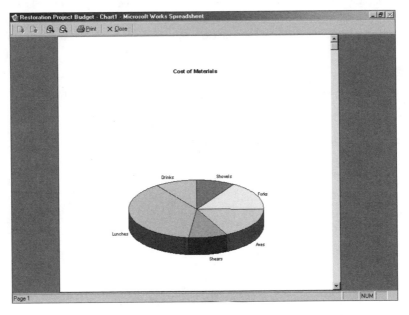

11   On the toolbar, click the Print button.

The Print dialog box appears.

12   Click OK.

Works Spreadsheet prints only the chart.

13   To return to viewing the spreadsheet, on the View menu, click Spreadsheet.

The spreadsheet is displayed.

tip
You can copy a chart from the Chart window and then paste it into another program, such as Microsoft Word. Click Copy on the Edit menu, switch to another program, and then click Paste on the Edit menu.

Previewing and Printing a Spreadsheet

Printing a spreadsheet can differ from printing documents in other types of programs. You can set a specific section of a spreadsheet as the **print area** so that only the information in that area is printed. For example, you can print only the portions of a large spreadsheet that you need to see by setting a print area.

Tracking a Budget

Before you print your spreadsheet, you can add a **header** or **footer**—text that appears in the top or bottom margin of every page. Just as you can add a header and a footer to a Word document, you can insert them in a spreadsheet to track page numbers, revision dates, and other file information. Headers and footers aren't displayed on your screen until you preview your spreadsheet.

In this exercise, you add a header to your spreadsheet, preview the results, and then specify a print area before printing the spreadsheet.

1   On the View menu, click Header And Footer.

The Header And Footer dialog box appears.

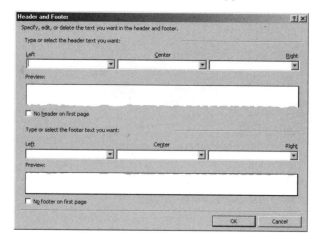

2   At the top of the Header And Footer dialog box, click the Right arrow.

A list of items you can add to your header appears.

3   Click «Current Date».

In the Preview area, Works Spreadsheet replaces the text «*Current Date*» with today's date.

4   Click OK.

The header is added to your spreadsheet, but until you preview or print it, you cannot see the header text.

5   To set the print area to show only the descriptions and prices, drag from cell A1 to cell B12.

6   On the File menu, point to Print Area, and then click Set Print Area.

A message box appears, asking if you want to set the print area to the highlighted cells.

7   Click OK.

The next time you print the spreadsheet, only the area you selected will be printed.

8   To print the spreadsheet, on the File menu, click Print.

The Print dialog box appears.

9   To see how the print area looks, click the Preview button.

The spreadsheet opens in the Print Preview window.

ZOOM

Zoom pointer

10   Click to zoom in.

Only the information in the specified print area appears in the Print Preview window. The header appears in the upper right corner.

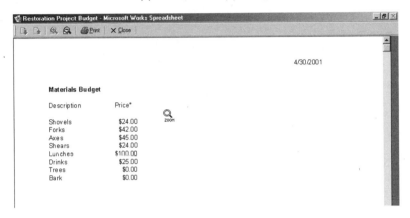

11   On the toolbar, click the Print button to display the Print dialog box again, and then click OK.

Works Spreadsheet prints the selected area of the spreadsheet.

12   To remove the specified print area, on the File menu, point to Print Area, and then click Clear Print Area.

The next time you preview or print the spreadsheet, the entire spreadsheet will be included.

Save

13   To save your changes, click the Save button on the toolbar.

tip

In a header and footer, you can type your own text as well as use one of the options from the drop-down boxes. For example, you can type *Printed On* in the Right box and then select «Current Date» from the drop-down list. To adjust the location of the header and footer with respect to the top and bottom edges of the paper, click Page Setup on the File menu, and then adjust the Header and Footer values on the Margins tab.

Tracking a Budget

6

Lesson Wrap-Up

To finish the lesson:

Close

1 On the File menu, click Exit. Or, on the title bar of the Works Spreadsheet window, click the Close button.

Works Spreadsheet closes, and the Task Launcher appears.

If the Task Launcher does not appear, click Microsoft Works Task Launcher on the taskbar.

2 In the Task Launcher, click Close.

Quick Reference

To create a spreadsheet using the Works Financial Wizard

Tasks

1 In the Task Launcher, click the Tasks tab.

2 Under Tasks, click Money Management, and then in the list of tasks, click Financial Worksheets.

3 Click Start This Task.

4 In the Works Financial Worksheets Wizard, choose a style, and then click Finish.

To start Works Spreadsheet and create a new spreadsheet from scratch

Programs

1 In the Task Launcher, click the Programs tab.

2 Click Works Spreadsheet, and then click Start A Blank Spreadsheet.

To save a spreadsheet

1 On the toolbar, click the Save button.

2 Specify a location, type a filename, and then click Save.

To select a cell

● Click a cell.

To select a range of cells

● Click a starting cell, and then drag to the ending cell.

To cancel a selection

● Click any other cell.

To move among cells in a spreadsheet

● Press an arrow key or the Tab key, or click with the mouse.

To add text or numbers

● Click a cell, type the text or numbers, and then click the Enter button on the formula bar.

To repeat text and numbers

1   Select a cell containing information you want to repeat.

FILL

2   Drag the fill handle on the selection border down rows or across columns.

To format a cell as currency

●   Click a cell, and then click the Currency button on the toolbar.

To calculate the total of a row or column

1   Click a cell at the end of the row or column in which you want the total to appear.

2   Click the AutoSum button.

To create a formula

1   Click the cell in which you want the formula to appear.

2   Type an equal sign (=) followed by the formula.

3   Click the Enter button on the formula bar.

To show formulas in the cells

●   On the View menu, click Formulas.

To show results in the cells

●   On the View menu, clear the Formulas check box.

To insert a function into a cell

1   Click a cell, and then click the Easy Calc button on the toolbar.

2   Select a function, and then follow the instructions in the Easy Calc dialog box to complete the formula.

To create a chart

1   Select a range of cells, and then click the New Chart button on the toolbar.

2   Choose a chart type, type a title, and then click OK.

To view a chart

●   On the View menu, click Chart.

To change a chart's type

1   In Chart view, click the Chart Type button on the toolbar.

2   Choose a chart type, and then click OK.

To preview a chart

- In Chart view, click the Print Preview button on the toolbar.

To print a chart

- In Chart view, click the Print button on the toolbar.

To view a spreadsheet

- On the View menu, click Spreadsheet.

To add headers or footers to a spreadsheet

1   On the View menu, click Header And Footer.

2   Type text or choose an option in the Left, Center, and Right boxes, and then click OK.

To specify a part of the spreadsheet to print

1   Select the range of cells you want to print.

2   On the File menu, point to Print Area, and then click Set Print Area.

To preview a spreadsheet

- In Spreadsheet view, click the Print Preview button on the toolbar.

To print a chart

- In Spreadsheet view, click the Print button on the toolbar.

To remove the print area

- On the File menu, point to Print Area, and then click Clear Print Area.

7

Creating a Mass Mailing

In this lesson, you will learn how to:

✔ *Set up a form letter.*

✔ *View and print merged data.*

✔ *Customize a letter in a mass mailing.*

✔ *Filter and sort a mailing list.*

✔ *Print labels and envelopes for a mass mailing.*

ESTIMATED TIME 40 min.

In Lesson 2, you explored simple word processing techniques using Microsoft Word to write a letter. When you want to write a letter intended for multiple recipients such as the members of a group or organization, you can merge a single form letter with a mailing list to create a mass mailing. For example, you can write your annual holiday greetings as a form letter that can be merged with a family address list. Sometimes this technique is called print merge or **mail merge**, after the Word command you use to do it. Word can address a form letter to each person on your mailing list and even print mailing labels and envelopes using the same mail merge technique. In the end, you save a considerable amount of time compared with the time it takes to manually address a stack of letters.

This lesson shows you how to do a mass mailing. You'll open a form letter intended to generate community interest in a volunteer park restoration project and then merge the letter with a mailing list. You'll use the same mailing list to create address labels for envelopes.

This lesson requires the sample mailing list (Oak Park Mailing List.doc) and form letter (Volunteer Solicitation Letter.doc) that you installed from this book's CD-ROM. For details about installing the practice files, see "Using the Book's CD-ROM" at the beginning of this book.

What Is a Mail Merge?

Many businesses and individuals rely on the mail merge feature in Word for their mass mailings. For example, you can create a single form letter containing all the latest family news and merge it with your mailing list of all the out-of-state cousins. To work smoothly, however, mail merging requires both the letter and the mailing list to be set up in a very specific manner. To get the results you want, you must take care to follow each step in the process exactly. In general, it works like this:

1	Create a form letter, which Word calls the **main document**. The form letter contains the text that you want to send to each person in your mass mailing. In this lesson, you'll use a sample letter.

2	Specify the location of your mailing list, which Word calls the **data source**. The data source can be a document created in Word or in another program that lists each name and address in a consistent format.

3	Add **merge fields** to the letter, which are placeholders that show Word where to insert the address information contained in the data source. For example, *First Name*, *Last Name*, and *Address* are typical merge fields that Word replaces with a person's name and address from your mailing list.

4	Merge the data source with the main document, which causes Word to create a new document that contains information from both the main document (your letter) and the data source (the names and addresses of the letter's recipients). For example, if your mailing list contains the names and addresses of 10 people, when you merge your letter and mailing list, Word creates a new document that contains 10 copies of the letter, each addressed to a different person from the mailing list. You can then personalize some of the resulting merged letters, save the new document that contains all the letters, or just print the results.

The following illustration shows an overview of the mail merge process.

Creating a Mass Mailing

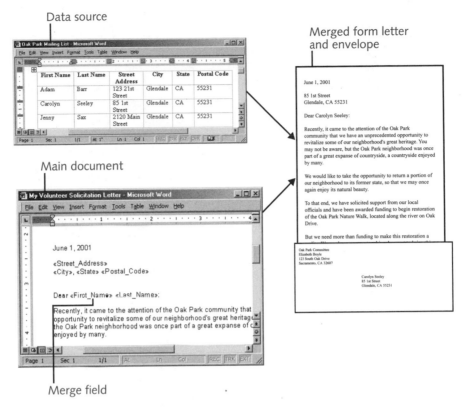

Data source

Merged form letter
and envelope

Main document

Merge field

In this exercise, you open an existing letter that tells community members how they can become involved in the Oak Park Nature Walk restoration project. This letter will be the main document for your mass mailing. You also open and view the Oak Park mailing list, which will be used as the data source.

Start

1   On the taskbar, click the Start button, point to Programs, and then click Microsoft Works.

    The Works Task Launcher opens.

Programs

2   Click the Programs tab.

    All Works programs are listed in the Task Launcher.

3   In the list of programs, click Word.

    Tasks for Word are listed on the right.

important

If you installed Microsoft Works 6.0 (rather than Microsoft Works Suite 2001), Microsoft Word does not appear in the Task Launcher. Instead, you'll see the Works Word Processor, which is the program that Works 6.0 uses for word processing tasks. For details about creating a form letter using Works Word Processor, search Works Help for *mail merge*.

To restore the Office Assistant, click Show The Office Assistant on the Help menu.

4   Click Start A Blank Word Document.

Word opens with a new, blank document.

5   If the Office Assistant appears, on the Help menu, click Hide The Office Assistant.

The Office Assistant is hidden.

Open

6   To open the sample form letter, click the Open button on the Standard toolbar.

The Open dialog box appears.

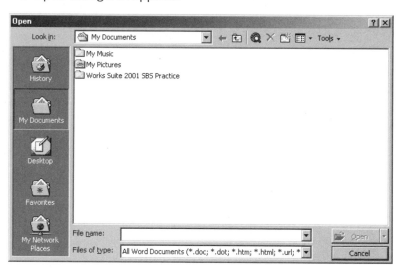

7   Make sure the Look In box shows My Documents.

For details about installing the practice files, see "Using the Book's CD-ROM" at the beginning of this book.

8   Double-click the Works Suite 2001 SBS Practice folder, and then double-click the Lesson07 folder.

If you do not see Works Suite 2001 SBS Practice in the list of folders, browse to the location where you installed the practice files.

9   Click Volunteer Solicitation Letter.doc, and then click Open.

A complete draft of the letter opens in a new window.

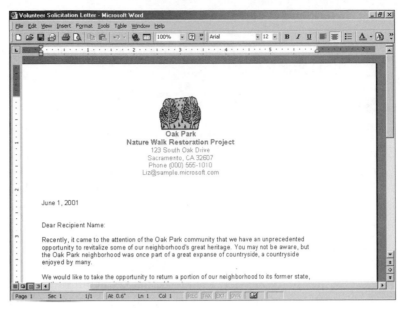

Open

10 To view the data source, click the Open button on the Standard toolbar.

The Open dialog box appears.

11 Make sure the Look In box shows Lesson07.

If you do not see the Lesson07 folder, locate and open this folder.

12 Click Oak Park Mailing List.doc, and then click Open.

Names and addresses for nine people are listed in a format that Word can use for a mail merge.

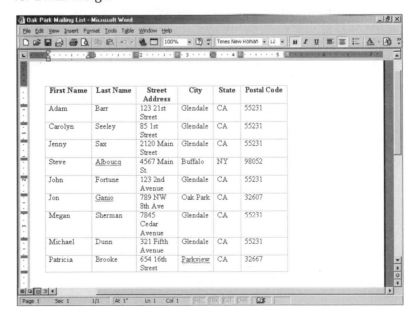

First Name	Last Name	Street Address	City	State	Postal Code
Adam	Barr	123 21st Street	Glendale	CA	55231
Carolyn	Seeley	85 1st Street	Glendale	CA	55231
Jenny	Sax	2120 Main Street	Glendale	CA	55231
Steve	Alboucq	4567 Main St.	Buffalo	NY	98052
John	Fortune	123 2nd Avenue	Glendale	CA	55231
Jon	Ganio	789 NW 8th Ave	Oak Park	CA	32607
Megan	Sherman	7845 Cedar Avenue	Glendale	CA	55231
Michael	Dunn	321 Fifth Avenue	Glendale	CA	55231
Patricia	Brooke	654 16th Street	Parkview	CA	32667

Close

If the letter does not appear, click Volunteer Solicitation Letter on the taskbar.

13 To close the mailing list data source, click the Close button on the Word title bar.

The data source is closed, and the window containing the Volunteer Solicitation Letter appears.

Setting Up a Form Letter

To tell Word where to insert names and addresses into your form letter, you add merge fields. When you merge the main document and the data source, Word replaces the merge fields with the actual names and addresses. You use the Mail Merge Helper dialog box to tell Word where to find your data source. Then Word reads the fields in your data source and lists them on the Mail Merge toolbar.

To add merge fields to your letter, you choose a field from the Mail Merge toolbar, and Word inserts it into your letter. You can insert a merge field anywhere in the text of your main document. Word will merge the data source information in exactly the spot you insert the merge field, so you might need to add spaces or punctuation around the field. Field names are enclosed in angle brackets (« ») in the main document.

To see a multi-media demo about creating a form letter, double-click the Create Form Letter icon in the Demos folder on the book's CD-ROM.

The names of the merge fields you see in Word vary depending on your data source. If your data source names the fields *First Name*, *Surname*, and *Address Block*, those are the names you'll see. Or the fields might be something like *First_Name*, *Last_Name*, *Street_Address*, *City*, and *Postal_Code*.

In this exercise, you use the Mail Merge Helper dialog box to set up the volunteer solicitation form letter you just opened as the main document. You also set up the mailing list as the data source. Then you add merge fields to the letter based on the fields in your data source.

important

Works Suite 2001 includes a version of Word 2000 that is modified so that it integrates well with Works. If you perform the steps in this lesson with a standard installation of Word 2000, you will notice some small differences.

1 On the Tools menu, click the down arrow to expand the menu, point to Mail Merge, and then click Options.

The Mail Merge Helper dialog box appears.

tip

Depending on your installation of Word, the Mail Merge option on the Tools menu might not have a submenu. In this case, to open the Mail Merge Helper dialog box, click Mail Merge on the Tools menu.

2   Under Main Document, click the Create button, and then click Form Letters.

A message box might appear, asking you to choose a document as the main document for the mail merge.

3   If the message box appears, click Active Window.

The message box closes, and the Mail Merge Helper dialog box now includes an Edit button under Main Document.

4   Under Data Source, click the Get Data button, and then click Open Data Source.

The Open Data Source dialog box appears.

5   Make sure the Look In box shows Lesson07.

If you do not see the Lesson07 folder, locate and open this folder.

6   Click Oak Park Mailing List.doc, and then click Open.

A message box might appear, indicating that Word found no merge fields in your main document.

7   If the message box appears, click Edit Main Document.

The Mail Merge Helper dialog box closes. Your document window now includes the Mail Merge toolbar, as shown in the following illustration.

Standard toolbar   Formatting toolbar

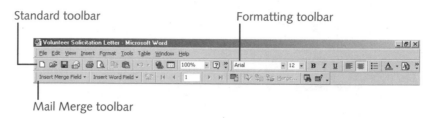

Mail Merge toolbar

8   To the right of the salutation, drag across the words *Recipient Name* to select them.

9   On the Mail Merge toolbar, click the Insert Merge Field button.

A list of all the fields from the mailing list data source is displayed.

10   Click First_Name, and then press the Spacebar.

The selected phrase is replaced by the First_Name merge field. Various buttons on the Mail Merge toolbar are enabled.

tip
Until you specify a data source that Word recognizes, the Insert Merge Fields button is dimmed on the Mail Merge toolbar. To set up or change the data source, point to Mail Merge on the Tools menu, and then click Options. In the Mail Merge Helper dialog box, click the Get Data button and select a data source option.

11   On the Mail Merge toolbar, click Insert Merge Field, and then click Last_Name.

Word inserts the Last_Name merge field to the right of the First_Name field.

12   Click the empty line below the date, and then press Enter.

You will insert merge fields for the recipient's address in this area.

13   On the Mail Merge toolbar, click Insert Merge Field, click Street_Address, and then press Enter.

14   On the Mail Merge toolbar, click Insert Merge Field, and then click City.

15   Type a comma (,), and then press the Spacebar.

16   On the Mail Merge toolbar, click Insert Merge Field, click State, and then press the Spacebar.

17 On the Mail Merge toolbar, click Insert Merge Field, click Postal_Code, and then press Enter.

The recipient address area should now look similar to the following:

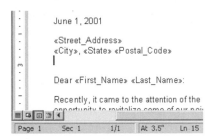

18 To save your changes as a form letter with a new name, on the File menu, click Save As.

The Save As dialog box is displayed.

19 In the Save In box, make sure that the Lesson07 folder is selected.

If you want to save your work in a different location, browse to the folder you want.

20 In the File Name box, click to the left of the filename, and then type **My**.

The filename is now My Volunteer Solicitation Letter.

21 Click Save to save the document.

The Word title bar changes to show the new filename.

Viewing and Printing Merged Data

After you add merge fields to your form letter, you can merge the real names and addresses from your data source and view the results. Word refers to each result, such as a letter or a label, as a **record** and includes the Mail Merge toolbar for viewing, editing, and navigating among records. Even after you specify a data source, you can add, edit, and delete entries in the data source from within the main document. Once you are satisfied that the main document is merging data correctly into the merge fields you created, you can print the results.

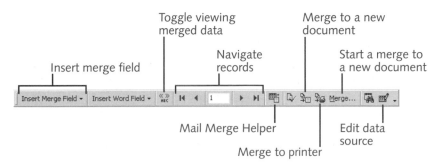

In this exercise, you view the merged data in the main document, navigate to different records, and learn how to modify information in the data source.

View Merged Data

1   On the Mail Merge toolbar, click the View Merged Data button.

Word replaces the merge fields with the actual names and addresses from the data source.

Next Record

Last Record

First Record

Edit Data Source

2   On the Mail Merge toolbar, click the Next Record button.

The second record in the data source is displayed.

3   On the Mail Merge toolbar, click the Last Record button.

The ninth record in the data source is displayed.

4   To move to the first record, click the First Record button on the Mail Merge toolbar.

5   To view and edit the information in the data source, click the Edit Data Source button on the Mail Merge toolbar.

The Data Form dialog box appears and displays the name and address for the current record. From this dialog box, you can add, edit, and delete records in the data source.

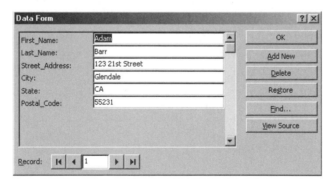

6   To close the Data Form dialog box, click OK.

7   To save the main document and the data source, on the Standard toolbar, click the Save button.

Save

Merge To Printer

8   To print all nine letters, on the Mail Merge toolbar, click the Merge To Printer button.

The Print dialog box is displayed.

9   Under Page Range, note that the All option is selected.

For a very large mailing with hundreds of letters, you could choose the Pages option and enter a page range, such as *1–100*, so that you print only the pages you want.

10   Click OK.

Word prints all nine form letters.

11   To view the merge fields again, click the View Merged Data button.

The merge fields in the letter are displayed.

View Merged Data

Working with Other Data Sources

The expression "data source" comes from the world of database development and is used by Word to describe the place to look for merge information. A data source file has to be formatted in a particular way so that Word knows how to merge the information it contains with your form letter or envelopes.

In this lesson, the data source is another Word document that contains names and addresses in a table. You can copy the practice file (Oak Park Mailing List.doc) to use as a template for your own mailing list by editing the names and addresses.

If you don't have an existing data source, you can use the Mail Merge Helper dialog box to set one up for you. Click the Get Data button, and then click Create Data Source. It suggests a list of fields for the data source, such as FirstName and LastName. You choose the fields you want and remove the ones you don't want, and the Mail Merge Helper dialog box creates a data entry form with those fields. You then enter the names and addresses into each data entry form. The entries are saved as a new Word document that you can use as a data source.

Word can also use a data source created in another program. For a list of the program file types that Word can use as a data source, see the "Data Sources You Can Use with Word" topic in Word Help. If your data source is not recognized by Word, you might be able to export the data in another format, such as comma-delimited text.

Customizing the Merge Results

As long as you want to send an identical form letter to each recipient in your data source, a mail merge is quite simple. But what if you want to customize the letter intended for one person? If you edit the main document, all copies of the form letter will include the change when you merge. Fortunately, Word provides an alternative: You can merge your main document and data source to create a new multiple-page document, each page of which is a copy of the form letter addressed to a different recipient. Then you can locate an individual letter and personalize it before printing. Because the new document contains all the merged information, the options on the Mail Merge toolbar will no longer apply.

In this exercise, you merge the information to a new document and edit the letter to John Fortune, a fictional city official.

1   On the Mail Merge toolbar, click the Merge button.

The Merge dialog box appears.

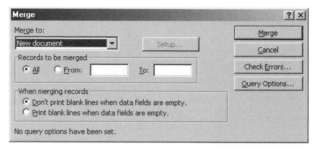

2   Make sure the Merge To box is set to New Document and Records To Be Merged is set to All.

3   Click Merge.

Word merges the mailing list entries in the data source with the merge fields in your letter and creates a new document named Form Letters1. The new document contains nine pages—one for each of the names in the data source. The new document does not display the Mail Merge toolbar.

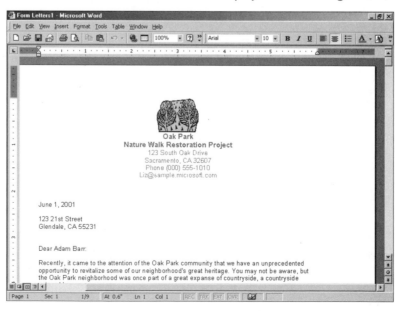

Next Page

4 To scroll through the pages and verify that the names and addresses were merged as expected, click the Next Page button at the bottom of the vertical scroll bar.

5 To return to the beginning of the document, hold down the Ctrl key and press the Home key.

6 On the Edit menu, click Find.

The Find And Replace dialog box appears.

7 In the Find What box, type **John Fortune**, and then click Find Next.

In the document behind the Find And Replace dialog box, Word finds the letter addressed to John Fortune.

8 Click Cancel to close the Find And Replace dialog box.

9 If necessary, scroll down in the letter, and then drag to select the paragraph that begins *To that end.*

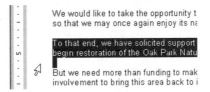

10 Press the Delete key.

The paragraph and the blank line are removed, and this letter now differs from the others in the mass mailing.

Save

11 To save the document containing the form letters for mass mailing, on the Standard toolbar, click the Save button.

The Save As dialog box opens.

12 In the Save In box, select the Lesson07 folder or browse to another folder.

13 In the File Name box, type **My Mass Mailing**.

14 Click Save to save the document.

The Word title bar changes to show the new filename.

Close

If the letter does not appear, click My Volunteer Solicitation Letter on the taskbar.

15 On the Word title bar, click the Close button.

The window containing My Volunteer Solicitation Letter appears.

Filtering and Sorting Names and Addresses

When you merge your form letter and mailing list, Word adds every field you specify in the order that it finds it in the data source. If you want to use only certain information from your data source or merge the field information in alphabetical or numeric order, you can **filter** and **sort** the data source before you merge.

For example, you can filter the addresses from your data source by selecting information that meets a certain criterion, such as all addresses in a particular city. Or you can sort the merge in ascending order by postal code (a requirement of the United States Postal Service for certain types of mass mailings).

In this exercise, you filter the addresses based on the City field and then view the results. Next you remove the filter, sort the addresses by postal code instead, and then view the results.

Mail Merge Helper

1   On the Mail Merge toolbar, click the Mail Merge Helper button.

The Mail Merge Helper dialog box appears.

2   Click Query Options.

The Query Options dialog box appears, and the Filter Records tab is displayed.

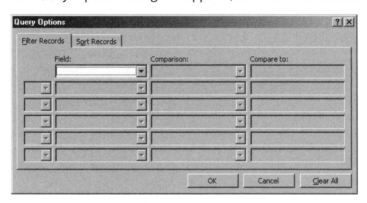

3   Click the first Field arrow, and then click City.

The insertion point moves to the Compare To box.

4   In the Compare To box, type **Glendale**.

Because the Comparison option is Equal To, Word will use only the addresses in the city of Glendale.

5   Click OK.

The Mail Merge Helper dialog box appears and indicates under Options In Effect that query options have been set.

6   Click Close.

The Mail Merge Helper dialog box closes.

View Merged Data

7   On the Mail Merge toolbar, click the View Merged Data button.

Word replaces the merge fields with the actual names and addresses from the data source. The first letter with a Glendale address appears.

Next Record

8   On the Mail Merge toolbar, click the Next Record button to view each record.

As you click the Next Record button, notice that there are now only six records and that all of them contain the Glendale address.

*Mail Merge
Helper*

9 On the Mail Merge toolbar, click the Mail Merge Helper button.

The Mail Merge Helper dialog box appears.

10 Click Query Options.

The Query Options dialog box appears, and the Filter Records tab is displayed.

11 Click the Clear All button.

The filter options you set are removed.

12 Click the Sort Records tab.

Options for sorting the fields in your data source appear.

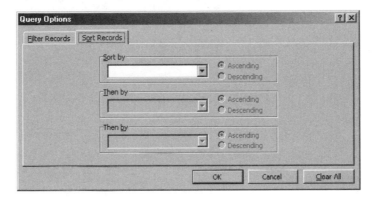

13 Click the Sort By arrow, and then click Postal_Code.

Options for ascending or descending order become available. Leave the Ascending option selected.

14 Click OK in the Query Options dialog box, and then click Close in the Mail Merge Helper dialog box.

15 On the Mail Merge toolbar, click the navigation buttons to view each record.

As you click the navigation buttons, notice that postal codes are in ascending order and that there are nine records.

Creating Labels and Envelopes

You can use the mail merge feature in Word to create and print mailing labels or envelopes just as you created form letters. You still need a main document and a data source. The only difference is that the main document is a label or an envelope; the data source is the same list of addresses you used before.

Mailing labels are available in a variety of types and sizes. Word can format your main document to match the size of various types of labels, such as Avery and AOne.

In this exercise, you use the Mailing Label Wizard to create labels using the same data source (Oak Park Mailing List) that you used for the form letter.

1   To create mailing labels using the same data source, on the File menu, point to New, and then click More Word Templates.

The New dialog box appears.

2   Click the Letters & Faxes tab.

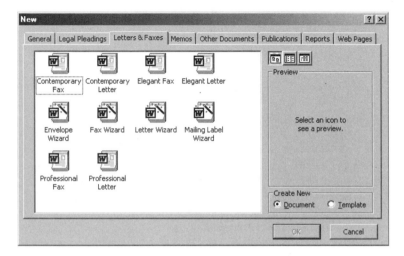

3   Click Mailing Label Wizard, and then click OK.

A new document is opened. The Office Assistant appears and includes a welcome to the Mailing Label Wizard. If the Office Assistant is disabled, you will see the Mailing Label Wizard dialog box.

4   Click Create Labels For A Mailing List.

The Mail Merge Helper dialog box appears. Merge Type is set to Mailing Labels, and Main Document is set to a new document.

5   Under Data Source, click Get Data, and then click Open Data Source.

The Open Data Source dialog box appears.

6   Make sure the Look In box shows Lesson07.

If you do not see the Lesson07 folder, locate and open this folder.

7   Click Oak Park Mailing List.doc, and then click Open.

The Label Options dialog box appears.

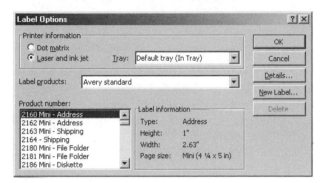

8   Click the Label Products arrow, and then click AOne.

Under Product Number, a list of AOne label types appears.

9   In the Product Number list, click AOne 28173 – Address.

Under Label Information, the Height and Width values change to indicate the size of this type of label.

10   Click OK.

The Create Labels dialog box appears.

11   Click Insert Merge Field, click First_Name, and then press the Spacebar.

In the Sample Label box, Word previews the merge field you inserted.

12   To complete the mailing label, do the following:

- ▪ Click Insert Merge Field, click Last_Name, and then press Enter.

- ▪ Click Insert Merge Field, click Street_Address, and then press Enter.

- ▪ Click Insert Merge Field, click City, type a comma (,), and then press the Spacebar.

- ▪ Click Insert Merge Field, click State, and then press the Spacebar.

- ▪ Click Insert Merge Field, and then click Postal_Code.

The Create Labels dialog box should now look similar to the following:

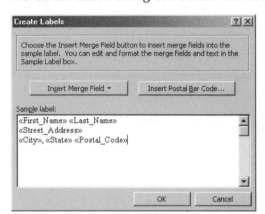

13 Click OK.

The Mail Merge Helper dialog box appears.

14 Click Close.

The Mail Merge Helper dialog box closes. The merge fields appear in the document and are positioned to fit the specified labels.

View Merged Data

15 To view the names and addresses instead of the fields, on the Mail Merge toolbar, click the View Merged Data button.

Word replaces the merge fields with the actual names and addresses from the data source. Your screen should look similar to the following:

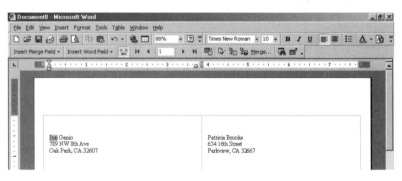

Merge To Printer

16 To print the labels, on the Mail Merge toolbar, click the Merge To Printer button.

The Print dialog box appears.

If you wanted to print actual labels, you would load AOne 28173 address labels (available at most office supply stores) into your printer's paper tray. For the purposes of this lesson, you can print the labels on regular laser printer paper to see what they look like.

17   Click OK.

Word prints a page of mailing labels.

Printing Envelopes

When it comes to printing envelopes, most laser printers include an adjustable feed tray or allow you to manually feed envelopes or other unusual sizes of paper. To set up an envelope as the main document in a mail merge, you can use the Envelope Wizard and follow the steps similar to ones used for creating labels. You can also follow the steps used for form letters.

1   To follow the steps used for form letters, first start a new, blank document.

2   On the Tools menu, point to Mail Merge, and then click Options.

3   In the Mail Merge Helper dialog box, click Create, and then click Envelopes. If a message box appears, click Active Document.

4   In the Mail Merge Helper dialog box, click Get Data and specify the source of your mailing list.

5   Set up the main document similar to the way that you did for mailing labels. In the Envelope Options dialog box, you can specify the envelope size, the fonts to use for the delivery and return addresses, and the feed method required by your printer.

6   After you've set the envelope options, click OK to insert the merge fields you want on your envelope.

7   When you've finished, click OK to return to the Mail Merge Helper dialog box.

8   To add a return address, click Edit under Main Document, and click Envelope: Document. You can type the return address that you want to appear on every envelope or insert merge fields for the return address.

9   To review the envelopes before printing, you can click the View Merged Data button on the Mail Merge toolbar and then use the navigation buttons on the Mail Merge toolbar. You can also merge the main envelope document with the data source to create a new document by clicking the Merge button on the Mail Merge toolbar.

Lesson Wrap-Up

To finish the lesson:

1   To close all open Word windows, click Exit on the File menu.

2   When message boxes appear, prompting you to save the Oak Park Mailing List.doc, click No.

3   When message boxes appear, prompting you to save changes, click No. The Task Launcher appears.

If the Task Launcher does not appear, click Microsoft Works Task Launcher on the taskbar.

4   In the Task Launcher, click Close.

Quick Reference

To set up a form letter for a mail merge

1   Start Word and open the document you want to use as the form letter.

2   On the Tools menu, point to Mail Merge, and click Options.

3   In the Mail Merge Helper dialog box, click Create and then click Form Letters.

4   In the Mail Merge Helper dialog box, click Get Data, and specify a data source.

5   In the main document, insert merge fields.

To open the Mail Merge Helper dialog box

●   Click the Tools menu, point to Mail Merge, and then click Options.

To open the Mail Merge Helper dialog box using the toolbar

●   Click the Mail Merge Helper button on the Mail Merge toolbar.

To view merged data

1   Click the View Merged Data button on the Mail Merge toolbar.

2   Use the navigation buttons on the Mail Merge toolbar to move to different records.

To save a mail merge document

●   Click the Save button on the Standard toolbar.

To print a mail merge document

●   Click the Merge To Printer button on the Mail Merge toolbar.

To create a Word document data source

1   Open the Mail Merge Helper dialog box.

2   Click the Get Data button, and then click Create Data Source.

3   In the Create Data Source dialog box, add and remove the appropriate field names and then click OK.

4   Specify a name for the document, and click Save.

To modify the information in a data source

1   Click the Edit Data Source button on the Mail Merge toolbar.

2   In the Data Form dialog box, modify the information in the data source.

To modify the information in a data source using the Mail Merge Helper dialog box

1   Open the Mail Merge Helper dialog box.

2   Under Data Source, click the Edit button and then click the data source.

3   In the Data Form dialog box, modify the information in the data source.

To merge the main document and the data source into a new document

1   In the main document that you've set up already, click Merge on the Mail Merge toolbar.

2   In the Merge dialog box, keep the Merge To New Document setting, and then click Merge.

To edit a letter in a mass mailing

1   In the new document created by the mail merge, click Find on the Edit menu.

2   In the Find And Replace dialog box, type the name of the recipient whose letter you want to edit, and then click Find Next.

3   Click Cancel to close the dialog box, and then edit the letter as necessary.

To filter a data source before merging

1   Open the Mail Merge Helper dialog box.

2   Click Query Options, and then click the Filter Records tab.

3   In the Field box, click the field to use in the comparison. In the Comparison box, click the operator you want. In the Compare To box, type a value to use in the comparison.

4   Click OK. In the Mail Merge Helper dialog box, click Close to return to editing the main document, or click Merge to proceed with the mail merge.

To sort a data source before merging

1   Open the Mail Merge Helper dialog box.

2   Click Query Options, and then click the Sort Records tab.

3   Under Sort By, click a field, click Ascending or Descending, and then click OK.

4   In the Mail Merge Helper dialog box, click Close to return to editing the main document, or click Merge to proceed with the mail merge.

Creating a Mass Mailing

To remove filter or sort criteria from a main document

1   Open the Mail Merge Helper dialog box.

2   Click Query Options, and then click Clear All.

3   In the Mail Merge Helper dialog box, click Close to return to editing the main document, or click Merge to proceed with the mail merge.

To create mailing labels using the Mailing Label Wizard

1   In Word, on the File menu, point to New, and then click More Word Templates.

2   In the New dialog box, click the Letters & Faxes tab.

3   Click Mailing Label Wizard, and then click OK.

4   In the Mailing Label Wizard welcome, click Create Labels For A Mailing List.

5   Under Data Source, click Get Data, click Open Data Source, and then specify a mailing list you want to use.

6   In the Label Options dialog box, click a label type in the Label Products box, click a label number in the Product Number list, and then click OK.

7   In the Create Labels dialog box, insert merge fields, and then click OK.

8   In the Mail Merge Helper dialog box, click Close to return to editing the main label document, or click Merge to proceed with the mail merge.

LESSON

8

Working with Databases

ESTIMATED TIME 30 min.

In this lesson, you will learn how to:

✔ *Understand and create a simple database.*

✔ *Find and view database information in different ways.*

✔ *Print reports of database information.*

Microsoft Works includes a database that you can use to collect, organize, and manage almost any kind of information, from names and addresses to recipes. Even if you don't know much about databases, this lesson will show you why they're useful and how easy it is to create one in Works. When do you need to create a database? For projects with a lot of details to track, a database gives you unique and powerful tools for looking at and filtering information in different ways. Plus, knowing how to create your own database makes it easier to work with the predefined database tasks that are included with Works.

In this lesson, you learn how to create a database from scratch that you'll use to manage information for the fictional Oak Park restoration project.

What Is a Database?

Any organized collection of similar information (data) is a database. For example, your phone book's white pages are a database, as are your checkbook register and your recipe file. You can think of a database that you create in Works as a super-organized filing system with built-in flexibility for viewing and printing information.

For example, if you have a database of recipes, you can quickly find all the recipes that use a particular ingredient, such as corn. Or in a database of movies, you can display only titles from one studio that were filmed in a particular year.

The most basic components of a database are fields and records. A **field** is a specific category of information that you want to store. For example, *First Name* is a field in a mailing list database, and *Ingredient* is a field in a recipe database. A **record** is the complete set of related fields about a person, place, item, or event. Together, all the records make up a database, which in Works Database looks like a table as shown below. The columns represent fields, and rows represent records.

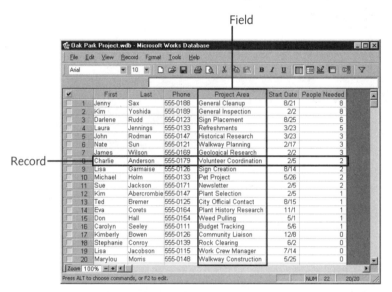

After you create fields in Works Database, you can enter information by typing directly into the table. This table format is called **List view**. Later in this lesson, you'll explore the power of databases when you learn how to view your database in different ways, sort fields, find specific records, and create reports that you can print.

Creating a Database

The quickest way to create a database is to start with a suitable Works task if there is one that matches what you want. If not, you'll need to know how to create a new database. For example, the recipe book task in Works actually creates a database. In this section, you'll learn how to create a database to manage the Oak Park restoration project.

For details about working with Works tasks, see Lesson 1, "Introducing Microsoft Works."

Before you create anything, it's best to plan how you want to organize your information. For example, if you need to collect addresses, you could create one big Address field to contain the street name, city, state, and zip code information. A better solution is to create four fields: Street, City, State, and Zip Code. By breaking information down into several discrete chunks, you make it easier down the road to sort, filter, and report on your data. Ultimately, your database is more flexible and therefore more useful. You can always make changes later, though, if you need to add, delete, move, or resize a field.

When you create fields for your database, you specify the type, or **format**, of information that will go in it—that is, whether you'll be entering text or numbers or something else. Works Database provides handy options for displaying the contents of your field based on its format so that you don't have to manually edit entries to get them to look the way you want. So, for example, if you create a field called Start Date and specify its format as Date, you can choose how you want dates to look in your database, such as *May 3*. Later, even if you type *5/3* when you're entering your information, Works Database displays the date as *May 3*.

In this exercise, you start Works Database and create a database from scratch.

1   On the taskbar, click the Start button, point to Programs, and then click Microsoft Works.

The Works Task Launcher appears.

2   Click the Programs tab.

All Works programs are listed in the Task Launcher.

3   Click Works Database.

Works displays a list of database tasks.

4   Click Start A Blank Database.

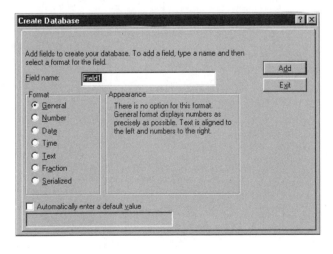

5   In the Create Database dialog box, type **First** in the Field Name box.

Under Format, the General option is already selected. For this field, keep this setting.

6   Click Add.

A field named First is created in your database. The Create Database dialog box remains open.

7   To create the other fields in your Oak Park project database, repeat steps 5 and 6 using the settings in the following table.

Field name	Format
Last	General
Phone	Text
Project Area	General

If you make a mistake while typing, press the Backspace key to delete the mistake and then type the correct text. You can also add and remove fields later if necessary.

8   When you finish adding the fields, click Done in the Create Database dialog box.

Works Database displays in List view with the fields that you created.

Your database should look something like this:

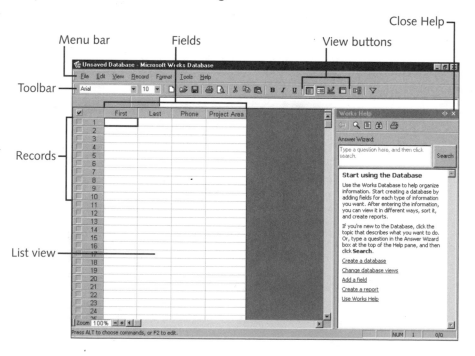

9 To add more fields, click the Project Area field name.

The Project Area column is selected.

10 On the Record menu, point to Insert Field, and then click After.

The Insert Field dialog box appears.

11 In the Field Name box, type **Start Date**.

12 Under Format, click the Date option.

A set of formatting options for dates is displayed under Appearance.

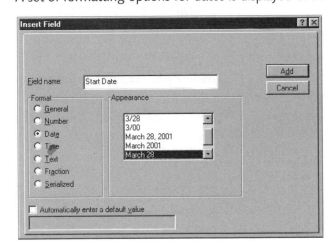

13 In the Appearance box, click the "month day" format, such as March 28.

14 Click Add.

The Start Date field appears in the database. The Insert Field dialog box remains open.

15 In the Field Name box, type **People Needed**.

16 Under Format, click the Number option.

A set of formatting options for numbers is displayed under Appearance. Leave the first option selected, which is 1234.56.

17 In the Decimal Places box, click the down arrow twice to change the value to **0**.

18 Click Add, and then click Done.

The People Needed field is added to the right of the Start Date field. Your database now looks something like this:

✔		First	Last	Phone	Project Area	Start Date	People Needed
☐	1						
☐	2						
☐	3						
☐	4						
☐	5						
☐	6						

Working with Databases   8

Save

For details about installing the practice files, see "Using the Book's CD-ROM" at the beginning of this book.

19   To save your database, click the Save button on the toolbar.

The Save As dialog box appears.

20   Make sure the Save In box shows My Documents.

21   Double-click the Works Suite 2001 SBS Practice folder, and then double-click the Lesson08 folder.

If you don't see the Works Suite 2001 SBS Practice folder, choose any convenient location to save your database.

22   In the File Name box, type **Oak Park Project**.

23   Click Save.

Your database is saved as a file called Oak Park Project.wdb and displays this name in the Microsoft Works Database title bar.

Entering Information

Fields form the backbone of your database, which you can fill out by entering information for each record. Data entry can be time-consuming, but Works Database offers some options that can ease your task. For example, you can enter and edit data in List view to see your entire database at once. Or you can work in Form view, which displays one record at a time. List view and Form view are simply two different ways of seeing the same information. Most people find Form view easier for data entry.

You can enter data into your fields in any order. The database keeps everything organized for you.

In this section, you'll learn how to switch between views and learn how to enter details about several people working on the Oak Park restoration project.

Form View

1   On the toolbar, click the Form View button.

Works Database displays one record in a form that looks like this:

Press Tab to move from one field to the next.

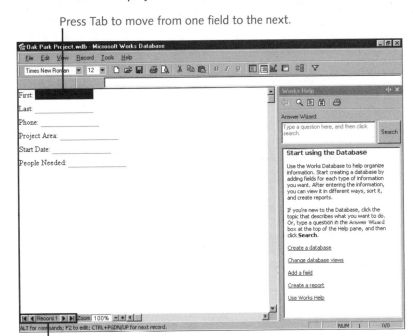

Click a navigation button to move among records in a database.

List View

2   On the toolbar, click the List View button.

Works Database displays all the records in a table.

Form View

3   To enter information into your database, click the Form View button on the toolbar again.

Works Database displays the form for the database.

4   Click in the First field, and then type **Sue**.

5   Press the Tab key to move to the Last field, and then type **Jackson**.

6   Press Tab to move to the Phone field, and then type **555-0171**.

7   Press Tab to move to the Project Area field, and then type **Newsletter**.

8   Press Tab to move to the Start Date field, and then type **2/5**.

When you pressed Tab, Works Database used the format that you specified earlier to display the Start Date field as February 05.

9   Press Tab to move to the People Needed field, and then type **2**.

10   Press Tab to advance to the next blank record.

11   Continue filling in the fields for all the records, using the following information:

First	Last	Phone	Project area	Start date	People needed
Kim	Abercrombie	555-0147	Plant Selection	2/5	1
Charlie	Anderson	555-0179	Volunteer Coordination	2/5	2
Laura	Jennings	555-0133	Refreshments Provision	3/23	5
Carolyn	Seeley	555-0111	Budget Tracking	5/6	1
Michael	Holm	555-0133	Pet Project	5/26	2

To go back to a record or move to a different one, use the following navigation buttons at the bottom of the window:

Button	Click to display
⏮	First record in the database
◀	Previous record in the database
▶	Next record in the database
⏭	Last record in the database

List View

12   When you are finished entering information, click the List View button on the toolbar.

All your records appear in List view, where you can quickly verify your entries.

If you see pound signs (#) in some fields, it means that the column is not wide enough to display all the information.

Close Help

13   To gain space for displaying fields, close Works Help by clicking the Close Help button.

ADJUST
Horizontal Adjust pointer

14   If you need to widen a field, position the pointer over the edge of the column headings until you see the horizontal Adjust pointer, and then drag the pointer to resize the column. Your database should look something like this:

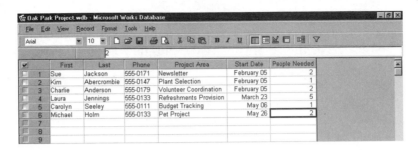

Save

15   On the toolbar, click the Save button to save your changes.

Formatting a Database Form

In a database with many records, you can spend a lot of time in Form view entering data. One way to lighten the task is to format your forms so that they're easier to read. In **Form Design view**, you can arrange fields and add borders, colors, text labels, and graphics—without changing the fields' contents. In fact, you cannot edit or enter field data in Form Design view. You can edit only the fields themselves.

To reposition fields in Form Design view, drag them to a new location. When you click a field, gray squares, called **resize handles**, appear on its sides and corners. Drag a resize handle to stretch the field in the direction that you want. To experiment with fonts, click a field, and then click Font And Style on the Format menu to choose a different look for the text.

Form Design

For details about designing your forms, search the Works Help index for *form* or *design*. To use your newly designed forms, click the Form Design button on the toolbar to change views.

Finding and Sorting Information

After you've added information to your database, how do you retrieve it? If you have only a handful of records, you can probably locate what you want at a glance in List view. Now imagine that your database contains details about dozens or even hundreds of records. What's the quickest way to change one person's phone number? What if you want to put all the names that you entered in alphabetical order? How can you see all the volunteers available to start in the spring? To manage the information that you've entered, you can **find, sort,** and **filter** your database. The method that you use depends on your goal, as the following table shows.

To see a multimedia demo about sorting and filtering database information, double-click the Work in Database icon in the Demos folder on the book's CD-ROM.

What you want to do	Method	Examples
Locate database records that contain specific information in a field or fields.	Find	Find the record for Michael Holm so that you can look up his phone number.
		Find out who's in charge of volunteer coordination.
Put all the database records in ascending or descending alphabetic or numeric order based on the entries in one or more fields.	Sort	Sort the records alphabetically by last name.
		Put the records in order by start date to see who begins first.
Show a set of records that meet the criteria that you set.	Filter	Show the people whose start date is between April 1 and June 1.
		Show everyone who starts after February and needs more than two people for the project.

None of these methods of organizing information changes the data that you entered. Instead, each presents an alternative way of viewing your database's contents. You can find, sort, and filter information in either List view or Form view. You can even print the results.

In this exercise, you'll find and sort your records to display different kinds of information from your Oak Park restoration project database. Then in the following exercise, you'll create and apply a filter to selectively view information.

1   On the Edit menu, click Find.

The Find dialog box appears.

2   In the Find What box, type **Michael**.

3   Under Match, click the All Records option, and then click OK.

Works Database displays just the record for Michael Holm.

4   To see all your records again, on the Record menu, point to Show, and then click All Records.

To repeat a search, press Shift+F4.

List View

If your sort results are not what you expected, immediately click Undo Sort on the Edit menu.

All the records appear. If you're in List view, you may need to scroll up to see all the records. If you're in Form view, you can use the navigation buttons to see all the records.

5   If Form view is displayed, click the List View button on the toolbar.

Works Database displays all the records in List view.

6   To sort your records, on the Record menu, click Sort Records.

The Sort Records dialog box appears.

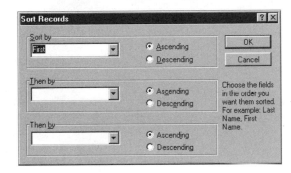

7   Click the Sort By arrow to show all the options, and then click Last.

The Ascending option is already selected.

8   Click OK.

The records are sorted by last name in alphabetical order.

tip

In the Sort Records dialog box, you can sort by more than one field when you want to sort by multiple criteria. For example, in a family database that contains parents, children, and the children's birthdays, you can sort by the Parent field and the Birthday field to sort the records alphabetically by the parents' name and then by birthday from oldest to youngest child.

Filtering Database Information

By using a filter, you can define specific criteria that fields must meet. The result is that you can display a particular subset of matching records. For example, if you want to see records for only the last year, you can filter out everything prior to the last year. The records that do not meet the criteria are temporarily hidden from view. When you no longer need to filter the view, you can display all the records again.

In this exercise, you create and apply a filter to your database.

Filters

1   On the toolbar, click the Filters button.

The Filter Name dialog box appears on top of the Filter dialog box.

> **tip**
> If you see only the Filter dialog box, click the New Filter button to display the Filter Name dialog box.

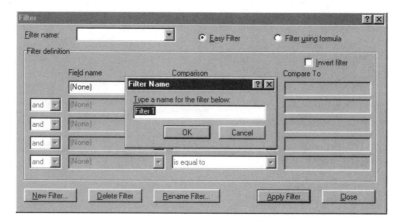

2   In the Filter Name box, type **Starts March** and then click OK.

The Filter Name dialog box closes so that you can work in the Filter dialog box.

3   Click the Field Name arrow, and then click Start Date.

4   Click the Comparison arrow, and then click Is Greater Than Or Equal To.

5   Under Compare To, type **March 1**.

The settings that you've chosen look like this:

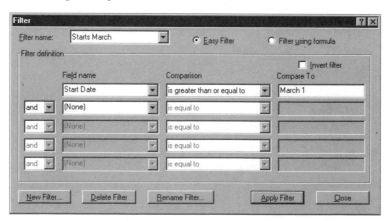

6 Click Apply Filter.

Works Database displays only the records that meet the criteria that you set—that is, all the records for people who start the project on or after March 1.

The other records have not been removed from the database; they are merely temporarily hidden while you view the filtered information.

Filters

7 To refine your filter and apply it to the database, on the toolbar, click the Filters button.

The Filter dialog box appears.

8 In the Filter Name box, make sure that Starts March is showing.

If other filters are listed, click the arrow, and then click Starts March.

9 In the second box under Field Name, click the arrow, and then click People Needed.

10 In the second box under Comparison, click the arrow, and then click Is Greater Than.

11 In the second box under Compare To, type **1**.

The settings that you've chosen look like this:

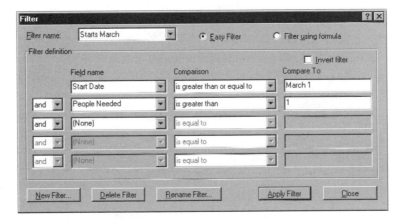

12 Click Apply Filter.

Works Database displays all the records that match the new criteria—that is, all the records for everyone who starts the project after March 1 and needs two or more people for his or her area.

Your database should look something like this:

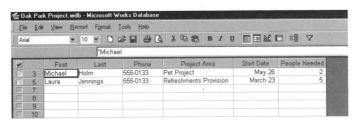

13   To restore the view to show all the records, on the Record menu, point to Show, and then click All Records.

Works Database displays all the records in List view.

Printing Database Information

To publish your database information, you can print a **report** that contains a neatly formatted summary of the contents you want. Although you can also print the contents of List or Form view, a report offers more flexibility and polished results. In a report, you can print only certain fields; sort, group, and filter the information for greater effectiveness; add titles and labels; and even calculate averages and other statistics for numeric information.

In this section, you'll use the ReportCreator, which contains options for defining the contents and format of your report. You can define up to eight different reports for one database. You'll create a report for the Oak Park restoration project to show the number of volunteers that you have and how many more that you need for the project.

In this exercise, you create and print a report:

1   On the Tools menu, click ReportCreator.

The Report Name dialog box appears.

2   In the Type A Name For The Report Below box, type **People Needed**, and then click OK.

The ReportCreator dialog box appears, and the Title tab is displayed.

3   In the Report Title box, type **Oak Park Project Volunteers**.

The title will appear at the top of the report. The report name in step 2 is used by Works Database to refer to this report.

4   Click Next to display the Fields tab.

5   In the Fields Available box, click First, and then click Add.

The First field appears in the Field Order box.

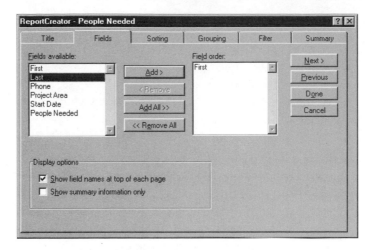

6   Repeat step 5 to add the Last, Project Area, and People Needed fields to the
     Field Order box.

7   Click Next to display the Sorting tab.

8   Click the Sort By arrow, and then click People Needed.

9   Click the Descending option.

     Your report will sort fields in order from the most people needed to the fewest.

10   Click Next to display the Grouping tab.

11   Under Group By, select the When Contents Change check box.

     This option inserts a blank line between groups of records that have a differ-
     ent value for People Needed. When you select it, the dimmed options under
     Group By become available.

12   Under Group By, select the Show Group Heading check box.

     This option adds a heading for each group based on the contents of the field:
     in this case, the number of people needed.

13   Click Next to display the Filter tab.

     Leave the settings unchanged to use the current records.

14   Click Next to display the Summary tab.

15   In the Select A Field box, click People Needed.

Working with Databases

16   Under Summaries, select the Sum check box.

A message box prompts you to preview or modify the report.

17   Click Done.

18   Click Preview.

The Print Preview window opens and displays your report.

---

tip

If you don't have a default printer selected, use Control Panel to specify a printer.

---

19   To magnify the view, click the Zoom In button or click anywhere on the report. From here you can click the Print button to print the report or click Cancel.

Click to see more of your report.

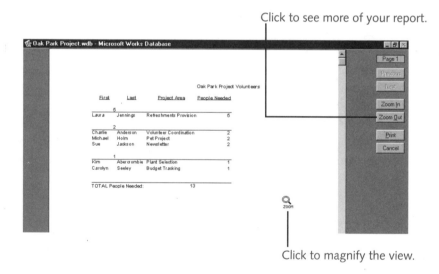

Click to magnify the view.

Modifying a Report

After you use the ReportCreator to define the contents of a report, the Print Preview window shows you whether your report contains everything that you expected. If it doesn't, you can close the window and then modify your report definition. Closing the preview returns the display to **Report view,** where you can see the report definition. In Report view, additional editing commands for working with reports are available on the Tools menu.

In this exercise, you return to List view to modify your report definition before previewing it again.

1   If the Print Preview window is still displayed, click the Cancel button.

The report definition is displayed in Report view.

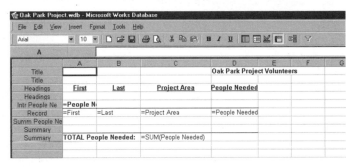

List View

Save

2   On the toolbar, click the List View button.

List view appears.

3   On the toolbar, click the Save button.

The database and the report definition are saved.

4   On the View menu, choose Report.

The View Report dialog box appears.

5   In the Select A Report box, click People Needed, and then click Modify.

The report definition appears in Report view.

6   On the Tools menu, click Report Sorting.

The Report Settings dialog box appears with the Sorting tab open.

7   Click the Then By arrow, and then click Last.

Leave the Ascending option selected so that your report will show the groups of people sorted in alphabetical order by last name.

8   Click Done.

The report definition is displayed again.

9   On the File menu, click Print Preview.

The Print Preview window opens and displays your modified report.

10   To print the report, click the Print button; otherwise, click the Cancel button.

Save

11   On the toolbar, click the Save button.

The modified report definition is saved.

List View

12   To see your database again, click the List View button on the toolbar.

Lesson Wrap-Up

To finish the lesson:

Close

If the Task Launcher does not appear, click Microsoft Works Task Launcher on the taskbar.

1   On the File menu, click Exit. Or on the title bar of the Works Database window, click the Close button.

The Task Launcher appears.

2   Click Close to exit the Task Launcher.

Quick Reference

To create a database

1   In the Task Launcher, click the Programs tab and then click Works Database.

2   Click Start A Blank Database, and then add fields.

To add a field

1   On the Record menu, point to Insert Field, and click After.

2   Enter field information, click Add, and then click Done.

To delete a field

1   Select the field.

2   On the Record menu, click Delete Field, and then click OK.

To move a field

1   Open List view or Form Design view.

2   Select a column field name.

3   Drag the field name, which will display the Move pointer.

MOVE

To change database views

●   Click the List View, Form View, or Form Design button on the toolbar.

To add a record in Form View

1   In the last record, click the last field.

2   Press Tab to add another record.

To move among records in Form View

●   Click a navigation button in the bottom-left corner of the screen.

To save a database

●   Click the Save button on the toolbar. Or on the File menu, click Save.

To open a database

●   Click the Open button on the toolbar. Or on the File menu, click Open.

To find a record

1   On the Edit menu, click Find.

2   Type the text that you want to find, and then click OK.

To sort records

1   On the Record menu, click Sort Records.

2   Specify sort criteria, and then click OK.

To find records using a filter

1   On the toolbar, click the Filters button.

2   Type a filter name and click OK.

3   Specify filter criteria, and then click Apply Filter.

To print records

●   On the toolbar, click the Print button. Or on the File menu, click Print.

To create a report

1   On the Tools menu, click ReportCreator.

2   Type a name, and click OK.

3   Specify title, field, sorting, grouping, filter, and summary information, and then click Done.

To modify a report

1   On the View menu, click Report.

2   Choose the report that you want, and then click Modify.

3   On the Tools menu, click the editing command that you want, specify changes, and then click Done.

To close a database

●   Click the Close button on the Works Database window. Or on the File menu, click Exit.

LESSON

9

Creating a Newsletter

**ESTIMATED
TIME
40 min.**

In this lesson, you will learn how to:

✔ *Create a newsletter with a Works wizard.*

✔ *Add text from another Word document.*

✔ *Change the appearance of a newsletter.*

✔ *Collect and manage pictures with the Works Portfolio.*

✔ *Add pictures and clip art to a newsletter.*

A custom-made newsletter, flyer, or brochure is a fun way to publish information about a club, an activity, a team, a business, or even your family. Together, Microsoft Works and Microsoft Word make it easy to create attractive, colorful documents that you can print or send as e-mail attachments. Works wizards, such as the Works Newsletters Wizard, create preformatted Word documents complete with clip art and placeholder text. All you have to do is write your own text or paste it from another source and add pictures.

In this lesson, you'll use the Works Newsletters Wizard to create a newsletter in Word. This lesson builds on the editing techniques you learned in Lesson 2, "Creating a Letter." Newsletters are typically more complex to lay out than letters, but by using the wizard, you'll have a template that shows you exactly where to place text. You'll also learn how to take advantage of the Works Portfolio to store and manage the pictures you want to use in other documents, including this lesson's newsletter.

**Practice files
for the lesson**

This lesson uses the practice files that you installed from this book's CD-ROM. For details about installing the practice files, see "Using the Book's CD-ROM" at the beginning of this book.

Creating a Newsletter Using a Wizard

The shortest route to a well-designed newsletter is through the Works Newsletters Wizard. It offers several audience-specific designs as well as a variety of layout, font, and color choices to provide custom results faster than you could create from scratch. The wizard creates a template in Word that contains a masthead, headlines, clip art, and placeholder text. Together, these elements give you a clear picture of the finished newsletter before you've added even the first article. To customize the newsletter, you replace the template's placeholder text with your own stories.

In this exercise, you'll see how Word actually creates the page design for the newsletter template. Behind the scenes, Word inserts hidden **formatting marks** into a document. For example, every time you press the Enter key, Word inserts a paragraph mark (¶), and every time you press the Spacebar, Word inserts a space mark (•). You can make these formatting marks visible to help you see exactly how a document is put together and to troubleshoot design problems, such as extra lines between paragraphs. You'll find it particularly useful to see the formatting marks when you work in a preformatted template because you can more easily retain the intended design as you add your own text and pictures. Formatting marks do not show up in your document when it is printed.

In this exercise, you create a newsletter using the Works Newsletters Wizard, which prompts you for formatting information before creating a newsletter template in Word. To better see how the newsletter's text is formatted, you make Word's formatting characters visible.

1   On the taskbar, click the Start button, point to Programs, and then click Microsoft Works.

The Works Task Launcher opens.

2   Click the Tasks tab.

All Works tasks are listed in the Task Launcher.

3   In the list of categories, click Newsletters & Flyers, and then click Newsletters.

A description of the Newsletters task appears.

4   Click Start This Task.

The Microsoft Word program window opens, and the Works Newsletters Wizard is displayed. The wizard asks you to choose a topic.

important

If you installed Microsoft Works 6.0 (rather than Microsoft Works Suite 2001), Works Word Processor appears behind the wizard instead of Word.

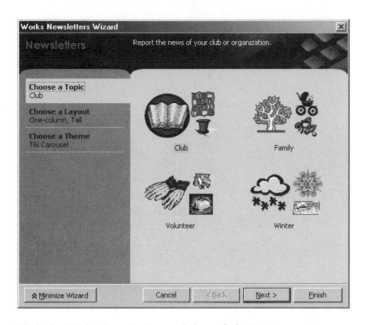

5 Click the Volunteer topic, and then click Next.

Options for choosing a layout appear.

6 Click the One-Column, Tall layout, and then click Next.

Options for choosing a theme appear.

7 Drag the Font Set slider to the left until the Simple font set is selected.

8 Drag the Color Set slider to the right until the Spring color set is selected, and then click Finish.

The wizard closes, and Word displays a one-column newsletter with place-holder text.

9 If the Office Assistant appears, on the Help menu, click Hide The Office Assistant.

To restore the Office Assistant, click Show The Office Assistant on the Help menu.

The Office Assistant goes away. For the purposes of this lesson, the Office Assistant is not shown in any illustrations.

Your screen should look similar to the illustration on the following page.

Masthead   Headline

"Lorem ipsum" placeholder text

10   To display the formatting characters that Word uses, on the Tools menu, click Options.

The Options dialog box appears and displays the View tab.

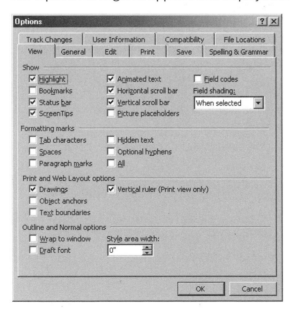

*To display for-
matting marks
using the tool-
bar, click the
Show/Hide ¶
button on the
Standard tool-
bar.*

11 Under Formatting Marks, select the All check box, and then click OK.

Word displays formatting marks in the document as shown below.

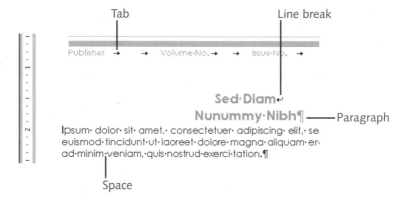

12 Double-click the word *Newsletter* in the masthead to select it.

Make sure that only the word is selected and not the paragraph mark after the word. Word selects the text, displays the Text Box toolbar, and highlights the entire masthead with a thick border, which shows that it is a separate text box from the rest of the newsletter.

The paragraph mark
is not selected.

*If you don't get
the results you
expected,
immediately
press Ctrl+Z to
undo the last
action.*

13 Type **Oak Park News**.

The new title appears in the masthead with the same formatting characteristics as the placeholder title.

Save

14 To save your work, on the Standard toolbar, click the Save button.

The Save As dialog box opens.

15 Make sure the Save In box shows My Documents.

16 Double-click the Works Suite 2001 SBS Practice folder, and then double-click the Lesson09 folder.

For details about installing the practice files, see "Using the Book's CD-ROM" at the beginning of this book.

If you do not see Works Suite 2001 SBS Practice in the list of folders, browse to the location where you installed the practice files.

17 In the File Name box, type **My Newsletter**.

18 Click Save to save the document.

The Word title bar changes to show the new filename.

What Is Lorem Ipsum?

When you start a newsletter with the Works Newsletters Wizard, Works inserts placeholder text to show you where to place your own stories. This text is sometimes called greeked text, or **lorem ipsum**, after the phrase *lorem ipsum dolor sit amet* that typically appears. Professional graphic designers have used lorem ipsum text for years to help them lay out pages before they had the final copy. The words are meaningless but let you see what the finished document will look like.

Adding Text to a Newsletter

To see a multimedia demo about formatting text, double-click the Format Text In Word icon in the Demos folder on the book's CD-ROM.

All the Works newsletter templates include sample text formatted with a theme that you choose. To add stories to your newsletter, select the sample text, and then type. The sample text acts as a placeholder so that you can visualize the overall design. As you type over it, the new text takes on the formatting of the sample text.

If you want to use text from a variety of sources or authors, you can add it to your newsletter by copying it. Copying text is a simple matter of selecting the text you want and then using the **Copy** command. The copied text is placed in a temporary storage area called the Clipboard. (If you are using a software product included in Microsoft Office, such as Word, the temporary storage area is a special Clipboard, called the Office Clipboard.) After you copy text to the Clipboard, you click to place the insertion point where you want the text to go, and use the **Paste** command. Word takes the text on the Clipboard and inserts it at the specified point. You can copy text and paste it elsewhere in the same document, in a new document, or even in several other documents.

The Office Clipboard can hold up to 12 items. To learn more about the Office Clipboard, search Word Help for Office Clipboard.

You can get unexpected results when the document from which you copied text is formatted differently from the document into which you're pasting the text. Word recognizes formatting and will paste the text, format and all, into your document. For example, if you copy text that is formatted as 10-point Times Roman into a document where all the text is formatted as 11-point Century Gothic, the pasted text will look different from the surrounding text. You'll want to avoid this problem because when you've gone to the effort of creating a cohesive page design with the Works wizard, naturally you want all the text to look the same.

One way that Word lets you quickly format text is to copy an existing format. You can do this with the **Format Painter**, which copies just the format of existing text and applies it to new text. You can also use the commands on the Format menu to manually reformat selected text. In this exercise, you'll use the Format Painter to apply the wizard's format to an article that you copy from another Word document. The article text is a sample file that you installed from this book's CD.

1 Select the first headline, *Sed Diam Nunummy Nibh*, but not its paragraph mark.

2 Type **Nature Walk Restoration Project Update**.

The new headline replaces the placeholder text.

3 Click immediately to the left of the word *Project*, and then hold down the Shift key and press Enter.

Word inserts a line break between the words *Restoration* and *Project*. A line break ends the current line and continues the text on a new line without creating a new paragraph, which adds extra space between lines.

Right-pointing arrow

4 Move the mouse in the margin just below the Nature Walk Restoration Project Update headline until you see a right-pointing arrow, and then drag down to select all the placeholder article text.

Three paragraphs of placeholder text are selected.

5 Hold down the Shift key and click the Left Arrow key once.

The ending paragraph mark is no longer selected, but the rest of the placeholder text remains selected.

6 Press the Delete key.

The placeholder article text is deleted, and one paragraph mark remains under the headline.

7 To open the sample article, click the Open button on the Standard toolbar.

The Open dialog box appears.

Open

8   Make sure the Look In box shows Lesson09.

If you do not see the Lesson09 folder, locate and open this folder.

9   Click Restoration Project Article.doc, and then click Open.

A new Word window opens and displays an article entitled *Nature Walk Restoration Project Update*. On the taskbar, two instances of Word are visible: one with My Newsletter and the current instance with Restoration Project Article.

10   Select just the article text. Do not select the headline or the final paragraph mark.

Copy

11   On the Standard toolbar, click the Copy button.

Word copies the selected text to the Office Clipboard.

Close

12   On the Restoration Project Article title bar, click the Close button.

The window closes, and the Word window containing My Newsletter.doc reappears.

Paste

13   On the Standard toolbar, click the Paste button.

Word pastes the article text, which retains its original formatting, as the following illustration shows.

To paste text without its formatting, on the Edit menu, click Paste Special, specify Unformatted Text, and click OK.

14   To format the pasted text, scroll down to the next article and select the second paragraph, including the paragraph mark.

Format Painter

15   On the Standard toolbar, click the Format Painter button. If the Format Painter button is not visible, click the More Buttons button and then click the Format Painter button.

When you point to text, the pointer changes to a paintbrush and an I-beam.

Format Painter pointer

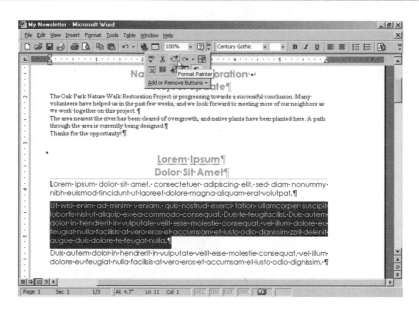

16 Select the pasted text, including the ending paragraph mark.

The formatting used in the second article is applied to the first article.

17 To save your changes, click the Save button on the Standard toolbar.

Save

Modifying Document Formatting

Although the Works Newsletters Wizard applies a formatting theme to the newsletter template, you can customize the look of your newsletter. The quickest way to change the overall appearance of any document created with a Works wizard is to use the **Format Gallery** to apply a new theme. When you apply a theme, you maintain a unified design that includes a set of fonts and colors for the headlines, article text, and other design elements.

In addition, you can change the overall look of your newsletter by adding columns. Earlier in this lesson, you used the Works Newsletters Wizard to select a one-column layout style for the newsletter. In Word, you can easily change a document to a multiple-column layout, in which text flows from the bottom of one column to the top of the next.

You can also customize the look of portions of a document without changing the overall format. To do this, you select just the text you want to change and then apply a new format. For example, you can add a shaded background behind a paragraph.

In this exercise, you use a sample file that continues where the last exercise left off. The sample newsletter includes several articles, which you format in a two-column style. Then you choose a new formatting theme for the entire newsletter and customize one section with a shaded background.

Open

1   To open the set of sample articles, click the Open button on the Standard toolbar.

The Open dialog box appears.

2   Make sure the Look In box shows Lesson09, and then double-click Oak Park News - One Column.doc.

Works opens the selected document.

3   To make a two-column newsletter, on the Format menu, click Columns.

The Columns dialog box appears. If the Columns command is not listed, click the arrows at the bottom of the Format menu to expand the menu.

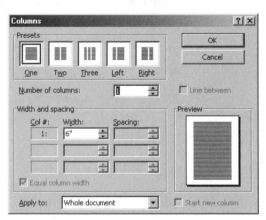

4   Under Presets, click Two, and then click OK.

Word flows the text of the newsletter into two columns.

Zoom

5   To see the entire document, on the Standard toolbar, click the Zoom arrow, and then click Whole Page.

Word zooms the view to show the entire page. Your screen should look similar to the one shown on the facing page.

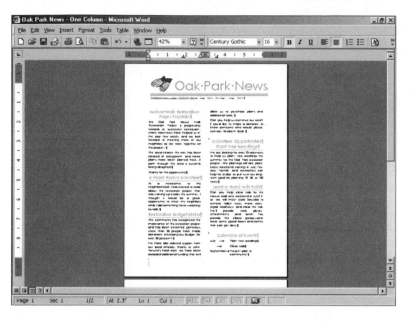

Format Gallery

6 To change the overall look of the newsletter, on the Formatting toolbar, click the Format Gallery button.

The Format Gallery appears and displays the Format All tab.

important

If the Format Gallery button does not appear on the Formatting toolbar, Word might not have been installed using the Works Suite setup.

7   Under Font Set, click the right arrow until the Newspaper font set is selected, and under Color Set, click the left arrow until the Summer color set is selected.

The preview area displays a sample of the Newspaper Summer font and color set.

8   Click Apply All.

After a few seconds, Word reformats the newsletter using the fonts and colors you chose. The Format Gallery remains open.

Close

9   On the Format Gallery title bar, click the Close button.

10   To see the new format close-up, on the Standard toolbar, click the Zoom arrow, and then click 100%.

100% ▾

Zoom

Word zooms in.

11   Scroll to the bottom of the newsletter until the Calendar of Events is visible, and then select the text of the calendar from *July* to *Winter hiatus*.

12   On the Format menu, click Borders And Shading.

The Borders And Shading dialog box appears and displays the Borders tab.

13   Click the Shading tab.

Options for adding fill color to the selection are shown. As you click a color in the Fill color palette, its name is displayed to the right of the palette.

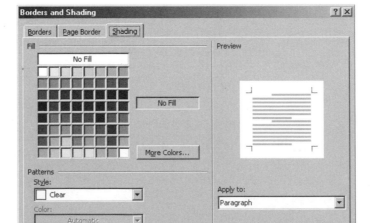

14 In the Fill color palette, click Light Orange, and then click OK.

Word fills the selected text with orange shading. The text remains selected.

15 To cancel the selection and see the results better, click the text of an article.

16 To save your changes as a new document, on the File menu, click Save As.

The Save As dialog box appears.

17 Make sure the Save In box shows Lesson09, and in the File Name box, type **My Oak Park Newsletter**, and then click Save.

Word saves your document and displays the new filename on the title bar.

Enhancing a Document with Pictures

Pictures add the finishing touch to any document. You can add pictures in the form of clip art images, graphics or drawings created in another program or copied from the Internet, and digital photographs. As you collect images that you want to use in your documents, you need a place to store them. One option is to use the Works Portfolio, a window that stays open on your desktop and into which you can copy all the pieces of information that you find and want to keep as you work on your computer.

The Portfolio stores the information and images you gather in a **collection**. You can copy, store, and organize pictures, text, and entire files from virtually any-where—the Internet, e-mail attachments, a scanner, files on a network, or documents you create. Each piece of information you add to a collection is called an **item**. Once you've added items to a collection, you can quickly insert one, several, or all items in a collection into other documents, including this lesson's newsletter. You can place the Portfolio along any edge of your computer's screen, where it remains conveniently open while you work in other program windows.

To add a picture to a document, you can drag an item from the Portfolio or use commands on the Insert menu to insert a picture file or clip art image. Word includes a large gallery of clip art from which to choose. When you insert a picture from any source, Word adjusts the text to flow around the image. You can drag the image to a new position in the document and even resize it to fit better if necessary.

A JPEG (.jpg) file is a compressed graphics file format. JPEG stands for Joint Photographic Experts Group.

In this exercise, you create a new collection in the Portfolio and add a sample photograph in JPEG format included with this book's CD. You then add clip art to the newsletter.

1 To expand Portfolio, click it.

The Portfolio expands to display a toolbar, a Tasks menu, and a Sample collection with an assortment of images, as shown in the illustration on the following page.

> **tip**
> If the Portfolio is not already open on your desktop, click Works Task Launcher on the taskbar. On the Programs tab, click Works Portfolio in the list of programs, and then click Start Works Portfolio.

Pushpin

2   To keep the Portfolio expanded, click the pushpin button.

> **tip**
> To move the Portfolio to the edge of the screen, drag it to a new location. If you move the Portfolio to a corner of the screen, it switches to Docked view, and surrounding windows are resized so that the Portfolio does not overlap them.

3   To create a place to store pictures for your newsletter, click the Tasks menu, and then click New Collection.

The Collection Name dialog box appears.

4   In the box, type **Volunteers** and then click OK.

Portfolio creates a new Volunteers collection and displays it.

5   To add pictures to the Volunteers collection, click the Tasks menu, and then click Insert File.

The Insert Files dialog box appears.

6   Make sure the Look In box shows My Documents.

7   Double-click the Works Suite 2001 SBS Practice folder, and then double-click the Lesson09 folder.

The practice files for Lesson 9 are displayed.

8 Click Friends.jpg, and then click Insert.

Portfolio displays the picture in the Volunteers collection.

9 Click the Actions menu below the picture, and then click Copy.

The picture is copied to the Clipboard.

Paste

10 In the newsletter, click just to the left of the headline *Restoration Budget Status*, and then click the Paste button on the Standard toolbar.

Word inserts the picture between the articles, as the following illustration shows.

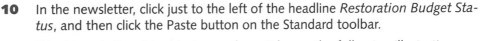

Pushpin

11 To display the Portfolio in Compact view, click the pushpin button.

12 To add clip art above the newsletter's calendar, click immediately to the left of the headline *Calendar of Events*, press the Enter key, and then press the Up Arrow key once.

Word inserts a paragraph mark above the headline.

13 On the Insert menu, point to Picture, and then click Clip Art.

The Insert ClipArt dialog box appears and displays the Pictures tab.

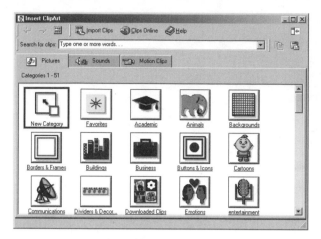

14   Scroll down the list of categories, and then click Plants.

Several plant images are displayed.

15   Click the tree image.

A toolbar appears with buttons for working with the selected image.

Insert Clip

Close

100%

Zoom

16   Click the Insert Clip button.

Behind the Insert ClipArt dialog box, Word inserts the selected clip art image at the insertion point.

17   On the title bar of the Insert ClipArt dialog box, click the Close button.

The size of the clip art image causes Word to flow the picture and the calendar of events onto the next page.

18   To see the entire document, on the Standard toolbar, click the Zoom arrow, and then click Two Pages. Your screen should now look similar to the one on the facing page.

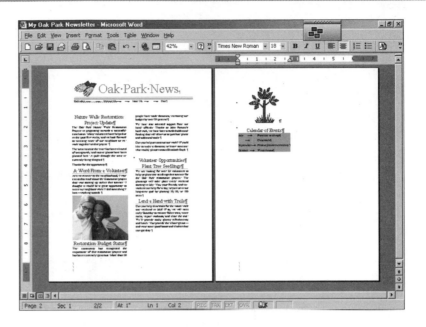

Working with Pictures

You can add pictures to Word documents from sources other than the Portfolio or Word's clip art. Perhaps you have a digital camera that saves pictures on your computer. Or maybe you've created a drawing in another program and saved it in a format that Word can insert (such as .jpg, .bmp, or .gif). You can add almost any picture that's saved as a file to a Word document:

1   Click the document where you want to insert a picture.

2   On the Insert menu, point to Picture, and then click From File.

3   Locate the file and then click Insert.

After you've inserted a picture, you can resize it in Word. Click the picture to display its selection handles, and then drag a corner handle until the picture is the size you want.

For added effect, you can flow the text of your document around the picture. To do this, right-click the picture, and then click Format Picture. Click the Layout tab, and then choose an option under Wrapping Style. You can give your documents a very professional look with this technique.

Lesson Wrap-Up

To finish the lesson:

1   To close the Portfolio, click it to expand it, click the Tasks menu, and click Close.

2   On the File menu, click Exit.

   If a message box appears, asking whether you want to save the changes you made to My Oak Park Newsletter, click Yes.

   If a message box appears, asking whether you want to save the changes you made to My Newsletter, click Yes.

   Word closes, and the Works Task Launcher appears.

3   In the Task Launcher, click the Close button on the title bar.

X

Close

If the Task Launcher does not appear, click Microsoft Works Task Launcher on the taskbar.

Tasks

Quick Reference

To start a newsletter with the Works Newsletters Wizard

1   In the Task Launcher, click the Tasks tab.

2   In the list of categories, click Newsletters & Flyers, click Newsletters, and then click Start This Task.

3   In the Works Newsletters Wizard, choose a topic, layout, and theme, and then click Finish.

To display formatting marks in a document

1   On the Tools menu, click Options.

2   On the View tab, under Formatting Marks, select the All check box, and then click OK.

To display formatting marks in a document using the toolbar

●   On the Standard toolbar, click the Show/Hide ¶ button.

¶

To replace the placeholder text added by the wizard

1   Select the placeholder text you want to replace, but don't select the ending paragraph mark.

2   Press Delete.

3   Type new text.

To copy text from one Word document into another

1   In the first Word document, click the Open button on the Standard toolbar.

2   Locate the document containing the text you want to copy, and then click Open.

3   In the second Word document, select the text you want, and then click the Copy button on the Standard toolbar.

4   Close the second Word document, and then switch to the first Word document.

5   Click the insertion point where you want to insert the text, and then click the Paste button on the Standard toolbar.

To reformat text using Format Painter

1   Select the text that's formatted the way you want. Include the paragraph mark if you also want to copy the paragraph formatting.

2   Click the Format Painter button on the Standard toolbar.

3   Select the text you want to format.

To change the number of columns in a document

1   On the Format menu, click Columns.

2   Under Presets, choose the number of columns you want, and then click OK.

To view an entire page

●   On the Standard toolbar, click the Zoom arrow, and then click Whole Page.

To change the overall look of a document

1   On the Formatting toolbar, click the Format Gallery button.

2   On the Format All tab, choose a font set, choose a color set, and then click Apply All.

To add shading to text

1   Select the text to which you want to add shading.

2   On the Format menu, click Borders And Shading, and then click the Shading tab.

3   In the Fill color palette, click a color, and then click OK.

To open the Portfolio

1   Click the Programs tab in the Task Launcher.

2   Click Works Portfolio in the list of programs, and then click Start Works Portfolio.

To close the Portfolio

●   Click the Tasks menu, and then click Close.

To expand the Portfolio

●   Click the Portfolio.

To keep the Portfolio open

●   Click the pushpin button.

To add a collection to the Portfolio

1   Click the Tasks menu, and then click New Collection.

2   Type a collection name, and then click OK.

To add pictures to a collection

1   Make sure the collection you want is visible.

2   Click the Tasks menu, and then click Insert File.

3   Locate the picture you want, and then click Insert.

To add a picture in the Portfolio to a Word document by dragging

●   With both the Portfolio and Word windows open, drag the picture from the Portfolio into the document.

To add a picture in the Portfolio to a Word document by using the Clipboard

1   Below the Portfolio picture, click Actions, and then click Copy.

2   Switch to Word, click where you want to insert the picture, and then click the Paste button on the Standard toolbar.

To add clip art to a document

1   Click where you want to insert the clip art.

2   On the Insert menu, point to Picture, and then click Clip Art.

3   Click the category you want, click the picture you want, and then click the Insert Clip button.

UNIT 3

Integrating Other Tasks

10

Managing Accounts and Investments

ESTIMATED TIME 60 min.

In this lesson, you will learn how to:

✔ *Set up your accounts in Microsoft Money.*

✔ *Enter common transactions.*

✔ *Schedule a recurring transaction.*

✔ *Keep track of investments.*

✔ *Report on personal finances.*

If you know how to write a check, you probably know all you need to take advantage of Microsoft Money 2001 Standard, a program for managing personal finances. Microsoft Works Suite includes Money, which you can use to balance your checkbook, pay bills, bank on line, create a budget, reduce debt, report on your financial status, and more. You don't have to be an expert with budgets or investments to make good use of Money. Its step-by-step wizards and forms help you set up your financial information quickly and correctly so that you can make informed decisions about short-term and long-term monetary goals.

There's much more to Money than this lesson can show. For example, you can use Money to bank and pay bills on line, track assets and liabilities, record real estate investments, and even manage a small business. This lesson merely introduces you to a few of the most common tasks you do in Money. For example, you'll set up a fictional checking account and investment portfolio. If you like, you can use the steps in this lesson as a model for entering your own account information in Money. Just substitute your account names and numbers for the fictional ones provided in the procedures.

Setting Up Accounts in Microsoft Money

To see a multimedia demo about setting up a new account, double-click the Create Account icon in the Demos folder on the book's CD-ROM.

Most people would probably agree that they could use a clearer picture of their financial status. Microsoft Money provides that picture. It helps you record your income and expenditures so that you can prioritize and meet financial goals as well as forecast trends. To make the most of Money, you need a certain amount of discipline: you must set up an **account** for each banking, investment, credit card, or other real-world account that you want to track in Money, and then enter your transactions. Then the fun begins as you use the information to create reports that measure your cash flow, net worth, tax status, and so on.

Fortunately, Money makes it easy to set up your accounts. The first time you start Money, the Setup Assistant asks a series of simple questions to walk you through the process of creating new accounts and personalizing the product for your use. After you've worked through the Setup Assistant, you'll see the Money home page, which summarizes account information and your financial status. It also provides access to accounts and bills, investing, planning, tax, and reporting features.

Money Setup Assistant

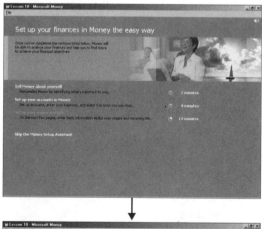

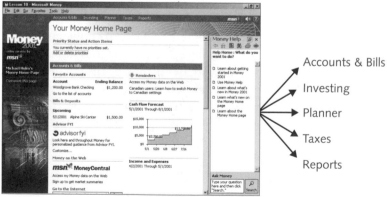

Accounts & Bills

Investing

Planner

Taxes

Reports

Money home page

Money often provides more than one way to accomplish a task. For example, commands on the menu bar typically echo links on the screen, and the navigation bar offers another way to access different areas in Money. If you thrive on flexibility, you'll like the versatility of the program, but at first it can seem a little confusing. This book introduces you to a couple of different ways to move through Money so that you can learn which method you like best.

Audio Help

Money also includes audio help that tells you about each new screen you encounter. If your computer can play sound files, you will hear the narration as you work through this lesson. If you find the audio help distracting, click the speaker icon and click Turn All Audio Help Off on the shortcut menu.

In this exercise, you use the Money Setup Assistant to create new, temporary checking and billing accounts for Michael Holm.

important

If you want to use this exercise to set up your own accounts, rather than entering fictional information, have your financial information handy, including your recent paycheck stubs, bank statements, and regular bills.

1 On the taskbar, click the Start button, point to Programs, and then click Microsoft Works.

The Works Task Launcher opens.

2 Click the Programs tab.

All Works programs are listed in the Task Launcher.

3 Under Programs, click Money.

Tasks for Money are listed on the right.

4 Click Start Microsoft Money.

If you've started Money before and walked through the Money Setup Assistant, the Money home page appears.

5 If this is the first time you've started Money, on the File menu, click New. If you've started Money before and you see the Money home page, on the File menu, point to New, and then click New File.

The New dialog box appears.

For details about installing the practice files, see "Using the Book's CD-ROM" at the beginning of this book.

6 In the Save In box, make sure that the My Documents folder is selected.

7 Double-click the Works Suite 2001 SBS Practice folder, and then double-click the Lesson10 folder.

If you did not install this book's practice files or you want to save your work in a different location, browse to the folder you want.

8   In the File Name box, type **Lesson 10**, and then click OK.

Money creates a new file with the extension .mny that will store the settings you create during this lesson. The Money Setup Assistant appears.

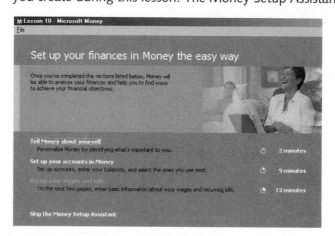

9   Click Tell Money About Yourself.

A page titled Whose Finances Do You Want To Track? appears.

10   In the First box, type **Michael**, and in the Last box, type **Holm**.

11   Leave the option selected to Track Only My Finances, leave US Dollar as the currency, and then click Next.

A page titled What Financial Priorities Are Most Important To You? appears.

12   Leave the priority check boxes unchecked and click Next.

A page titled Describe Your Internet Connection appears.

13   For the first question, check Yes, I Have Connected.

The dimmed options become available. Answer as follows:

- For the second question (Do You Use America Online…), leave the No, I Don't Use AOL option selected.

- For the third question (Do You Want to Get Up-To-Date Information…), click No.

- For the fourth question (Do You Want Links To Financial Services…), click No.

14   Click Done.

The Money Setup Assistant home page appears.

15   Click Set Up Your Accounts In Money.

A page titled Which Accounts Do You Want To Track? appears.

16   Select the Checking Account check box, leave the default value for How Many Accounts (1), and then click Next.

A page titled Enter The Basic Details Of Each Account appears.

17 Enter the following account information:

■ Click the Bank Name down arrow, and then click Woodgrove Bank.

■ Click in the Your Account Name box to accept the name that Money suggests: Woodgrove Bank Checking.

■ In the Starting Balance box, type **1200**.

18 Click Next.

A page titled Select The Accounts You Use Most appears.

19 Select the Woodgrove Bank Checking check box, and then click Next.

A page titled Is Your Account Information Accurate? appears.

20 Click Done.

A message box appears, asking if you are finished setting up your accounts.

21 Click Yes.

The Money Setup Assistant home page appears.

22 Click Set Up Your Wages And Bills.

A page titled Which Paychecks Do You Want To Track In Money? appears.

23 Under Paycheck #1, enter the following information:

■ In the Who Pays You? box, type **Alpine Ski Center**.

■ In the Take-Home Pay box, type **1500**.

■ Click the Next Pay Date arrow to display a calendar, and then click the first day of the month.

■ Click the How Often Are You Paid? arrow, move the scroll bar up, and then click Twice A Month.

Your paycheck information should look similar to the following:

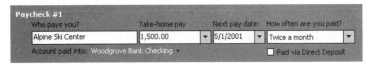

24 Click Next.

A page titled Which Bills Do You Pay Regularly? appears.

25 In the list of Common Bills, select Rent, select Electricity, and then click Next.

A page titled Enter The Basic Details Of Each Bill appears.

26 Leave the bill details blank for now, and then click Next.

A message box appears, asking whether to skip this section. Click Yes. A page titled Is Your Paycheck And Bill Information Accurate? appears.

27 Click Done.

A message appears, asking if you are finished adding your bills and paychecks. Click Yes.

The Money Setup Assistant home page appears.

28   Click Start Using Money Now.

The Money home page appears.

Navigation buttons

Menu bar   Navigation bar   Money Help pane

Current page

Options for current page

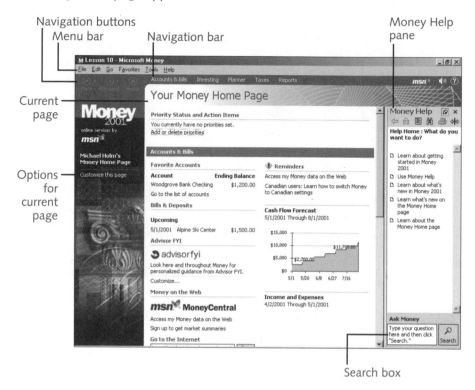

Search box

Close Money Help

To open the Money Help pane, click Help Topics on the Help menu.

29   If the Money Help pane is open, click the Close Money Help button to close the pane.

Entering Transactions

The accounts you set up in Money mirror the real accounts you hold at a bank, credit union, or other institution. When you withdraw cash from an ATM, deposit a paycheck, or take care of other financial business, you can record the action in Money as a **transaction**. Each account you create has its own **account register** that looks similar to a checkbook register and shows you all the transactions for your account. You can type directly in the account register or use a **transaction form** to record your transactions in Money. Transaction forms display fields for the amount, date, and so forth, so that you can fill in the blanks. Money then enters the transaction into the account register.

When you enter transactions, you can assign them to specific income and expense **categories**, such as car payments and bills. Money includes many category groups and subcategories within these groups. By assigning your transactions to categories, you can later track your expenses in a personalized report or create an accurate budget. You can even create your own categories and subcategories. For example, when you record the amount of money withdrawn from an ATM, you can assign it to the Cash Withdrawal category. To track the money more precisely, you can create an Entertainment or a Dining Out subcategory.

In this exercise, you enter a withdrawal and a deposit using the account register and transaction forms. For each transaction, you assign a category and a subcategory to use later in a report.

1   On the Accounts & Bills menu, click Account List.

The accounts list home page appears.

2   Under Bank Accounts, click Woodgrove Bank Checking.

The account register and transaction form for this account appear, as shown below.

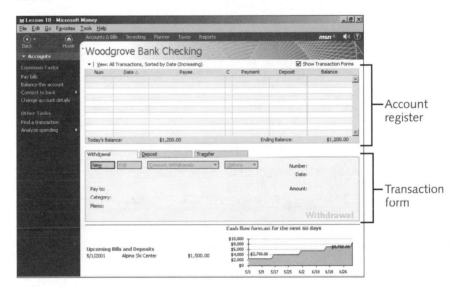

3   On the Withdrawal tab of the transaction form, click New.

Options for entering a new withdrawal appear.

4   Click Common Withdrawals, and then click ATM.

Money inserts *Cash* in the Pay To box, and then the insertion point appears in the Amount box.

5   In the Amount box, type **250**, and then press the Tab key.

The insertion point moves to the Category box.

6   Click Cash Withdrawal.

7   Press Tab to move the insertion point to the subcategory box.

8   Click Add New Subcategory.

The New Category dialog box appears.

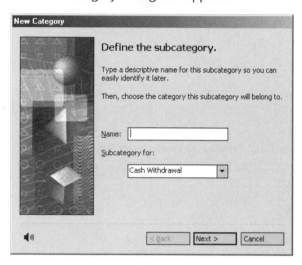

9   In the Name box, type **Dining Out**, and then click Next.

Money asks you to indicate the group that this subcategory falls under. Cash Withdrawal is already selected.

10   Click Finish.

In the subcategory box, Dining Out now appears.

11   Click Enter.

Money enters the withdrawal transaction in the account register.

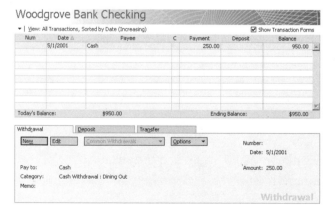

12 At the top of the screen, clear the Show Transaction Forms check box.

Money removes the transaction form and enlarges the account register.

13 To enter a deposit, in the Num column, double-click the empty box below the withdrawal you just entered.

Money displays options for entering a new transaction in the account register.

Num	Date △	Payee	C	Payment	Deposit	Balance
	5/1/2001	Cash Cash Withdrawal : Dining Out		250.00		950.00
	5/1/2001	Payee Category: Category Subcategory Memo: Memo		Withdrawal Deposit		
Common Transactions				Enter Split	Cancel	

14 In the Payee box, type **Bonus**.

15 In the Deposit box, type **1000**.

16 Click the Category arrow, and then click Other Income.

17 Click the Subcategory arrow, and then click Gifts Received.

Enter

18 Click Enter.

Money enters the deposit transaction directly into the account register and starts a new transaction on the next line.

Tips for Entering Transactions

As you enter transactions in an account register, the AutoComplete feature works in the background to remember your entries. Then, the next time you type a payee name that the AutoComplete feature recognizes, it fills in the rest of the name for you.

Another way to enter dates and amounts in an account register is to use the miniature calendar and calculator built into date and amount fields. Click the date arrow to enter a date using a small calendar. Click the amount arrow to enter numbers or calculations with a calculator.

Scheduling a Recurring Transaction

Money can help you remember when bills are due, such as the monthly rent payment, and when to expect recurring deposits, such as direct-deposit paychecks. You can enter a **recurring transaction** to record bills and deposits that occur regularly. Money then displays the transactions on a convenient calendar.

When you're working in your checking account register, you can use the Common Withdrawals or Common Deposits button to set up a recurring transaction of those types. You can also track recurring payments from the Bills & Deposits page of Money, which lists all the bills and recurring deposits that you specified in the Money Setup Assistant. You can also add new bills on this page, forecast your cash flow, and even set up bills to be paid on the Internet.

In this exercise, you work in the bills and deposits area to specify a monthly rent payment as a recurring transaction.

1   On the Accounts & Bills menu, click Bills & Deposits Setup.

The Bills & Deposits home page appears.

2   Click New.

The Create New Scheduled Transaction Wizard appears.

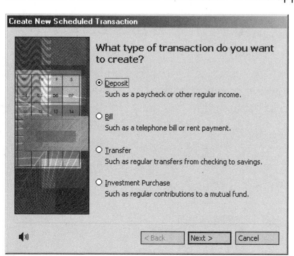

3   Click the Bill option, and then click Next.

The wizard asks you how often this payment occurs.

4   Keep the current settings for More Than Once, At Regular Intervals with a frequency of Monthly, and click Next.

The wizard asks you how you plan to make this payment in the future.

5   Keep the current Payment Method setting of Write Check, and then click Next.

The wizard asks you if the bill is usually the same amount each time.

6   Click the Yes, It's Typically The Same Amount option, and then click Next.

The Create New Scheduled Payment dialog box appears.

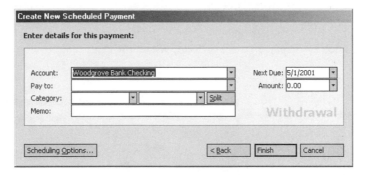

7   In the Pay To box, type **John Fortune**.

8   Click the Category arrow, and then click Bills.

9   Click the Subcategory arrow, and then click Rent.

10   In the Amount box, type **550**, and then click Finish.

Money enters the transaction into your account register and displays it in the bills and deposits list as shown.

Payee	Account	Frequency	Amount
Scheduled Paychecks & Deposits			
⏲ Alpine Ski Center	Woodgrove Bank Checking	Twice a month	$1,500.00 ~
Scheduled Bills & Withdrawals			
⏲ John Fortune	Woodgrove Bank Checking	Monthly	($550.00)
Scheduled Transfers			
Click New to schedule a recurring transfer			
Scheduled Investment Purchases			
Click New to schedule a recurring investment purchase			

11   Click Done.

To see upcoming bills and deposits in a calendar, on the Accounts & Bills menu, click Calendar.

Money displays the account register and lists the upcoming bills and deposits.

Tracking Investments

To keep an eye on your investments, you can add investment accounts to your Money portfolio. You can set up accounts for investments you own, such as stocks, bonds, and mutual funds, and then let Money help you anticipate tax implications, such as capital gains and losses. Your Money portfolio can also include investments that you want to watch. Money can even update prices automatically from the stock quotes that are available on the Internet.

To set up and monitor your investment accounts, you work in Your Portfolio, the Investing Center area that lists your individual accounts. Investment accounts have an account register like the one you used in an earlier exercise to record checking transactions. You perform the day-to-day record-keeping for an investment in its account register.

In this exercise, you use the New Account Wizard to set up a new investment account for a brokerage firm and add one investment, a fictional stock. Then you work in the new investment's account register to record changes to the stock.

1   On the Investing menu, click Portfolio.

Money displays Your Portfolio, which includes a list of common stock indices.

Investments that you want to track

Investing Center navigation bar

Options for working with Your Portfolio

2   On the Investing Center navigation bar, click Accounts.

The Accounts page of the Investment Center appears. On the left side of the screen under Common Tasks, options for working with accounts are listed.

3   Under Common Tasks, click Set Up Accounts.

Money asks you what you want to do and displays a list of options.

4   Click Add A New Investment Account.

The New Account Wizard appears.

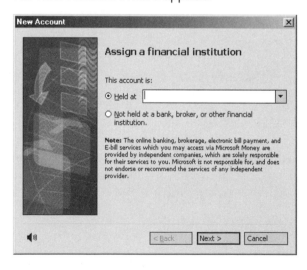

5   In the Held At box, type **Northwind Traders**, and then click Next.

The wizard asks you to choose an institution name.

6   Leave the Use Northwind Traders option selected, and then click Next.

The wizard asks you what kind of account you would like to set up.

7   Leave the current setting to set up an Investment account, and then click Next.

The wizard asks you what you want to call the account and supplies the name Northwind Traders Investment.

8   Leave the current settings, and then click Next.

The wizard asks you whether to add investments right now and selects the Yes option.

9   Click Next.

The wizard asks you to type a name for the investment.

10   In the Investment Name box, type **Inspired Technologies**, and then click Next.

The wizard asks you what type of investment it is.

11   In the list of investments, click Stock, and then click Next.

The wizard asks you for the stock symbol.

12   In the Symbol box, type **IJK**, and then click Finish.

The wizard asks you for the quantity of shares.

13   Type the following information:

  ▪   In the Quantity box, type **200**.

  ▪   In the Date Acquired box, type **6/20/99**.

  ▪   In the Price box, type **12.25**.

14   Click Next.

The wizard asks if you want to add another investment and selects the No option.

15   Click Next.

The wizard asks if you have other accounts at this institution and selects the No option.

16   Click Next, and then click Finish.

The Accounts page of the Investment Center appears.

17   On the Investing Center navigation bar, click Portfolio.

Your Portfolio appears and lists the investment account you just created as shown on the following page.

18   To edit an investment transaction, under Northwind Traders Investment, click Inspired Technologies.

Money displays details for this investment.

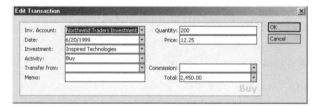

19   Click Edit.

The Edit Transaction dialog box appears.

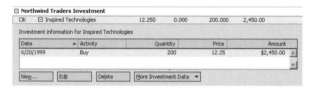

20   Click the Transfer From arrow, and then click Northwind Traders Investm (Cash).

21   In the Commission box, type **10**,and then click OK.

Money updates the Your Portfolio page with the information.

22   To hide the investment details, click Inspired Technologies.

tip

Depending on the type of Internet connection you have, you might want to have Money retrieve online quotes for your portfolio investments. To specify this, you must first register your copy of Money. Then under Common Tasks on the Your Portfolio page, click Update Prices, and then click Update Price Automatically. Online quotes are typically delayed by about 20 minutes.

Reporting Financial Health

What better way to see where your money has gone than to create a report? The Reports Gallery in Money lets you see and summarize your financial status in a multitude of ways. Built-in reports can depict net worth, cash flow, debts, and more in tabular or graphic format. You can produce reports on the screen, customize them easily, and then print them for your records. You can even include your favorite reports on the My Favorites page. Money includes six general types of reports: Spending Habits, What I Have, What I Owe, Investments, Taxes, and Monthly Reports.

In this exercise, you view a report that details checking account transactions and a report that summarizes account balances. You customize one report, save it on the My Favorites page, and then print it.

1   On the Reports menu, click Reports Gallery.

The Reports Gallery home page appears, and the Spending Habits reports are displayed under Pick A Report Or Chart.

2   In the list of Spending Habits reports, click Account Transactions.

Money highlights the report in the list.

3   At the bottom of the screen, click the Date Range arrow, click Last 30 Days, and then click the Go To Report/Chart button.

Money displays a history of transactions for all accounts during the last 30 days.

4   In the upper left corner, click the Back button.

The Reports Gallery home page appears and displays the Spending Habits reports.

5   In the list of reports on the left, click What I Have.

A list of net worth reports appears on the right.

6   Click Account Details, and then click the Go To Report/Chart button at the bottom of the screen.

Money provides a summary of all your accounts.

7   At the bottom of the screen, click Customize.

The Customize Report dialog box appears and displays the Rows & Columns tab.

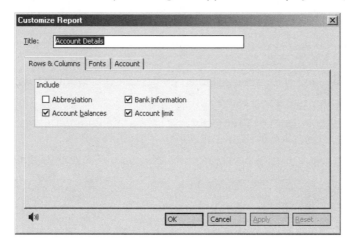

8   In the Title box, type **My Account Balances**.

9   Clear the Bank Information and Account Limit check boxes, and then click OK.

The customized report is displayed.

Account	Opening Balance	Current Balance
Northwind Traders Investm (Cash)	$0.00	($2,460.00)
Northwind Traders Investment		$2,450.00
Woodgrove Bank Checking	$1,200.00	$1,950.00

10   Right-click the white area of the report page to display a shortcut menu, and then click Add To Favorites.

The Add To Favorites dialog box appears and suggests the current report title as the report name.

11 Click OK.

Money saves the customized report and adds it to the list of My Favorites.

12 On the Reports menu, click My Favorites.

The customized My Account Balances report appears in the list.

13 Double-click My Account Balances.

Money displays the report.

14 To print the report, on the File menu, click Print.

The Print Report dialog box appears.

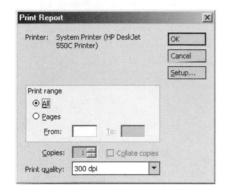

15 Click OK to print the report.

Lesson Wrap-Up

To finish the lesson:

Close

1 On the Microsoft Money title bar, click the Close button.

A message appears, asking if you want to back up to a floppy disk.

2 Click Don't Back Up.

Money closes, and the Task Launcher appears.

3 In the Task Launcher, click the Close button on the title bar.

tip
The next time you start your computer, Money Express automatically starts. With Money Express, you can quickly enter transactions without starting Money, get reminders about upcoming bills, and receive automatic updates from the Internet for stock quotes, mortgage rates, and tax rates.

Using Money Files

If you entered the fictional account information for Michael Holm, the next time you start Money, you can create a new file for your own accounts as described in "Setting Up Microsoft Money" at the beginning of this lesson. If you uninstall the practice files or if you delete Lesson 10.mny, the next time you start Money, a message is displayed indicating that Lesson 10.mny could not be opened.

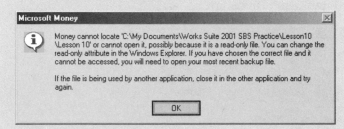

When you click OK in the message box, the Open A File Wizard is displayed.

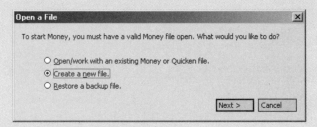

To specify the name and location for a new Money file, click the Create A New File option and click Next.

Quick Reference

To set up a new account in Money

1   Start Microsoft Money.

2   On the File menu, point to New, and then click New File.

3   In the New dialog box, choose a location and specify a filename.

4   In the Money Setup Assistant, follow the instructions to set up accounts for the file.

To add an account

1   On the File menu, point to New, and then click New Account.

2   In the New Account Wizard, follow the instructions to create the type of account you want.

Accounts and Investments

To enter a withdrawal

1   On the Accounts & Bills menu, click Account List. Under Bank Accounts, click an account to display the account register.

2   Make sure the Show Transaction Forms check box is selected, and then in the transaction form, click the Withdrawal tab.

Enter

3   If necessary, click New, type the withdrawal information, and then click Enter.

To enter a deposit

1   On the Accounts & Bills menu, click Account List. Under Bank Accounts, click an account to display the account register.

2   Make sure the Show Transaction Forms check box is selected, and then in the transaction form, click the Deposit tab.

Enter

3   If necessary, click New, type the withdrawal information, and then click Enter.

To create a category group

1   In an account register or a transaction form, click the Category down arrow, and then click Add New Category.

2   In the New Category Wizard, follow the instructions to define the category.

To schedule a recurring withdrawal

1   On the Accounts & Bills menu, click Account List. Under Bank Accounts, click an account to display the account register.

2   Make sure the Show Transaction Forms check box is selected, and then in the transaction form, click the Withdrawal tab.

3   Click Common Withdrawals, point to Upcoming Bills, and then click Create New Recurring Bill.

4   Follow the instructions in the Create New Scheduled Payment Wizard.

To schedule a recurring deposit

1   On the Accounts & Bills menu, click Account List. Under Bank Accounts, click an account to display the account register.

2   Make sure the Show Transaction Forms check box is selected, and then in the transaction form, click the Deposit tab.

3   Click Common Deposits, point to Recurring Deposits (Paychecks), and then click Create A New Recurring Deposit.

4   Follow the instructions in the Create New Scheduled Deposit Wizard.

To create an investment account

1   On the Investing menu, click Portfolio, and then click Accounts on the navigation bar.

2   Under Common Tasks, click Set Up Accounts, and then click Add A New Investment Account.

3   Follow the instructions in the New Account Wizard.

To add an investment to an account

1   On the Investing menu, click Portfolio.

New

2   In Your Portfolio, click an account name to display its account register, and then click New.

3   In the Date box, type the date you made the transaction. In the Investment box, type a name for the transaction, and then click the Activity box.

4   In the Create New Investment Wizard, follow the instructions to complete the details of this transaction.

5   Enter the rest of the account information and click OK.

To edit account details in Your Portfolio

1   On the Investing menu, click Portfolio.

2   In Your Portfolio, click the name of the investment you want to edit to display its details in the account register.

3   Edit the information as necessary. To close the detail fields, click the account name.

To view a report

1   On the Reports menu, click Reports Gallery.

2   Click a report type on the left, and then choose the report you want from the list on the right.

3   Click Go To Report/Chart.

To customize a report

1   View a report as explained above, and then click Customize.

2   In the Customize Report dialog box, make the changes you want.

To save a report on the My Favorites page

1   View a report as explained above.

2   Right-click the report, and then click Add To My Favorites.

3   In the Add To Favorites dialog box, type a report name, and then click OK.

To print a report

1   View a report as explained above.

2   On the File menu, click Print.

LESSON

11

Creating an Invitation

ESTIMATED TIME 30 min.

In this lesson, you will learn how to:

✔ *Start a project in Picture It! Publishing.*

✔ *Work with pictures and apply special effects.*

✔ *Edit and add text in a design.*

✔ *Save and print a project.*

If you want to use digital photographs in your publishing projects, Microsoft Picture It! Publishing has the tools you need. Both Microsoft Works and Picture It! Publishing include handsome predesigned templates for creating professional-quality cards, newsletters, flyers, brochures, and so on, but Picture It! Publishing is specially tailored for home projects that require photo editing.

With Picture It! Publishing, you can easily create eye-catching paper, photo, e-mail, and Web projects that even include sound effects and animation. Picture It! Publishing does more than this lesson can cover, but you'll get an introduction to the print publishing and photo editing tools. You'll create a flyer-style invitation to an Oak Park community event and then add and edit photographs for a customized touch.

Practice files for the lesson

This lesson uses a practice file that you installed from this book's CD-ROM. For details about installing the practice files, see "Using the Book's CD-ROM" at the beginning of this book.

Starting with a Built-In Design

Whether you're looking for inspiration or just don't have time to start from scratch, you can start a publishing **project** with a built-in **design.** Like the templates you use with Works and Microsoft Word, designs set up everything you need for quick results: text, pictures, and sometimes even multimedia extras. Picture It! Publishing includes many designs for print, photo, e-mail, and multimedia projects organized by theme such as crafts, business, and family. Print projects include flyers, newsletters, and cards, and their designs are formatted to fit standard sizes of paper.

As you work on a project, Picture It! Publishing displays only those commands and options you need for the area you're working on. For example, if you select a picture in a print project, the Picture Options commands are displayed on the left side of the screen. Along the bottom of the screen, a **thumbnail**—a miniature picture—of your project appears in the **Tray**. All the pictures and projects you've opened are shown in the Tray so that you can easily switch among your projects.

Task-specific commands change
according to the current selection.   Open project

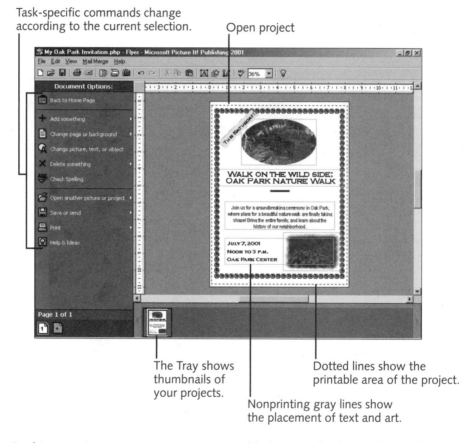

The Tray shows
thumbnails of
your projects.

Dotted lines show the
printable area of the project.

Nonprinting gray lines show
the placement of text and art.

In this exercise, you start Picture It! Publishing and select a design for a print project. The project is a flyer-style invitation that advertises the groundbreaking ceremony for the fictional Oak Park nature walk.

1   On the taskbar, click the Start button, point to Programs, and then click Microsoft Works.

The Works Task Launcher opens.

2   Click the Programs tab.

All Works programs are listed in the Task Launcher.

3   Under Programs, click Picture It! Publishing.

Tasks for Picture It! Publishing are listed on the right.

4   Click Start Picture It! Publishing.

Picture It! Publishing opens.

5   Click the Pick A Design tab.

A list of all the types of designs is displayed.

6   Click Flyers/Brochures, and then click Flyer Invitations.

Design themes are listed on the left, and thumbnails of all the selected design themes are displayed on the right.

7   In the Themes box, click Other Occasions.

Thumbnails of assorted invitation designs are displayed.

8   Click the Join The Neighborhood Block Party flyer thumbnail, and then click the Open button.

The flyer invitation is displayed, reduced to show the entire page.

Save File

9   To save this invitation before proceeding, click the Save File button on the toolbar.

The Save As options appear on the left, and the contents of the currently selected folder appear on the right.

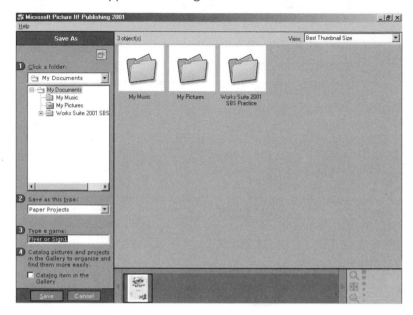

10   In the Click A Folder box, make sure that the My Documents folder is selected.

11   In the list, double-click Works Suite 2001 SBS Practice, and then double-click the Lesson11 folder.

For details about installing the practice files, see "Using the Book's CD-ROM" at the beginning of this book.

If you do not see Works Suite 2001 SBS Practice in the list of folders, browse to the location where you installed the practice files.

12   In the Save As This Type box, leave Paper Projects selected.

13   In the Type A Name box, type **Oak Park Invitation**.

14   Make sure the Catalog Item In The Gallery check box is unselected, and then click Save.

The new filename appears on the title bar, and the invitation is again displayed.

Starting a Print Project from Scratch

When you want free reign to create a design, you can start a blank project in Picture It! Publishing.

1   Click the Pick A Design tab.

Picture It! Publishing lists all the designs by type.

(continued)

continued

> **2**   Click Blank Projects, and then click a subcategory that most closely fits the size of the project you're creating:
>
>   ■ Click Standard Paper if you want to create a design on 8-1/2-by-11-inch paper.
>
>   ■ Click Cards if you want to create a folded card on 8-1/2-by-11-inch paper.
>
>   ■ Click Signs/Banners if you intend to print your project on large paper.
>
> **3**   In the Themes box, click a theme, click the thumbnail you want, and then click the Open button.
>
> Picture It! Publishing starts a new, blank project of the specified size.

Working with Pictures

Pictures in Picture It! Publishing include clip art, graphics from other programs, and photos that you captured from a digital camera, a scanner, the Internet, or another source. The **Gallery** in Picture It! Publishing houses a large searchable collection of clip art, photos, and other multimedia files that you can use in your projects. Pictures are listed in the Gallery by category, such as Nature and Sports, and also by keyword. For example, you can type *tree* to find all the pictures associated with that keyword. The Gallery also helps you organize your own items with its My Collection category.

There's a lot you can do with the pictures in your projects. When you want to edit a picture or add a special effect, Picture It! Publishing guides you through every step. To work with a picture, you must first select it, which displays selection **handles**, the black squares at the edge of the picture. Then you can move, size, or rotate the picture or apply a special effect. When you select a picture, the Picture Options list is displayed, which includes commands to apply the effects contained in the following table.

Type of Effect	What It Does
Cutouts & Pictures	Cuts holes in a picture, crops away parts of a picture, or inserts pictures within pictures
Edge Effect	Changes just the edges by creating a text edge around a picture, softening the edges, or highlighting the edges of an image in a collage

(continued)

Creating an Invitation
11

continued

Type of Effect	What It Does
Effects & Illusions	Stretches, shrinks, blurs, sharpens, or distorts all or part of a picture; or lets you choose from over 150 illusions, such as watercolor or finger paint, to change the texture of a picture
Paint & Color Effects	Applies artistic brush strokes or shapes to a picture or stamps color on a picture

In this exercise, you change the pictures on the invitation by adding a photo from the Picture It! Publishing clip art gallery and adding a photo from the practice files. Then you apply special effects to dress up the pictures.

1   In the invitation, click the top picture to select it.

Handles appear around the picture. In the left navigation area, the Picture Options list is displayed.

2   In the Picture Options list, click Change Picture, and then click Replace Picture.

Browse options appear, and the Browse tab is displayed.

3   At the bottom of the Browse tab, click Find A Specific Item.

The Find tab is displayed.

To view more pictures at once, in the View list, click Small Thumbnails.

4   In the Find box, type **poppy** and then click Find.

Picture It! Publishing locates clip art from the gallery that is associated with the keyword "poppy" and displays thumbnails of matching pictures in the display area.

*If this picture is
not displayed,
select another
picture that
you like.*

5   Right-click the picture of a field of orange poppies labeled PH02919J.jpg, and
then click Add To My Favorites.

The picture is added to the My Favorites collection and remains selected.

6   In the Browse options on the left, click Look Elsewhere.

The items in the My Documents folder are displayed.

7   In the list, double-click Works Suite 2001 SBS Practice, and then double-click
the Lesson11 folder.

If you do not see Works Suite 2001 SBS Practice in the list of folders, browse
to the location where you installed the practice files.

8   Click the picture labeled Trail.jpg to select it.

9   Click the Add button.

Picture It! Publishing replaces the original flyer invitation artwork with the
trail picture. Selection handles appear around the picture.

10 To crop the picture to an oval, in the Picture Options list, click Cutouts & Pictures, and then click Crop.

Creating an Invitation

A new display area showing just the picture appears, and cropping options are displayed on the left. The crop area is highlighted in magenta on the picture, and a thumbnail is displayed in the **Stack**, which shows the order in which images are layered in your project.

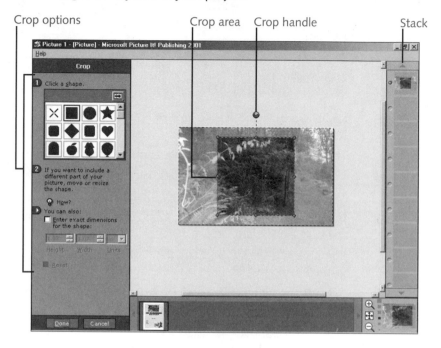

Crop options   Crop area   Crop handle   Stack

11   In the Click A Shape box, click the circle.

On the picture, a circle-shaped selection area appears that shows where the picture will be cropped.

12   To resize the area to crop, drag the side, top, and bottom selection handles until the selection circle touches the edges of the picture.

As you point to a selection handle, the pointer changes to indicate that you can drag. When you're finished, an oval-shaped selection area fills the rectangular picture as shown.

13 Click the Done button.

The cropped picture is displayed on the invitation.

14 Click the picture in the lower right corner of the invitation, click Change Picture, and then click Replace Picture.

The Browse options appear, and the Browse tab is displayed.

15 In the Click A Collection box, make sure that My Collection is selected, and then, in the My Collection box, click My Favorites.

In the display area, the poppy picture that you added to My Favorites is displayed.

16 Click the close-up poppy picture (PH02919J.JPG), and then click the Open button.

Picture It! Publishing replaces the original flyer invitation artwork with the poppy picture. Selection handles appear around the picture.

Zoom

17 To zoom in for a better view, on the toolbar, click the Zoom arrow, and then click 100%.

The selected picture is magnified to full size.

18 To apply an edge effect to the picture, in the Picture Options list, click Edge Effects, and then click Cool Edges.

Edge categories are displayed.

19 Under Click An Edge Category, click Designer.

A list of edge effects appears.

20 In the list, click Mesh and select the Stretch Edge To Fit Picture check box.

The mesh edge effect is applied to the picture.

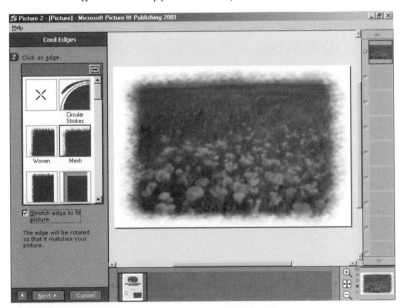

21   Click the Next button.

Edge color options are displayed.

22   Leave the current edge color and click the Next button.

Handles appear around the picture, and in the options list on the left, a help link appears that describes how to move or resize the picture.

23   Leave the size and position of the picture as is and click the Done button.

The invitation appears and the picture includes the Mesh edge effect.

Zoom

24   To cancel the selection, click the white area of the page, and then, in the Zoom box, click Entire Page.

The entire invitation is displayed.

Formatting Text

If you like to play with words, Picture It! Publishing provides a host of interesting tools for formatting text. You can create 3-D text effects, apply fancy borders and backgrounds, and shape text along a curve, wave, or triangle.

Picture It! Publishing handles text a little differently from other programs, such as Microsoft Word. You type text in a **text box**, which is outlined on the screen with a nonprinting gray box. Most Picture It! Publishing designs include text boxes that are designed for an attractive layout. Yet even when you start with a design that includes text, you can type your own text and change its position and format.

To work with text, you click a text box to select it. On the left, Picture It! Publishing displays the Text Options list, which includes commands for changing the format of the text as well as the appearance, size, and position of the text box. When you select a text box, handles appear around it. You can resize a text box by dragging a side, corner, or top handle. To move a text box, drag the gray border. When you want to add text to a project, you insert a new text box and type the text you want.

tip

In a longer document, such as a newsletter or a school report, you can link text boxes so that the text flows from column to column and page to page. For details, see Picture It! Publishing Help and search for *text box links*.

In this exercise, you customize the text supplied by the flyer invitation design and then add a new text box and format it. You also change the page background and add a page border.

1   Drag across the text *Join the Neighborhood Block Party!* to select it.

When you select text or a text box, Picture It! Publishing displays the Text Options list on the left and adds text formatting buttons to the toolbar.

2   Type **Walk on the wild side:**, press the Enter key, and then type **Oak Park Nature Walk**.

The new text replaces the old and retains the design's format, which uses a font with all capital letters.

3   In the text box in the middle of the invitation, select the words *Your Text Here*, and then type the following:

Join us for a groundbreaking ceremony in Oak Park, where plans for a beautiful nature walk are finally taking shape! Bring the entire family, and learn about the history of our neighborhood.

As you type, the text box expands to fit all the text and wraps the lines. If you can't see the third line of text, drag the bottom center handle on the text box down until all the text appears.

The text box now overlaps the Date Time Place text box.

Creating an Invitation

11

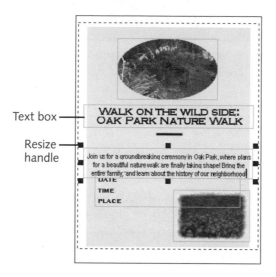

Text box ——

Resize —— handle

4 Point to the left, center handle on the text box you just typed in.

A double-headed arrow pointing east and west appears.

Double-headed arrow

5 Drag the text box to the right about one half inch so that its left edge is aligned with the left edge of the Date Time Place text box.

6 Perform the same steps and drag the right edge of the text box to the left the same distance.

7 Select the Date Time Place text box and then point to one of its gray borders.

A four-headed arrow pointer appears.

Four-headed arrow

8 Drag the Date Time Place text box down about one inch so that it is centered vertically with the poppy picture.

Although the text box border still overlaps the poppy picture, its text does not, so the invitation will be printed correctly.

9 To replace the Date Time Place text:

- Double-click the word *Date* to select it, and then type **July 7, 2001**.

- Double-click the word *Time*, and then type **Noon to 3 p.m**.

- Double-click the word *Place*, and then type **Oak Park Center**.

The new text replaces the old and retains the original's formatting.

10 To add a new text box to the invitation, click the Add Text button on the toolbar.

Add Text

A text box with *Your Text Here* appears in the middle of the invitation. The text is selected.

11 Drag the new text box to the upper left corner of the invitation.

The text box can overlap the cropped picture.

Zoom

12 On the toolbar, click the Zoom arrow, and then click 100%.

The text is shown at full size and remains selected.

Font Size

13 On the toolbar, click the Font Size arrow, scroll up, and then click 22.

The font size of the selected text is reduced, and the text remains selected.

14 Type **This Saturday!**

The new text replaces *Your Text Here* but does not fill the text box.

15 To resize the text box to fit the text, drag the right-side handle to the left until the box is just wide enough to fit the text without wrapping.

Rotate handle

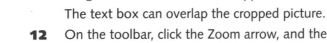

Rotate pointer

16 Point to the rotate handle on the text box until you see the Rotate pointer, and then drag counterclockwise until the text box is approximately at a 45-degree angle.

If the text moves off the page, drag the rotated text box by an edge until all the text appears on the colored background. The text box remains selected.

17 To fill the text box with color, in Text Options, click Change Text Box, and then click Text Box Background Color.

A color palette appears.

18 Click yellow.

The text box is filled with a yellow background.

19 To cancel the selection, click off the page.

Handles no longer appear on the text box, and the Document Options list is displayed on the left.

Zoom

20 To zoom out for a better view, in the Zoom box, click Entire Page.

The entire invitation is displayed.

21 To delete the gradient background, click Delete Something in the Document Options list, and then click Page Background.

22 To add a border around the invitation, click Add Something in the Document Options list, and then click Page Border.

The Border dialog box appears.

Creating an Invitation

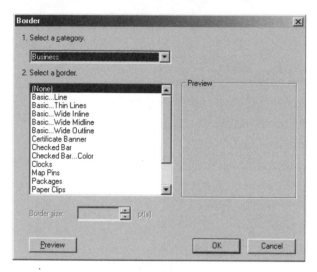

23 In the Select A Category list, click Nature, and in the Select A Border list, click Earth...One.

A preview of the border appears in the Preview box.

24 In the Border Size box, change the size to 24 points.

25 Click OK.

The invitation is displayed with a border.

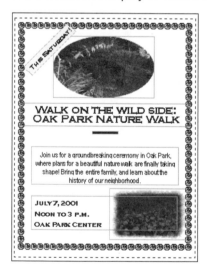

Saving and Printing Your Invitation

You can save the projects you create with Picture It! Publishing much as you save a document in any program. You can also save the pictures you create and edit as new files that can be reused in other programs. For example, after cropping a picture, you can save it as a new Windows bitmap (.bmp) file. When you save a project or a picture, you can add it to the Gallery and choose a category and key-words to use in cataloging it.

Print projects, such as this lesson's invitation, are intended to be printed in color. If you don't have a color printer, you can print in black and white. Picture It! Publishing displays a gray dotted line around the printable area of your project. Before you print, make sure that all text and pictures appear inside the dotted line.

In this exercise, you save your project as a new file and print it.

1   Make sure that nothing is selected in the invitation.

   The Document Options list is displayed on the left.

2   Click Save Or Send, and then click Save As.

   Save As options are displayed on the left.

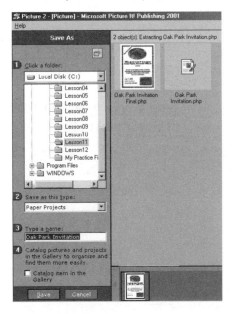

3   In the Click A Folder list, make sure that the Lesson11 folder is selected.

4   Leave the Save As This Type box set to Paper Projects.

5   In the Type A Name box, type **My Oak Park Invitation**.

6 Select the Catalog Item In The Gallery check box, and then click the Save button.

Edit Gallery options are displayed on the left. On the right, My Oak Park Invitation.php is selected.

7 In the Edit Gallery area, select the My Favorites check box in the Categories box.

8 Click in the Keywords box, type **nature walk**, and then click the Add button.

The words *nature walk* are added to the list of keywords for this project.

Delete

9 In the Keywords list, click My, and then click the Delete button.

The word *My* is removed from the list of keywords for this project.

10 Leave the Date options as is, and then click the Apply button.

Picture It! Publishing adds the invitation to the My Favorites category and applies the suggested keywords.

11 Click the Done button.

The invitation project appears with the new filename on the title bar, and the Document Options list is displayed on the left.

Print

12 On the toolbar, click the Print button.

The Print dialog box appears.

13 Click OK.

A message box appears, telling you to wait until printing is finished before you continue. When the invitation is finished being printed, click OK.

The invitation is printed.

14   On the File menu, click Close.

If a message asks you to save changes, click Yes. The Pick A Design tab appears.

15   Click the Show My Pictures & Projects tab.

Picture It! Publishing displays options for opening existing pictures or projects, importing pictures, and organizing pictures. Under Recent Files, the two files you saved during this lesson appear.

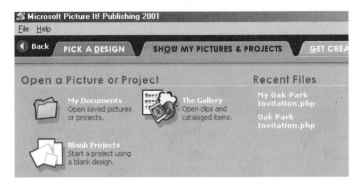

16   Under Open A Picture Or Project, click The Gallery.

Browse options appear, and the Browse tab is displayed.

17   Click the Find tab.

18   In the Find box, type **nature walk** and then click the Find button.

Picture It! Publishing displays thumbnails of all projects and clips associated with the keywords *nature walk*, including the My Oak Park Invitation.php project.

19   Click the Cancel button.

The Show My Pictures & Projects tab appears.

tip

You can save a picture you edit in Picture It! Publishing as a file in another format, including bitmap (.bmp) and JPEG (.jpg). To do this, select the picture. In the Picture Options list, click More Options, and then click Save Picture As. Choose a location for the file, and then click a file format in the Save As This Type list. Type a filename, and then click Save. For details about saving pictures, search in Picture It! Publishing Help for the topic *Which File Format Should I Use To Save My Picture?*

Lesson Wrap-Up

To finish the lesson:

Close

1   On the Microsoft Picture It! Publishing title bar, click the Close button.

Picture It! Publishing closes, and the Works Task Launcher appears.

2   In the Task Launcher, click the Close button on the title bar.

Quick Reference

To start Picture It! Publishing and choose a project design

1   In the Task Launcher, click the Programs tab, click Picture It! Publishing, and then click Start Picture It! Publishing.

2   On the Pick A Design tab, click a design category and then click a subcategory.

3   Click a theme, click the thumbnail you want to open, and then click Open.

To save a new project

1   On the toolbar, click the Save File button.

2   In the Click A Folder box, choose a location in which to save the project.

3   In the Save As This Type box, click Paper Projects.

4   In the Type A Name box, type a name for the project.

5   If you want to add Gallery keywords for cataloging the project, select the Catalog Item In The Gallery check box.

6   Click Save.

To replace an existing graphic

1   Click the picture in your project that you want to change.

2   In Picture Options, click Change Picture, and then click Replace Picture.

To add a new picture to a project

1   Click the Add Picture Or Animation button on the toolbar.

2   Browse the Gallery to locate the picture you want, click the thumbnail, and then click Open.

To locate a picture in the Gallery by keyword

1   In the Browse options, click the Find tab.

2   Type keywords in the Find box, and then click Find.

3   Click the thumbnail you want, and then click Open.

To save a Gallery item in the My Favorites collection

●   Right-click a thumbnail, and then click Add To My Favorites.

To crop an existing picture

1   Click the picture you want to crop.

2   In Picture Options, click Cutouts & Pictures, and then click Crop.

3   Choose the crop shape you want, adjust the position and size of the crop area on the picture, and then click Done.

To apply an edge effect to an existing picture

1   Click the picture you want to change.

2   In Picture Options, click Edge Effects, and then click the effect you want.

3   Follow the instructions on the left to refine the edge effect, and then click Done.

To resize a picture proportionally

1   Click the picture to display its handles.

2   Drag a corner handle until the picture is the size you want.

To change existing text

1   Select the text you want to change.

2   Type new text.

To add text to an existing text block

●   Click in a text box, and then type.

To change text font formatting

1   Select the text you want to format.

2   In Text Options, click Change Formatting, and then click Font.

3   Click a font, style, and size, and then click OK.

To move a text box

●   Drag the text box by its gray border to a new position.

To resize a text box

1   Click the text box to display its handles.

2   Drag a handle until the text box is the size you want.

To rotate a text box

1   Click the text box to display its handles.

2   Drag the rotate handle in the direction you want.

ROTATE

To change the view

●   On the toolbar, click the Zoom arrow, and then click a zoom option.

To print a project

1   Click the Print button on the toolbar.

2   In the Print dialog box, click OK.

LESSON 12

Planning Trips and Finding Information

ESTIMATED
TIME
20 min.

In this lesson, you will learn how to:

✓ *Search for information in Microsoft Encarta Encyclopedia.*

✓ *Locate places on a map in Microsoft Streets & Trips.*

✓ *Discover the best route between two places on a map.*

Microsoft Works puts the world at your fingertips with Microsoft Encarta Encyclopedia Standard 2001, a multimedia reference program, and Microsoft Streets & Trips 2001, a mapping and trip planning resource. Encarta Encyclopedia makes research fun with its audio and video clips, photos and illustrations, and interactive learning tools. You'll use the straightforward search tools to find just the information you want among tens of thousands of lively articles. To add a geographic dimension to your research, you can use Streets & Trips to display highly detailed street and topographical maps. Backed by a database containing information about hotels, restaurants, and other businesses and attractions, Streets & Trips is also a great resource for researching travel routes.

In this lesson, you'll learn to use the search capabilities in Encarta Encyclopedia to locate information about a botanical garden. Then you'll use Streets & Trips to find your way around a city and locate additional attractions.

Locating Information in Encarta Encyclopedia

Encarta Encyclopedia makes it easy to explore the world around you, whether you're researching a report or just browsing for fun. Interactive audio and video clips enliven thousands of articles about everything from air to Zen, and links to relevant topics encourage deeper exploration.

Encarta Encyclopedia can help you find what you're looking for, even if you aren't exactly sure what that is. You can search for articles and multimedia clips with the **Pinpointer**, which is both a search tool that lets you conduct text searches and an index that lists types of information, such as maps and interactive media.

Back

Working in Encarta Encyclopedia is a lot like surfing the Web with a browser. When you browse articles in Encarta Encyclopedia, you can use the Back button to review articles or media you already viewed. To find favorite articles or multimedia again, you can bookmark them by adding them to the Favorites menu.

tip

A fun and interactive way to browse Encarta Encyclopedia when you have no particular goal in mind is to use Encarta Explorer. Encarta Explorer organizes a subset of Encarta Encyclopedia's best content by topic, such as history or science. You can graphically zoom in on a category that interests you to view specially selected articles, media, and features. To use Encarta Explorer, on the Features menu, click Encarta Explorer.

In this exercise, you locate information about a botanical garden that the fictional members of the Oak Park nature walk restoration project heard about.

1   On the Start menu, point to Programs, and then click Microsoft Works.

The Works Task Launcher opens.

2   Click the Programs tab.

All Works programs are listed in the Task Launcher.

3   Under Programs, click Encarta Encyclopedia.

Tasks for Encarta Encyclopedia are listed on the right.

4   Click Start Encarta Encyclopedia.

The Encarta Encyclopedia home screen appears, and the Pinpointer is displayed on the left.

The Pinpointer, where
you can search for
specific information   Back and Forward buttons   Encarta Encyclopedia
home screen

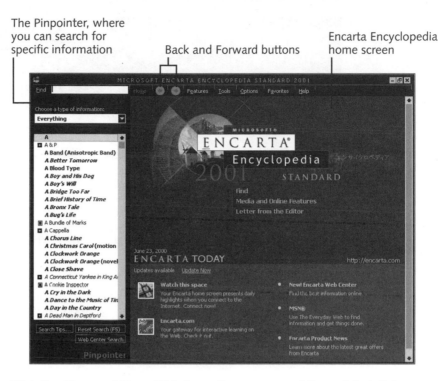

5   Click the Choose A Type Of Information arrow, and then click Articles.

The Pinpointer lists all the articles in Encarta Encyclopedia.

6   To narrow the scope of the search, type **garden** in the Find box.

The Pinpointer lists all the article titles that contain the word *garden* followed
by a list of other items that contain the word *garden*.

7   Click Royal Botanic Gardens, Kew.

Encarta displays the article with that title and hides the Pinpointer.

8   Click the Find button in the upper left corner.

The Pinpointer reappears.

9   In the Find box, type **san francisco garden**.

The Pinpointer lists everything that contains the words *san francisco garden*.

10   In the results list, click San Francisco.

Encarta Encyclopedia displays the article titled *San Francisco* and scrolls to the
section containing the search words, which are highlighted in yellow.

Notice that the article mentions the Strybing Arboretum and Botanical Gardens, which you will locate on a map in the next exercise.

Find

12

Trips and Information

11   In the blue area at the top of the article, click the Contents Page button.

Encarta Encyclopedia displays the table of contents for this article, which includes links to related information and multimedia content.

To scroll through the images at the top of the Contents page, hover the mouse over one of the blue arrows.

12   In the article outline, click I. Introduction.

The article's first section is displayed. Words in blue are links to related information.

13   In the first sentence, click the California link.

Encarta Encyclopedia displays an article about California.

Back

14 On the toolbar, click the Back button.

The San Francisco introduction reappears.

15 Use the scroll bar along the right side of the window to scroll to the third paragraph in the introduction.

In the left margin, the San Francisco Climate Chart label appears.

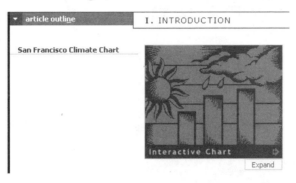

Expand

16 To explore this interactive item, click the Expand link below the Interactive Chart picture.

An interactive chart labeled City Climate appears. A brown bar representing San Francisco's annual average temperature appears in the chart.

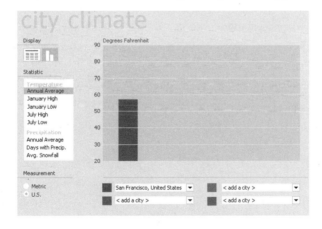

You can view statistics for other cities by clicking the Add A City arrow and clicking a city.

17 In the Statistic box, click Days With Precip.

The chart displays the number of days in a year with precipitation in San Francisco.

18 To return to the San Francisco article, click the Back button on the toolbar.

Back

Trips and Information 12

19   To bookmark this page, on the Favorites menu, click Add To Favorites.
The Add To Favorites dialog box appears.

20   Click OK.
Encarta Encyclopedia adds the San Francisco article to the Favorites menu.

21   To return to the Encarta Encyclopedia home screen, click Home on the toolbar.
The Encarta Encyclopedia home screen is displayed and the Pinpointer is hidden.

22   On the Favorites menu, click Article – San Francisco.
The introduction of the San Francisco article is displayed.

Close

23   To close Encarta Encyclopedia, click the Close button on the title bar.
The Task Launcher appears.

> **tip**
> Test your wits against the Encarta Mindmaze, an interactive quiz game in
> which you must supply the correct answers to find your way out of the maze.
> To play, on the Features menu, click Mindmaze.

Planning a Route with Streets & Trips

With Streets & Trips, you can find cities, countries, businesses, natural features,
and other places on a map that you can save and print. You can locate specific
addresses in the United States and Canada and even pinpoint exact latitude and
longitude coordinates. Streets & Trips can display either road or terrain maps, in
which you can move and zoom by using the tools on the Navigation toolbar.

You can find an address based on all or most of a street address and the zip code; city and state aren't necessary.

You can also locate useful resources for your travels. Streets & Trips includes a database of thousands of attractions and businesses across North America, such as hotels, restaurants, and gas stations, that you can display on a map. If you want to plan a driving route, or just see the shortest path from point A to point B, you can use the Route Planner. You provide a starting and a final destination, and the Route Planner calculates a route that best meets your needs. For example, you can designate stops that you want to make along the way and specify driving times, and Route Planner factors your preferences into its driving directions.

In this exercise, you locate the Strybing Arboretum and Botanical Gardens on a street map and then locate nearby points of interest. You use Route Planner to calculate the best driving routes between points and then print the directions and save the street map.

Programs

1   In the Task Launcher, click the Programs tab.

All Works programs are listed in the Task Launcher.

2   Under Programs, click Streets & Trips.

Tasks for Streets & Trips are listed on the right.

3   Click Start Streets & Trips.

Streets & Trips displays a map of North America. On the toolbar, the Find box is already highlighted, so you can type the name of a place or an address.

To see the Legend symbols for a category, click the plus sign (+) next to a category name.

Navigation toolbar

Standard toolbar

Location And Scale toolbar

Overview map

Legend

Drawing toolbar

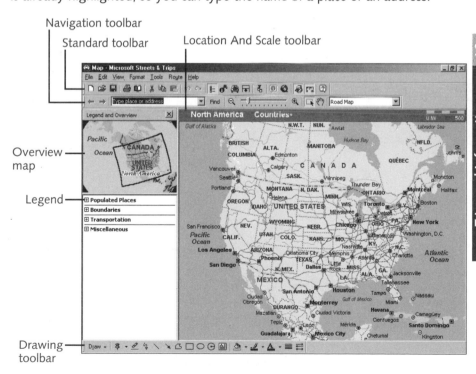

Trips and Information

12

4   In the Find box on the Navigation toolbar, type **Strybing**, and then press the Enter key.

The Find dialog box appears and lists potential matches for the search text on the Place tab. The first item, Strybing Arboretum & Gardens, San Francisco, is selected and displayed on the map behind the dialog box.

tip
To find a place based on its address or its latitude and longitude values, use the Address tab or the Lat/Long tab in the Find dialog box.

5   Click OK.

The dialog box is closed, and the map view is centered on Strybing Arboretum & Gardens.

6   To get information about nearby attractions, on the Edit menu, click Find Nearby Places.

A list of places within a one-mile radius is displayed on the left and highlighted on the map.

7 In the list of results, click the plus sign (+) next to Landmarks.

The list expands to show nearby landmarks.

Zoom Out

8 To see more of the city map, click the Zoom Out button on the Navigation toolbar.

The view is zoomed out, but Strybing Arboretum & Gardens remains at the center of the map.

9 To calculate the driving route from the arboretum to Alcatraz, on the Route menu, click Route Planner.

The Route Planner appears to the left of the map, replacing the Legend And Overview information. In the Type A Place Or Address box, Strybing Arboretum & Gardens already appears.

10 Click the Add To Route button.

The place is added to the results list and labeled 1 in green. On the map, the starting point for the route is also labeled with a green 1.

11 In the Find box on the Navigation toolbar, type **Alcatraz** and then press Enter.

The Find dialog box appears and selects the first match, Alcatraz, New Mexico, which is displayed on the map behind the dialog box.

12 In the Find dialog box, click Alcatraz (Island(s)), California, United States, and then click OK.

The view in the map is centered on Alcatraz island.

13 Click Add To Route.

In the results list and on the map, Alcatraz is labeled 2 in red.

14 In the Route Planner, click the Get Directions button.

A driving map appears on the right with the route highlighted in green. Driving directions are shown in a separate pane above the map.

12

Trips and Information

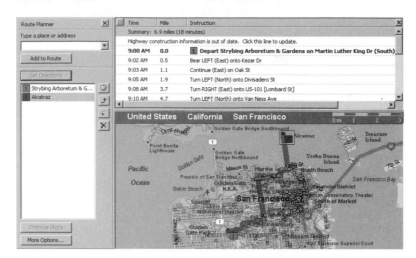

15   To print the map and directions, on the File menu, click Print.

The Print dialog box appears.

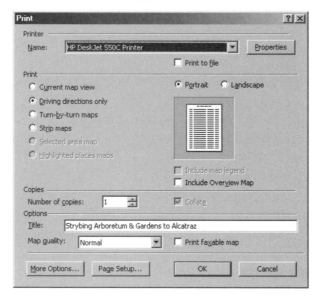

16   Click Strip Maps, select the Include Overview Map check box, and then click OK.

Two pages are printed: one showing a strip map of the route with driving directions, and the other showing the entire route. This route is so short that it fits on one strip map, but if the route were longer, a separate strip map for each driving segment would be printed.

Save

17   To save this view of Streets & Trips containing the driving map, click the Save button on the Standard toolbar.

The Save As dialog box appears.

18 In the Save In box, make sure that the My Documents folder is selected.

19 Double-click the Works Suite 2001 SBS Practice folder, and then double-click the Lesson12 folder.

If you did not install this book's practice files or you want to save your work in a different location, browse to the folder you want.

20 In the File Name box, type **My Strybing Trip**, and then click Save.

The map view is saved as a Streets & Trips format (.est) file.

---

tip

You can copy a map that you create in Streets & Trips for use in other documents and Web pages by clicking Copy Map on the Edit menu. When you copy a map, Streets & Trips automatically adds copyright information at the bottom of the map. You must include this copyright information when you use the map.

Lesson Wrap-Up

To finish the lesson:

Close

1 To close Microsoft Streets & Trips, click the Close button on the title bar.

Streets & Trips closes, and the Task Launcher appears.

2 In the Task Launcher, click the Close button on the title bar.

Quick Reference

To start Encarta Encyclopedia from the Task Launcher

● Click the Programs tab, click Encarta Encyclopedia, and then click Start Encarta Encyclopedia.

To display the Pinpointer

● Click the Find button.

To locate an item containing specific text

1 In the Find box, type the text you want to find.

2 In the results list, click an item to display it.

To locate specific text within an article

1 On the Tools menu, click Find In This Article.

2 Type the text you want to locate, and then click Find.

12

Trips and Information

To follow a link

● In the text of an article, click a blue word.

To browse with Encarta Explorer

1   On the Features menu, click Encarta Explorer.

2   Click a category, and then click a subcategory or a picture for more options.

To save a link to an article or item on the Favorites menu

1   Display the article or item you want, and on the Favorites menu, click Add To Favorites.

2   Type a name, and then click OK.

To start Streets & Trips from the Task Launcher

Programs

● Click the Programs tab, click Streets & Trips, and then click Start Streets & Trips.

To find a place on the map

1   In the Find box, type a place, and then press Enter.

2   In the Find dialog box, click the place you want, and then click OK.

To zoom to a specific area

1   On the Navigation toolbar, click the Select tool.

2   Draw a box around the area you want to enlarge, and then click in the box.

To identify an attraction on the map

● Click a symbol on the map.

To display information about an attraction on the map

● Right-click a symbol, and then click Show Information.

To create a route

1   On the Route menu, click Route Planner.

2   Type the name of the starting place, and then click Add To Route. If the Find dialog box appears, click a place name, and then click OK.

3   Type the name of the destination, and then click Add To Route. If the Find dialog box appears, click a place name, and then click OK.

4   Click Get Directions.

To print a map

1   On the File menu, click Print.

2   Click the options you want, and then click OK.

To save a map

1   Click the Save button on the Standard toolbar.

2   Choose a location, type a filename, and then click OK.

Index

Note: italicized page numbers indicate figures or tables.

Special characters

<<>> (angle brackets), 134
, (comma), 80
/ (division symbol), 115
= (equal sign), 115, 116, 127
- (minus sign), 115
* (multiplication symbol), 115
+ (plus sign), 77, 115, 239
(pound signs), 158
; (semicolon), 80

A

account registers, Money, 198
accounts and investments, 193–212.
    See also Microsoft Money
  creating new files, 210, *210*
  entering transactions, 198–201, *199,*
    200, 201, 211
  quick reference, 210–12
  reports, 207–9, *207, 208, 209,* 212
  scheduling recurring transactions, 202–3,
    202, 203, 211

accounts and investments, *continued*
  setting up accounts, 194–98, *194, 196,*
    197, 198, 210
  tracking investments, 203–6, *204, 206,*
    211–12
active cells, Spreadsheet, 112, *112*
Add Printer Wizard, 41
Address Book. *See* Windows Address Book
addresses
  entering e-mail, 47
  filtering and sorting, 141–43, *142, 143,*
    149–50
  finding and mapping, 238–43, *239, 240,*
    241, 242
  Web page, 65, 70
aliases, Address Book, 51, 52–54, *52, 53,*
  60–61
alignment, Spreadsheet, 114, 118
angle brackets (<<>>), 134
anniversaries, Calendar, 92, 97
Answer Wizard, 15, 16–17, *16,* 18, *18,* 21
appointments, Calendar. *See* schedules
attachments, e-mail, 79, 81, *81,* 82, 86
audio help, Money, 195
AutoComplete feature, Money, 201, *201*
AutoCorrect feature, Word, 32
AutoSum button, Spreadsheet, 118, 127

B

Back button, 16, 234, 237

Backspace key, 27, 29, 30, 154

birthdays
adding, to calendars, 97–98, *98,* 105
adding Address Book, to calendars, 92, 97
as events, 99

blank databases, 153

blank documents, 4, 12, *13,* 24, 25, *25,* 132

blank projects, 216–17

blank spreadsheets, 13–14, *13,* 109, 111, *111*

.bmp format, 229

browsers, Web, 64. *See also* Microsoft Internet Explorer

budget spreadsheets, 107–28. *See also* Works Spreadsheet
calculations, 115–20, *116, 117, 118, 119, 120,* 127
charts, 120–23, *121, 122, 123,* 127–28
components, 107–9, *108*
creating and saving, 109–11, *110, 111,* 126
entering text and numbers, 112–15, *112, 113, 114, 115,* 126–27
previewing and printing, 123–25, *124, 125,* 128
quick reference, 126–28

bulleted lists, Word, 36–37, *36, 37,* 43

Business Card style, Address Book, 58

C

calculations, Spreadsheet, 115–20, *116, 117, 118, 119, 120,* 127

calendars. *See* schedules; Works Calendar

canceling selections, Spreadsheet, 126

case of characters, 16, 34

categories
appointment, 98–101, *99, 100, 101,* 105–6
Money, 198–99, *199,* 211
task, 6

cell ranges, Spreadsheet, 112, 126

cell references, Spreadsheet, 112, *112*

cells, Spreadsheet, 108, *108,* 112, *112,* 126, 127

characters. *See also* fonts
case of, 16, 34
formatting, 172, 174–75, *175,* 188
special, 34

charts, Spreadsheet, 120–23, *121, 122, 123,* 127–28

checkbooks. *See* Microsoft Money

clip art. *See* pictures

Clipboard, 176

Clippit character, 19

closing
Address Book, 60
Calendar, 104
Database, 11, 168
databases, 169
e-mail messages, 82

closing, *continued*
    Internet Explorer, 69, 75
    Money, 209
    Outlook Express, 85
    Picture It! Publishing, 230
    Portfolio, 7, *7,* 20, 21, 188
    Spreadsheet, 14, 126
    Streets & Trips, 243
    Task Launcher, 20, 41, 60
    Windows Explorer, 79
    Word, 13, 15, 19, 82, 141, 147
    Word Help, 19
    Works, 20
    Works Help, 20, 92, 158
collections, Portfolio, 183, 190
colors
    printing, 122, 227
    of Word fonts, 35, 43
    Word shading, 182–83, *182*
    Word themes and, 8, 24, 27
columns
    newsletter, 180, *180,* 189
    Spreadsheet, 108, *108,* 113, 127
comma (,), 80
contacts, 45–61. *See also* **Windows Address Book**
    creating and editing, 46–49, *46, 47, 48,* 60
    identities, 58
    inserting, into Word documents, 27
    maps and, 49
    organizing, 51–55, *52, 53, 54, 55,* 60–61

contacts, *continued*
    printing, 58–59, *59,* 61
    quick reference, 60–61
    sending e-mail to, 79, 81
    sharing, 55–57, *56, 57,* 61
    sorting, 49–51, *50, 51,* 60
Content Advisor, Internet Explorer, 72–74, *74,* **86**
Contents
    Word Help, 18, *18*
    Works Help, 17, 21
copying
    appointments, *96,* 105
    charts, 123
    e-mail messages, 84
    maps, 243
    Spreadsheet formulas, 117, *117*
    text, 176, 178, 189
copyright information, map, 243
Create New Scheduled Transaction Wizard, 202–3, *202, 203*
cropping pictures, 219, 231
Ctrl key, 52, 61, 78, 84, 96, 105
Ctrl+Z key combination, 30, 175
Currency format, Spreadsheet, 114
customizing
    Internet Explorer, 70–72, *71, 72,* 86
    Money reports, 207–9, *207, 208, 209,* 212
    Word mail merge results, 139–41, *140, 141*
    Word menus and toolbars, 28

D

data
  entering Database, 156–59, *157, 158, 159*
  Money (*see* transactions, Money)
  Spreadsheet chart, 120–23, *121, 122, 123,* 127–28

databases, 151–69. *See also* Works Database
  components, 151–52, *152*
  creating, 152–56, *153, 154, 155,* 168
  entering information, 156–59, *157, 158, 159,* 168
  filtering information, 161–64, *162, 163,* 169
  finding and sorting information, 159–61, *160, 161,* 169
  forms, *159*
  printing information, 164–66, *165, 166,* 169
  quick reference, 168–69
  reports, 166–67, *167,* 169
  starting, from History list, 156

data sources, Word mail merge
  changing, 136
  creating, 148
  defined, 130
  editing, 138, *138,* 149
  mailing label, 145
  opening, 133–34, *133*
  specifying, 135
  working with other, 139

dates
  Database, 155
  Spreadsheet, 124

day calendar, 92, *92*
Deleted Items folder, Outlook Express, 84, 85
deleting
  appointments, *96,* 104, 105
  contacts, 51, 53–54, 60
  Database fields, 156, 168
  documents from History list, 14, 15
  e-mail messages, 84, 85
  groups, 54, 60
  holidays, 98
  text, 30, 42
demos. *See* multimedia demos
designs, Picture It! Publishing, 213–14, 230
digital photographs. *See* pictures
division symbol (/), 115
documents
  deleting, from History list, 14, 15
  spreadsheet (*see* budget spreadsheets)
  starting with, from History list, 14–15, *14,* 20
  Word, 24 (*see also* letters; mass mailings; newsletters)

E

Easy Calc tool, Spreadsheet, 116, 119–20, *119, 120,* 127
effects, Picture It! Publishing, *217–18,* 221–22, *221,* 231
e-mail addresses, 47. *See also* Microsoft Outlook Express
Encarta. *See* Microsoft Encarta Encyclopedia

Encarta Explorer, 234, 244

End User License Agreement, 6–7

envelopes, Word, 143–47, *144, 145, 146,* 150

Envelope Wizard, 147

equal sign (=), 115, 116, 127

error correction, Word, 29, 31–32

errors, Spreadsheet, 115

events, Calendar
adding, 93–97, *94, 95, 96,* 105
birthdays as, *99*

expanding
folders, 77
menus and toolbars, 28, 30, 43

F

Favorites
Encarta, 238
Internet Explorer, 70–72, *71, 72,* 86
Money, 207–9, *207, 208, 209,* 212
Picture It! Publishing, 219, 231

fields
Address Book, 49
Database, *152, 152,* 153, 155, 159, 168
Word merge, 130, 134, 136–37, *136, 137,* 145, *145*

files
Address Book, 49–50, *50*
Calendar, 102–4, *102, 103*
Money, 210, *210*
Outlook Express e-mail attachments, 79, 81, *81,* 82, 86

fill handle, Spreadsheet, 117

filtering
appointments by category, 98, 101, *101,* 104
Database information, 160, *160,* 161–64, *162, 163*
Word mail merge names and addresses, 141–43, *142, 143,* 149–50

financial matters. *See* accounts and investments; budget spreadsheets; Microsoft Money; Works Spreadsheet

Financial Worksheets Wizard, 109–10, *110,* 126

finding. *See* searching

flyers, garage sale, 6–10, *7, 8, 9,* 15, 18. *See also* invitations

Flyers Wizard, 8, *8*

folders
Address Book, 52, 54–55, *54, 55,* 61
e-mail, 77, 83–85, *84,* 87
Internet Explorer Favorites, 71–72, *71,* 86

Folders And Groups view, Address Book, 48, 57

FoneSync, *5*

fonts
Word, 34, 35, 43
Word themes and, 8, 24, 27, 173

footers, Spreadsheet, 124, *124,* 125, 128

Format Gallery, 179–83, *180, 181, 182,* 189

Format Painter, 177, 178, 189

formats
Address Book, 58
Calendar file, 102

formats, *continued*
  Database field, 153
  Picture It! Publishing picture, 229
formatting
  Database fields, 155
  Database forms, 159
  Picture It! Publishing text, 222–26, *224,*
    225, 226, 231–32
  searching for Word, 34
  Spreadsheet cells, 112, 114–15, *115,* 116,
    118, 127
  Word text, 34–37, *35, 36, 37,* 43, 177,
    178, 179–83, *180, 181, 182,* 189
  Word themes, 8, 24, 27, 173
formatting marks, Word, 172, 174–75, *175,*
  188
Form Design view, Database, 159
form letters, Word, 130, 132–33, *132,*
  134–37, *135, 136, 137,* 148.
    See also mass mailings
formula bar, Spreadsheet, 112, *112,* 115,
  116
formulas, Spreadsheet, 115–20, *116, 117,*
  118, 119, 120, 127
Form view, Database, 156, 157, *157*
functions, Spreadsheet, 116, 127

G

Gallery
  Picture It! Publishing, 217–22, *217–18,*
    219, 220, 221, 222, 228–29, *228, 229,*
    230–31
  Word, 19

garage sale flyer project, 6–10, *7, 8, 9,* 15, 18
grammar errors, Word, 29, 31–32, *31*
graphics. *See* pictures
groups, Address Book, 51, 52–54, *52, 53,*
  60–61

H

handles, selection, 217
headers, Spreadsheet, 124, *124,* 125, 128
Help
  Money, 195
  quick references (*see* quick references)
  Word, 18–19, *18*
  Works, 15–19, *16, 17, 18,* 20–21, 92,
    111, 120, 158
hiding formatting marks, 175, 188
hiding Office Assistant, 19, 21, 26, 173
History list, 14–15, *14,* 20, 156
holidays, Calendar, 97–98, *98,* 105
home pages
  Internet Explorer, 72, *72,* 86
  Microsoft, 70
  Money, *194, 198*
  MSN, 66, *66*
  Task Launcher, 4, *4,* 7, *7*
  Web, 64
.htm file extension, 102
HTML (Hypertext Markup Language)
  format
  calendars, 102–4, *102, 103*
  Web pages, 64
HTTP (Hypertext Transfer Protocol), 65

I

I-beam pointer, 30
icons
    Connect To Internet, 65, *65*
    Outlook Express, 76, *76*
    Works Suite, 6, *6*
identities, Address Book, 55–58, *56, 57,* 60
images. *See* pictures
importing
    Address Book contacts, 49–50, *50*
    Calendar files, 102
Inbox folder, Outlook Express, 77, 84
Index
    Word Help, 18, *18*
    Works Help, 17, *17,* 21
insertion point, Word, 24
installing printers, 41
Internet. *See also* Microsoft Internet
    Explorer; Microsoft Network (MSN);
    Microsoft Outlook Express; Web
    connecting, 64–65
    online stock quotes, 206
Internet Connection Wizard, 65, 66, 76
Internet Explorer. *See* Microsoft Internet
    Explorer
Internet service providers, 63, 64–65
investments, tracking, 203–6, *204, 206,*
    211–12. *See also* accounts and
    investments
invitations, 213–32. *See also* Microsoft
    Picture It! Publishing
    formatting text, 222–26, *224, 225, 226,*
        231–32

invitations, *continued*
    pictures, 217–22, *217–18, 219, 220, 221,*
        222, 230–31
    quick reference, 230–32
    saving and printing, 227–29, *227, 228,*
        229, 232
    starting from scratch, 216–17
    starting with a built-in design, 213–16,
        214, 215, 216, 230
items, Portfolio, 183

J

JPEG format, 183, 229

K

keyboard shortcuts, Spreadsheet, 115

L

labels
    mailing, 143–47, *144, 145, 146,* 150
    Spreadsheet, 113, 116
latitude, 240
layouts, Word, 26–27, *26,* 34, 37, 43
letters, 23–43. *See also* Microsoft Word
    creating, 24–27, *25, 26, 28,* 42
    entering and editing text, 29–32, *29, 31,*
        32, 42
    finding and replacing text, 32–34, *33,* 42
    forms (*see* mass mailings)
    formatting text, 34–37, *35, 36, 37,* 43
    installing printers, 41
    quick reference, 42–43

letters, *continued*
   saving and printing, 38–40, *38, 39, 40,* 43
   Word menus and toolbars, 28, 43
Letter Wizard, 26–27, *26, 28,* 42
links, Web, 64
List view, Database, 152, *152,* 156–59, *159,* 167
logon information, 76
longitude, 240
lorem ipsum text, 176
lowercase, 16

M

magnifying windows, 39, 122–23, *123,* 125, 166, 180, 182, 186, 221–22
mailing labels, Word, 143–47, *144, 145, 146,* 150
Mailing Label Wizard, 144–46, *144, 145, 146,* 150
mail merge, Word. *See* mass mailings
Mail Merge Helper, Word, 134–37, *135,* 142–43, *142, 143,* 148–50
Mail Merge toolbar, Word, 134, 136–39, *136, 137, 138*
main document, Word mail merge, 130, 132–33, *132,* 134–37, *135, 137*
Main Identity's Contacts folder, Address Book, 52, 53, 55
maps
   Expedia Maps, 49
   Streets & Trips, 238–43, *239, 240, 241, 242,* 244

margins, Word, 37, *37,* 43
mass mailings, 129–50
   creating labels and envelopes, 143–47, *144, 145, 146,* 150
   customizing results, 139–41, *140, 141,* 149
   filtering and sorting names and addresses, 141–43, *142, 143,* 149–50
   filtering data sources before merging, 149
   form letters, 134–37, *135, 136, 137,* 148
   mail merge overview, 129–34, *131, 132, 133*
   printing envelopes, 147
   quick reference, 148–50
   viewing and printing merged data, 137–39, *137, 138,* 148
   working with other data sources, 139, 148–49
maximizing windows, 67, 79
memo style, Address Book, 58–59, *59*
menus
   Address Book, 59
   Internet Explorer Favorites, 70–72, *71, 72,* 86
   Windows Start, 6, *6,* 12, 24, 65, 131, 153, 172, 214, 234
   Word, 28, 30, 43
merge fields, Word, 130, 134, 136–37, *136, 137,* 145, *145*
Microsoft Encarta Encyclopedia, *5,* 233–38, *235, 236, 237, 238,* 243–44
Microsoft End User License Agreement, 6–7
Microsoft Insider Web page, 70–71, *71*

Microsoft Internet Explorer, 63–75
  controlling security in, 72–75, *74*, *75*, 86
  finding people and information, 65–69, *66*, *67*, *68*, *69*, 85–86
  personalizing, 70–72, *71*, *72*, 86
  quick reference, 85–86
  as Web browser, 64
  as Works component, *5*, *5*

Microsoft Money
  accounts and investments (*see* accounts and investments)
  AutoComplete feature, 201, *201*
  home page, *194*, *198*
  Money Express, 209
  quick reference, 210–12
  as Works component, *5*

Microsoft Network (MSN), *5*, 64, 66–69, *66*, *67*, *68*, *69*, 85

Microsoft Office, 176

Microsoft Outlook Express, 76–85
  Address Book and, *56*
  attaching files to e-mail, 79, 86
  copying sample e-mail messages to, 76–79, *76*, *77*, *78*, *79*
  deleting e-mail messages, 85
  establishing Internet connections, 64–65
  managing e-mail messages, 82–84, *83*, *84*, 87
  quick reference, 86–87
  sending calendars in e-mail, 102–4, *102*, *103*, 106
  sending messages, 79–82, *80*, *81*, 86–87
  as Works component, *5*

Microsoft Picture It! Publishing
  invitations (*see* invitations)
  quick reference, 230–32
  as Works component, *5*

Microsoft Product Registration, 7

Microsoft Streets & Trips, *5*, 238–43, *239*, *240*, *241*, *242*, 244

Microsoft Web site, 64, 70–71, *71*

Microsoft Windows
  Address Book (*see* Windows Address Book)
  default printer, 166
  installing printers, 41
  Internet connections, 64–65
  Internet options, 73
  Start menu, 6, *6*, 12, 24, 46, 65, 92, 109, 131, 153, 172, 195, 214, 234
  Windows Explorer, 77–79, *78*

Microsoft Word
  AutoCorrect feature, 32
  e-mail attachments and, 82
  garage sale flyer, 6–10, *7*, *8*, *9*, 15, 18
  Help, 16, 18–19, *18*
  inserting Address Book information into documents, 27
  letters (*see* letters)
  lorem ipsum text, 176
  mass mailings (*see* mass mailings)
  menus and toolbars, 28, 43
  Office Assistant (*see* Office Assistant)
  newsletters (*see* newsletters)
  quick references, 42–43, 148–50, 188–90
  spelling and grammar errors, 29, 31–32

Microsoft Word, *continued*

starting, from Task Launcher, 12–13, *12, 13,* 20, 24, 131

starting document from History list, 14–15, *14*

views, 39, *39,* 40

Works versions and, 4, *5,* 24, 134

Microsoft Works 6.0

components, 5, *5*

Word Processor, 4, 5, *5,* 24, 132, 173

Microsoft Works Suite 2001, 3–21

Address Book (*see* contacts; Windows Address Book)

Calendar (*see* schedules; Works Calendar)

closing, 20

components, 4–5, *5*

Database (*see* databases; Works Database)

Encarta (*see* Microsoft Encarta Encyclopedia; trip planning)

exploring, 3–5, *4, 5*

Help, 15–19, *16, 17, 18,* 20–21

Internet communication (*see* Internet; Microsoft Internet Explorer; Microsoft Network (MSN); Microsoft Outlook Express; Web)

Money (*see* accounts and investments; Microsoft Money)

Office Assistant, 18–19, *18,* 21, 26

Picture It! Publishing (*see* invitations; Microsoft Picture It! Publishing)

Portfolio (*see* newsletters; Works Portfolio)

quick reference, 20–21 (*see also* quick references)

Microsoft Works Suite 2001, *continued*

registration, 6–7, 8

Spreadsheet (*see* budget spreadsheets; Works Spreadsheet)

starting, from Windows (*see* Start menu, Windows)

starting, with Task Launcher (*see* Works Task Launcher)

Streets & Trips (*see* Microsoft Streets & Trips; trip planning)

versions, 4, 5, *5,* 24, 132, 173 (*see also* Microsoft Works 6.0)

Web site, 69

wizards (*see* wizards)

Word (*see* letters; mass mailings; Microsoft Word; newsletters)

Mindmaze game, 238

minimizing dialog boxes, 119

minus sign (-), 115

Money. *See* **Microsoft Money**

Money Express, 209

month calendar, 93, *93*

More button, 28

More Buttons button, 34, 35

mouse operations, 29–30

moving

contacts into subfolders, 54–55, *55,* 61

Database fields, 168

e-mail messages into folders, 84, 87

MSN. *See* **Microsoft Network (MSN)**

multimedia demos

creating documents using wizards, 24

creating form letters, 134

multimedia demos, *continued*
   editing spreadsheets, 112
   formatting text, 176
   sending e-mail messages, 79
   setting up accounts, 194
   sorting and filtering database information, 160
   Task Launcher, 6
multiplication symbol (*), 115

N

names, filtering and sorting, 141–43, *142, 143,* 149–50
National Weather Service Web site, 72
navigation
   Address Book, 49
   Database, 158, *158,* 168
   Spreadsheet, 126
   Word mail merge records, 138, *138,* 141
network connections, 64–65
New Account Wizard, 204–6, *204, 206,* 212
newsletters, 171–90. *See also* **Microsoft Word; Works Portfolio**
   adding pictures, 183–86, *184, 185, 186, 187,* 189–90
   adding text, 176–79, *177, 178, 179,* 189
   creating, using wizard, 172–76, *173, 174, 175,* 188
   formatting, 179–83, *180, 181, 182,* 189
   lorem ipsum text and, 176
   pictures, 187
   quick reference, 188–90

Newsletters Wizard, 172–76, *173, 174, 175,* 188
numbers, Spreadsheet, 114–15, *114, 115,* 126–27

O

Office Assistant
   changing, 19
   hiding, 19, 21, 26, 173
   showing, 18, 26, 132
   Word Help and, 16, 18–19, *18*
Open A File Wizard, 210, *210*
orientation, Word paper, 37
Outlook Express. *See* **Microsoft Outlook Express**

P

page margins, Word, 37, *37,* 43
pages, Web, 64, 65
paper size and orientation, Word, 37
paragraph marks, 172, 174–75, *175,* 188
passwords, Internet Explorer, 73, 74
Paste command, Word, 176, 178
Paste Special command, Word, 178
people, searching Internet for, 65–69, *66, 67, 68, 69,* 85–86
personal finances. *See* **Microsoft Money**
personalizing. *See* **customizing**
Phone Number style, Address Book, 58, 59
photographs. *See* **pictures**
Picture It! Publishing. *See* **Microsoft Picture It! Publishing**

pictures

Picture It! Publishing, 217–22, *217–18, 219, 220, 221, 222,* 230–32

Portfolio, 183–87, *184, 185, 186, 187,* 189–90

pie charts, 121–23, *121, 122, 123*

Pinpointer, Encarta, 234–35, *235,* 243

planning trips. *See* trip planning

plus sign (+), 77, 115, 239

portals, Web, 64. *See also* Microsoft Network (MSN)

Portfolio. *See* Works Portfolio

portfolio, Money, 203–6, *204, 206,* 211–12

pound signs (##), 158

previewing

Database reports, 166–67, *167*

spreadsheets, 122, 123–25, *124, 125,* 128

Word documents, 38, 39, *39,* 43

print area, Spreadsheet, 123, 124, 125, 128

printers

default, 166

installing, 41

printing

contacts, 58–59, *59,* 61

Database information, 164–66, *165, 166,* 169

maps, 242, *242,* 244

Money reports, 209, *209,* 212

previewing (*see* previewing)

Picture It! Publishing projects, 228–29, *229,* 232

spreadsheets, 123–25, *124, 125,* 128

printing, *continued*

Word documents, 38–40, *38, 39, 40,* 43

Word envelopes, 147

Word mailing labels, 146

Word mail merge data, 137–39, *137, 138,* 148

print layout view, Word, 39, 40

product key dialog box, 8

product registration, 7

programs, starting, 11–14, *12, 13,* 20

projects, Picture It! Publishing, 213–14, *214,* 230–32. *See also* invitations

properties, Address Book, 54

Q

quick references

Address Book, 60–61

Calendar, 105–6

Database, 168–69

Encarta Encyclopedia, 243–44

Internet Explorer, 85–86

Money, 210–12

Outlook Express, 86–87

Picture It! Publishing, 230–32

Portfolio, 21, 189–90

Spreadsheet, 126–28

Streets & Trips, 244

Word letters, 42–43

Word mass mailings, 148–50

Word newsletters, 188–90

Works startup, 20–21

R

ranges of cells, Spreadsheet, 112, 126

ratings, Internet Explorer, 72–74, *74*, 86

reading e-mail messages, 77, *77*, 87

Recipe Book Wizard, 10–11, *10, 11*

records
    Database, 152, *152*, 161, 168, 169
    printing Database, 164–66, *165, 166*, 169
    Word mail merge, 137–39, *137, 138*

recurring appointments, Calendar, 94, 96–97, *96*, 105

recurring transactions, Money, 202–3, *202, 203*, 211

Redo command, Word, 30, 42

registers, Money, 198

registration, 6–7, 8

reminders, Calendar, 99, 100–101, *101*

repeating text and numbers, Spreadsheet, 127

replacing
    pictures, 230
    Word text, 32–34, *33*, 42

replying to e-mail messages, 82–83, *83*, 87

ReportCreator, Database, 164–66, *165, 166*

reports, Database
    creating and printing, 164–66, *165, 166*, 169
    modifying, 166–67, *167*, 169

Reports Gallery, Money, 207–9, *207, 208, 209*, 212

Report view, Database, 166–67, *167*

resizing
    Address Book window, *50*
    Database columns, 158
    Database fields, 159
    pictures, 220, 231
    Spreadsheet columns, 113, 118
    text boxes, 231
    Works Help window, 17

restricted sites, 75

right-pointing arrow, 29, 177

rotating text, Picture It! Publishing, 225, 231

Route Planner, 239–43, *239, 240, 241, 242*, 244

rows, Spreadsheet, 108, *108*, 127

S

saving
    calendar items in other formats, 104
    charts, 122
    Database reports, 167
    databases, 11, 156, 169
    maps, 242–43, 244
    Money reports, 212
    Picture It! Publishing projects, 216, 227–28, *227, 228*, 230, 232
    spreadsheets, 111, 125, 126
    Word documents, 9–10, *9*, 38–40, *38*, 43, 175–76, 179
    Word mail merge documents, 137, 138, 141, 148

schedules, 91–106. *See also* Works Calendar
appointments and events, 93–97, *94, 95, 96,* 105
birthdays and holidays, 97–98, *98,* 105
managing calendars, 98–101, *99, 100, 101,* 105–6
quick reference, 105–6
saving calendar items in other formats, 104
sharing calendars, 102–4, *102, 103,* 106
starting and viewing calendars, 91–93, *92, 93,* 105
scrolling
Encarta, 236
Word, 42
search engines, 65–66
searching
databases, 159–61, *160, 161,* 169
Encarta (*see* Microsoft Encarta Encyclopedia)
Gallery for pictures, 230
Internet for people and information, 65–69, *66, 67, 68, 69,* 85–86
Streets & Trips (*see* Microsoft Streets & Trips)
tasks, 10
Word Help, 18
Word text, 32–34, *33,* 42
Works Help, 16, 17, *17*
security zones, Internet Explorer, 72–73, 74–75, *75,* 86

selecting
contacts, 52–53, *53, 54, 59,* 61
e-mail messages, 78
Spreadsheet cells, 126
Word text, 29–30, 42, 177, *177*
selection handles, picture, 217
semicolon (;), 80
Sent Items folder, Outlook Express, 85
Setup Assistant, Money, 194–98, *194, 196, 197, 198.* 210
shading text, Word, 182–83, *182,* 189
Shared Contacts folder, Address Book, 52, 55, 57
sharing
calendars, 102–4, *102, 103,* 106
contacts, 55–58, *56, 57,* 61
Shift+F4 key combination, 161
Shift key, 59, 78, 177
shortcuts, Spreadsheet, 115
showing formatting marks, 175, *175,* 188
showing Office Assistant, 18, 26, 132
sites, Web. *See* Web
sorting
contacts, 49–51, *50, 51,* 60
Database information, 159–61, *160, 161,* 169
document history, 14–15, *15*
Word mail merge names and addresses, 141–43, *142, 143,* 149–50
space marks, 172, 174–75, *175,* 188
special effects, picture, *217–18,* 221–22, *221,* 231

spelling errors, Word, 29, 30–31

spreadsheets. *See* budget spreadsheets; Works Spreadsheet

Stack, Picture It! Publishing, 220, *220*

Start menu, Windows, 6, *6*, 12, 24, 46, 65, 92, 109, 131, 153, 172, 195, 214, 234

startup, Works. *See* Works Task Launcher

street maps. *See* maps

Streets & Trips. *See* Microsoft Streets & Trips

strip maps, 242, *242*

styles, Word, 34

subfolders, Address Book, 52, 54–55, *54, 55*, 61

SUM function, Spreadsheet, 118

T

tab-delimited format, Calendar, 104

Tab key, 49, 126, 157

tables of contents. *See* Contents

Task Launcher. *See* Works Task Launcher

tasks, starting, 6–11, *6, 7, 8, 9, 10, 11*, 20

templates, 5, 24

text

   adding, to Word newsletters, 176–79, *177, 178, 179*, 189

   deleting Word, 30, 42

   entering and editing Word, 29–32, *29, 31*, 42

   entering Spreadsheet, 112–15, *112, 113, 114, 115*, 126–27

   exporting calendars as, 104

   finding and replacing Word, 32–34, *33*, 42

text, *continued*

   formatting Picture It! Publishing, 222–26, *224, 225, 226*, 231–32

   formatting Word, 34–37, *35, 36, 37*, 43

   lorem ipsum, 176

   selecting Word, 29–30, 42

   shading, in Word, 182–83, *182*, 189

   Spreadsheet header and footer, 125

text boxes, Picture It! Publishing, 222–26, *224, 225*, 231

themes, Word, 8, 24, 27, 173

thumbnails, Picture It! Publishing, 214, *214*

tips, Calendar, 95

toolbars

   Database, 11

   Word, 28

   Word Formatting, 34–35, *35*

   Word Mail Merge, 134, 136–39, *136, 137, 138*

   Works Help, 16–17

transaction forms, Money, 198

transactions, Money, 198. *See also* accounts and investments

   entering, 198–201, *199, 200, 201*, 211

   recurring, 202–3, *202, 203*, 211

Tray, Picture It! Publishing, 214, *214*

trip planning, 233–44

   locating information in Encarta Encyclopedia, 233–38, *235, 236, 237, 238*

   planning routes with Streets & Trips, 238–43, *239, 240, 241, 242*, 244

   quick reference, 243–44

trusted sites, 75
typographic errors, Word, 29

U

underlines, Word, 31–32, *31*
Undo command
    Database, 156, 161
    Word, 29, 30, 42, 175
Uniform Resource Locators (URLs), 65
uppercase, 16

V

vCalendar format, 102
.vcs file extension, 102
versions, Works, 4, 5, *5*, 24, 132, 173.
    See also Microsoft Works 6.0;
    Microsoft Works Suite 2001
views. *See also* windows
    Address Book, 48, 57
    Calendar, 91–93, *92, 93*, 105
    Database, 152, *152*, 156–59, *157, 158,*
       159, 166–67, *167*, 168
    Picture It! Publishing, 232
    Portfolio, 185
    Spreadsheet, 115, *122*, 127
    Word, 39, *39*, 40, 189
    Word mail merge, 137–39, *137, 138,*
       146, *146*, 148

W

wavy underlines, Word, 31–32, *31*

Web. *See also* Internet
    addresses, 65, 70
    browsers, 64 (*see also* Microsoft Internet
      Explorer)
    Microsoft site, 64, 70–71, *71*
    Microsoft Works site, 69
    MSN home page, 66, *66* (*see also*
      Microsoft Network (MSN))
    National Weather Service site, 72
    search engines, 65
    sites and pages, 64, *65*
week calendar, 93, *93*
windows. *See also* views
    maximizing, 67, 79
    resizing, 17, *50*
    tiling, 78
    zooming, 39, 125, 166, 180, 182, 186,
      221–22
Windows Address Book
    Calendar and, 92
    contacts (*see* contacts)
    maps and, 49
    Outlook Express and, 79, 81
    quick reference, 60–61
    Word documents and, 27
    as Works component, *5*
Windows Explorer, 77–79, *78*
wizards
    Add Printer, 41
    Answer, 15, 16–17, *16*, 18, *18*, 21
    Create New Scheduled Transaction,
      202–3, *202, 203*

wizards, *continued*

defined, 5, 24, 109

Envelope, 147

Financial Worksheets, 109–10, *110,* 126

Flyers, 8, *8*

Internet Connection, 65, 66, 76

Letter, 26–27, *26, 28,* 42

Mailing Label, 144–46, *144, 145, 146,* 150

New Account, 204–6, *204, 206,* 212

Newsletters, 172–76, *173, 174, 175,* 188

Open A File, 210, *210*

Recipe Book, 10–11, *10, 11*

Word. *See* **Microsoft Word**

Word Help, 16, 18–19, *18*

word processors. *See* **Microsoft Word; Works Word Processor**

Works. *See* **Microsoft Works 6.0; Microsoft Works Suite 2001**

Works Calendar

quick reference, 105–6

schedules (*see* schedules)

as Works component, 4, *5*

Works Database

components, 151–52, *152*

databases (*see* databases)

quick reference, 168–69

Recipe Book Wizard, 10–11, *10, 11*

as Works component, 4, *5*

worksheets, 109. *See also* **budget spreadsheets; Works Spreadsheet**

Works Help, 15–19, *16, 17, 18,* 20–21, 92, 111, 120, 158. *See also* **Help**

Works Portfolio

opening and closing, 7, *7,* 20, 21

pictures, 183–86, *184, 185, 186, 187*

quick references, 21, 189–90

as Works component, 5, *5*

Works Spreadsheet

budget spreadsheets (*see* budget spreadsheets)

components, 107–9, *108*

quick reference, 126–28

starting, from Task Launcher, 13–14, *13,* 109, *110,* 111, *111*

as Works component, 4, *5*

Works Task Launcher

closing, 20, 41, 60

home page, 4, *4,* 7, *7*

quick reference, 20

starting, 6, *6,* 20, 24

starting Address Book, 46

starting Calendar, 92, *92*

starting documents in History list, 14–15, *14,* 20

starting Encarta Encyclopedia, 234

starting Internet Explorer, 70

starting MSN, 66–67, *66, 67*

starting Picture It! Publishing, 214

starting Portfolio, 20

starting programs, 11–14, *12, 13,* 20

starting Spreadsheet, 108, *108,* 109, *110,* 111, *111,* 126

starting Streets & Trips, 244

starting tasks, 6–11, *6, 7, 8, 9, 10, 11,* 20

Works Task Launcher, *continued*
   starting Word, 20, 172
   as Web portal, 64
Works Word Processor, 4, *5*, 24, 132, 173
World Wide Web. *See* Web

Z

zooming, 39, 125, 166, 180, 182, 186, 189,
   221–22

The manuscript for this book was prepared and submitted to Microsoft Press in electronic form. The content was structured using XML. Text files were prepared using Microsoft Word 2000. Pages were composed by Microsoft Press using Adobe FrameMaker+SGML 5.5.6 for Windows, with text in Sabon and display type in Syntax. Composed pages were delivered to the printer as electronic prepress files.

Cover Graphic Designer
Patrick Lanfear

Cover Illustrator
Daman Studio

Interior Graphic Artist
Joel Panchot

Principal Compositor/
Structured Content Specialist
Barbara Norfleet

Manuscript Editor
Shawn Peck

Principal Copy Editor
Cheryl Penner

Indexer
Shane-Armstrong Information Systems

Media Production
Jim Larkin
Terry Brandli
Tycen Hopkins

up! Step by Step

STEP BY STEP books provide quick and easy self-training—to help you learn to use the powerful features and tools in Microsoft Office 2000, Microsoft Windows Professional, and Microsoft Windows Me. The easy-to-follow lessons present clear objectives and real-world business examples, with numerous screen shots and illustrations. Put Office 2000 and Windows 2000 Professional, and Windows Me to work today with STEP BY STEP learning solutions, made by Microsoft.

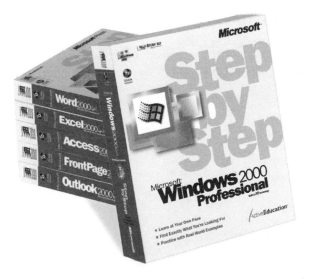

- MICROSOFT® OFFICE 2000 PROFESSIONAL 8-IN-1 STEP BY STEP
- MICROSOFT WORD 2000 STEP BY STEP
- MICROSOFT EXCEL 2000 STEP BY STEP
- MICROSOFT POWERPOINT® 2000 STEP BY STEP
- MICROSOFT INTERNET EXPLORER 5 STEP BY STEP
- MICROSOFT PUBLISHER 2000 STEP BY STEP
- MICROSOFT ACCESS 2000 STEP BY STEP
- MICROSOFT FRONTPAGE® 2000 STEP BY STEP
- MICROSOFT OUTLOOK® 2000 STEP BY STEP
- MICROSOFT WINDOWS® 2000 PROFESSIONAL STEP BY STEP
- MICROSOFT WINDOWS ME STEP BY STEP

Microsoft®

mspress.microsoft.com

Stay in the *running* for maximum productivity.

These are *the* answer books for business users of Microsoft software. They are packed with everything from quick, clear instructions for new users to comprehensive answers for power users—the authoritative reference to keep by your computer and use every day. The RUNNING series—learning solutions made by Microsoft.

- RUNNING MICROSOFT® EXCEL 2000
- RUNNING MICROSOFT OFFICE 2000 PREMIUM
- RUNNING MICROSOFT OFFICE 2000 PROFESSIONAL
- RUNNING MICROSOFT OFFICE 2000 SMALL BUSINESS
- RUNNING MICROSOFT WORD 2000
- RUNNING MICROSOFT POWERPOINT® 2000
- RUNNING MICROSOFT ACCESS 2000
- RUNNING MICROSOFT INTERNET EXPLORER 5
- RUNNING MICROSOFT FRONTPAGE® 2000
- RUNNING MICROSOFT OUTLOOK® 2000
- RUNNING MICROSOFT WINDOWS® 2000 PROFESSIONAL

Microsoft®

mspress.microsoft.com

Get fast answers—
at a glance!

Here's the easy, *visual* way to find fast answers for using the Microsoft Windows family of operating systems and Microsoft Office 2000 applications. Microsoft Press® AT A GLANCE books help you focus on specific tasks and show you, with clear, numbered steps, the easiest way to get them done now. Put Microsoft software to work for you with AT A GLANCE!

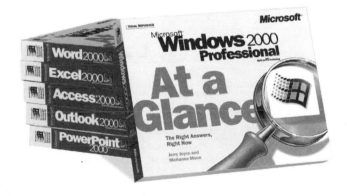

- MICROSOFT® OFFICE 2000 PROFESSIONAL AT A GLANCE
- MICROSOFT WORD 2000 AT A GLANCE
- MICROSOFT EXCEL 2000 AT A GLANCE
- MICROSOFT POWERPOINT® 2000 AT A GLANCE
- MICROSOFT ACCESS 2000 AT A GLANCE
- MICROSOFT FRONTPAGE® 2000 AT A GLANCE
- MICROSOFT PUBLISHER 2000 AT A GLANCE
- MICROSOFT OFFICE 2000 SMALL BUSINESS AT A GLANCE
- MICROSOFT PHOTODRAW™ 2000 AT A GLANCE
- MICROSOFT INTERNET EXPLORER 5 AT A GLANCE
- MICROSOFT OUTLOOK® 2000 AT A GLANCE
- MICROSOFT WINDOWS® 2000 PROFESSIONAL AT A GLANCE
- MICROSOFT WINDOWS ME AT A GLANCE

mspress.microsoft.com

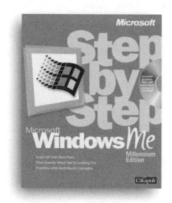
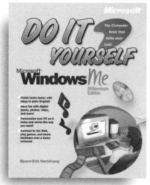

MICROSOFT LICENSE AGREEMENT

Book Companion CD

IMPORTANT—READ CAREFULLY: This Microsoft End-User License Agreement ("EULA") is a legal agreement between you (either an individual or an entity) and Microsoft Corporation for the Microsoft product identified above, which includes computer software and may include associated media, printed materials, and "online" or electronic documentation ("SOFTWARE PROD-UCT"). Any component included within the SOFTWARE PRODUCT that is accompanied by a separate End-User License Agreement shall be governed by such agreement and not the terms set forth below. By installing, copying, or otherwise using the SOFTWARE PRODUCT, you agree to be bound by the terms of this EULA. If you do not agree to the terms of this EULA, you are not authorized to install, copy, or otherwise use the SOFTWARE PRODUCT; you may, however, return the SOFTWARE PROD-UCT, along with all printed materials and other items that form a part of the Microsoft product that includes the SOFTWARE PRODUCT, to the place you obtained them for a full refund.

SOFTWARE PRODUCT LICENSE

The SOFTWARE PRODUCT is protected by United States copyright laws and international copyright treaties, as well as other intellectual property laws and treaties. The SOFTWARE PRODUCT is licensed, not sold.

1. GRANT OF LICENSE. This EULA grants you the following rights:

   a. **Software Product.** You may install and use one copy of the SOFTWARE PRODUCT on a single computer. The primary user of the computer on which the SOFTWARE PRODUCT is installed may make a second copy for his or her exclusive use on a portable computer.

   b. **Storage/Network Use.** You may also store or install a copy of the SOFTWARE PRODUCT on a storage device, such as a network server, used only to install or run the SOFTWARE PRODUCT on your other computers over an internal network; however, you must acquire and dedicate a license for each separate computer on which the SOFTWARE PRODUCT is installed or run from the storage device. A license for the SOFTWARE PRODUCT may not be shared or used concurrently on different computers.

   c. **License Pak.** If you have acquired this EULA in a Microsoft License Pak, you may make the number of additional copies of the computer software portion of the SOFTWARE PRODUCT authorized on the printed copy of this EULA, and you may use each copy in the manner specified above. You are also entitled to make a corresponding number of secondary copies for portable computer use as specified above.

   d. **Sample Code.** Solely with respect to portions, if any, of the SOFTWARE PRODUCT that are identified within the SOFT-WARE PRODUCT as sample code (the "SAMPLE CODE"):

   i. **Use and Modification.** Microsoft grants you the right to use and modify the source code version of the SAMPLE CODE, *provided* you comply with subsection (d)(iii) below. You may not distribute the SAMPLE CODE, or any modified version of the SAMPLE CODE, in source code form.

   ii. **Redistributable Files.** Provided you comply with subsection (d)(iii) below, Microsoft grants you a nonexclusive, royalty-free right to reproduce and distribute the object code version of the SAMPLE CODE and of any modified SAMPLE CODE, other than SAMPLE CODE, or any modified version thereof, designated as not redistributable in the Readme file that forms a part of the SOFTWARE PRODUCT (the "Non-Redistributable Sample Code"). All SAMPLE CODE other than the Non-Redistributable Sample Code is collectively referred to as the "REDISTRIBUTABLES."

   iii. **Redistribution Requirements.** If you redistribute the REDISTRIBUTABLES, you agree to: (i) distribute the REDISTRIBUTABLES in object code form only in conjunction with and as a part of your software application product; (ii) not use Microsoft's name, logo, or trademarks to market your software application product; (iii) include a valid copyright notice on your software application product; (iv) indemnify, hold harmless, and defend Microsoft from and against any claims or lawsuits, including attorney's fees, that arise or result from the use or distribution of your software application product; and (v) not permit further distribution of the REDISTRIBUTABLES by your end user. Contact Microsoft for the applicable royalties due and other licensing terms for all other uses and/or distribution of the REDISTRIBUTABLES.

2. DESCRIPTION OF OTHER RIGHTS AND LIMITATIONS.

   • **Limitations on Reverse Engineering, Decompilation, and Disassembly.** You may not reverse engineer, decompile, or disassemble the SOFTWARE PRODUCT, except and only to the extent that such activity is expressly permitted by applicable law notwithstanding this limitation.

   • **Separation of Components.** The SOFTWARE PRODUCT is licensed as a single product. Its component parts may not be separated for use on more than one computer.

   • **Rental.** You may not rent, lease, or lend the SOFTWARE PRODUCT.

   • **Support Services.** Microsoft may, but is not obligated to, provide you with support services related to the SOFTWARE PRODUCT ("Support Services"). Use of Support Services is governed by the Microsoft policies and programs described in the user manual, in "online" documentation, and/or in other Microsoft-provided materials. Any supplemental software code provided to you as part of the Support Services shall be considered part of the SOFTWARE PRODUCT and subject to the terms and conditions of this EULA. With respect to technical information you provide to Microsoft as part of the Support Services, Microsoft may use such information for its business purposes, including for product support and development. Microsoft will not utilize such technical information in a form that personally identifies you.

- **Software Transfer.** You may permanently transfer all of your rights under this EULA, provided you retain no copies, you transfer all of the SOFTWARE PRODUCT (including all component parts, the media and printed materials, any upgrades, this EULA, and, if applicable, the Certificate of Authenticity), **and** the recipient agrees to the terms of this EULA.

- **Termination.** Without prejudice to any other rights, Microsoft may terminate this EULA if you fail to comply with the terms and conditions of this EULA. In such event, you must destroy all copies of the SOFTWARE PRODUCT and all of its component parts.

3. **COPYRIGHT.** All title and copyrights in and to the SOFTWARE PRODUCT (including but not limited to any images, photographs, animations, video, audio, music, text, SAMPLE CODE, REDISTRIBUTABLES, and "applets" incorporated into the SOFTWARE PRODUCT) and any copies of the SOFTWARE PRODUCT are owned by Microsoft or its suppliers. The SOFTWARE PRODUCT is protected by copyright laws and international treaty provisions. Therefore, you must treat the SOFTWARE PRODUCT like any other copyrighted material **except** that you may install the SOFTWARE PRODUCT on a single computer provided you keep the original solely for backup or archival purposes. You may not copy the printed materials accompanying the SOFTWARE PRODUCT.

4. **U.S. GOVERNMENT RESTRICTED RIGHTS.** The SOFTWARE PRODUCT and documentation are provided with RESTRICTED RIGHTS. Use, duplication, or disclosure by the Government is subject to restrictions as set forth in subparagraph (c)(1)(ii) of the Rights in Technical Data and Computer Software clause at DFARS 252.227-7013 or subparagraphs (c)(1) and (2) of the Commercial Computer Software—Restricted Rights at 48 CFR 52.227-19, as applicable. Manufacturer is Microsoft Corporation/One Microsoft Way/Redmond, WA 98052-6399.

5. **EXPORT RESTRICTIONS.** You agree that you will not export or re-export the SOFTWARE PRODUCT, any part thereof, or any process or service that is the direct product of the SOFTWARE PRODUCT (the foregoing collectively referred to as the "Restricted Components"), to any country, person, entity, or end user subject to U.S. export restrictions. You specifically agree not to export or re-export any of the Restricted Components (i) to any country to which the U.S. has embargoed or restricted the export of goods or services, which currently include, but are not necessarily limited to, Cuba, Iran, Iraq, Libya, North Korea, Sudan, and Syria, or to any national of any such country, wherever located, who intends to transmit or transport the Restricted Components back to such country; (ii) to any end user who you know or have reason to know will utilize the Restricted Components in the design, development, or production of nuclear, chemical, or biological weapons; or (iii) to any end user who has been prohibited from participating in U.S. export transactions by any federal agency of the U.S. government. You warrant and represent that neither the BXA nor any other U.S. federal agency has suspended, revoked, or denied your export privileges.

DISCLAIMER OF WARRANTY

NO WARRANTIES OR CONDITIONS. MICROSOFT EXPRESSLY DISCLAIMS ANY WARRANTY OR CONDITION FOR THE SOFTWARE PRODUCT. THE SOFTWARE PRODUCT AND ANY RELATED DOCUMENTATION ARE PROVIDED "AS IS" WITHOUT WARRANTY OR CONDITION OF ANY KIND, EITHER EXPRESS OR IMPLIED, INCLUDING, WITHOUT LIMITATION, THE IMPLIED WARRANTIES OF MERCHANTABILITY, FITNESS FOR A PARTICULAR PURPOSE, OR NONINFRINGEMENT. THE ENTIRE RISK ARISING OUT OF USE OR PERFORMANCE OF THE SOFTWARE PRODUCT REMAINS WITH YOU.

LIMITATION OF LIABILITY. TO THE MAXIMUM EXTENT PERMITTED BY APPLICABLE LAW, IN NO EVENT SHALL MICROSOFT OR ITS SUPPLIERS BE LIABLE FOR ANY SPECIAL, INCIDENTAL, INDIRECT, OR CONSEQUENTIAL DAMAGES WHATSOEVER (INCLUDING, WITHOUT LIMITATION, DAMAGES FOR LOSS OF BUSINESS PROFITS, BUSINESS INTERRUPTION, LOSS OF BUSINESS INFORMATION, OR ANY OTHER PECUNIARY LOSS) ARISING OUT OF THE USE OF OR INABILITY TO USE THE SOFTWARE PRODUCT OR THE PROVISION OF OR FAILURE TO PROVIDE SUPPORT SERVICES, EVEN IF MICROSOFT HAS BEEN ADVISED OF THE POSSIBILITY OF SUCH DAMAGES. IN ANY CASE, MICROSOFT'S ENTIRE LIABILITY UNDER ANY PROVISION OF THIS EULA SHALL BE LIMITED TO THE GREATER OF THE AMOUNT ACTUALLY PAID BY YOU FOR THE SOFTWARE PRODUCT OR US$5.00; PROVIDED, HOWEVER, IF YOU HAVE ENTERED INTO A MICROSOFT SUPPORT SERVICES AGREEMENT, MICROSOFT'S ENTIRE LIABILITY REGARDING SUPPORT SERVICES SHALL BE GOVERNED BY THE TERMS OF THAT AGREEMENT. BECAUSE SOME STATES AND JURISDICTIONS DO NOT ALLOW THE EXCLUSION OR LIMITATION OF LIABILITY, THE ABOVE LIMITATION MAY NOT APPLY TO YOU.

MISCELLANEOUS

This EULA is governed by the laws of the State of Washington USA, except and only to the extent that applicable law mandates governing law of a different jurisdiction.

Should you have any questions concerning this EULA, or if you desire to contact Microsoft for any reason, please contact the Microsoft subsidiary serving your country, or write: Microsoft Sales Information Center/One Microsoft Way/Redmond, WA 98052-6399.

PN 097-0002296

Proof of Purchase

0-7356-1035-5

Do not send this card with your registration.
Use this card as proof of purchase if participating in a promotion or rebate offer on *Microsoft® Works Suite 2001 Step by Step*. Card must be used in conjunction with other proof(s) of payment such as your dated sales receipt—see offer details.

Microsoft® Works Suite 2001 Step by Step

WHERE DID YOU PURCHASE THIS PRODUCT?

CUSTOMER NAME

Microsoft®

mspress.microsoft.com

Microsoft Press, PO Box 97017, Redmond, WA 98073-9830

OWNER REGISTRATION CARD

Register Today!

0-7356-1035-5

Return the bottom portion of this card to register today.

Microsoft® Works Suite 2001 Step by Step

FIRST NAME | MIDDLE INITIAL | LAST NAME

INSTITUTION OR COMPANY NAME

ADDRESS

CITY | STATE | ZIP

E-MAIL ADDRESS | ( ) PHONE NUMBER

U.S. and Canada addresses only. Fill in information above and mail postage-free.
Please mail only the bottom half of this page.

**For information about Microsoft Press®
products, visit our Web site at
mspress.microsoft.com**

Microsoft